T0369230

My Impressions

A few thoughts on life and travel

August 2009

Order this book online at www.trafford.com
or email orders@trafford.com

Most Trafford titles are also available at major online book retailers.

Printed in Victoria, BC, Canada.

ISBN: 978-1-4269-1458-4 (sc)

Our mission is to efficiently provide the world's finest, most comprehensive book publishing service, enabling every author to experience success. To find out how to publish your book, your way, and have it available worldwide, visit us online at www.trafford.com

Trafford rev. 11/11/09

www.trafford.com

North America & international
toll-free: 1 888 232 4444 (USA & Canada)
phone: 250 383 6864 • fax: 812 355 4082

Contents

1st part: Short stories.....

2nd part: Travel notes

1. *Amanda*

Up at 6.30am. Showered, put on my casual clothes and blue sports jacket, the tramping boots I bought a few days earlier on Madison, and went down to the hotel entrance on 42nd Street. Cold, clear morning 25°F, a few degrees below freezing. Now, do I go uptown to Central Park, or do I go downtown - east or west? As the sun is coming up I decide east. I cross 3rd and when I come to 2nd I turn right thinking I normally go uptown so why not go the other way.

Busy streets and lots of people looking determined to get to work on time. Also a few people standing around - one guy who looked like he was hard done by, one father pushing twins in a pram and an elegant old lady with sunglasses and a sweet little lap dog. I shoot a few street pictures with my pocket camera and reflect on how nice some of the streets look between 2nd and 3rd with townhouses and trees right in the middle of Manhattan.

I am looking for a deli to have a quick breakfast before my morning pick up to JFK for my flight to LA and Auckland. I turn right on 28th and then right again on 3rd and find a nice little deli between 29th and 30th. A bagel with ham and mustard, a small bottle of orange juice and a cup of American coffee - white with one sugar.

I prefer to eat my breakfast in town for more excitement and half the price compared to the hotel. While eating my breakfast I write a few postcards to people who I think will appreciate a greeting. I always think that the joy of receiving a personal greeting by far exceeds the two to three minute effort of putting a postcard together. Twenty minutes to eight, six dollars, sixty for the breakfast, seven dollars handed over the counter - keep the change!

Uneventful walk back to 42nd, up to the 28th floor, pack my things and down to the lobby for my 9.00 o'clock pick up. Four limousines parked outside but none with my name. The doorman asks me if I want a taxi but I tell him I am being picked up. Now 9.10am and still no car. I think I'll wait until 9.15 and then take a cab, checking I have enough money for a cab, and yes, no problem. Knowing my friends have gone through the effort of pre arranging and prepaying for a car, I am reluctant to walk away from it.

At 9.15am another doorman asks if I want a taxi and I tell him I am waiting to be picked up. He asks my name - I say Olsson - and he says my car is waiting for me at the Park Avenue entrance - do I want him to take me there? Yes, that would be appreciated.

I had no idea the hotel has a second entrance but sure enough - there was my black leather upholstered limousine waiting for me. The sign in the window says Frank Olssong, which I find amusing since one of my favourite pastimes is singing. I had just completed six singing lessons with an opera singer back home - a present from a customer of mine. The driver put my bags in the booth, I pay a few dollars to the helpful doorman and take a seat in the back of the car. The front seat is pulled way forward to give me maximum leg space, very comfortable.

The driver, a tall good-looking African American in a pinstriped suit, asks me: what time is your flight? and I say 12.00 noon - plenty of time as it is now about 9.30am. He asks me where I am from and I say I live in New Zealand but I am Swedish from Stockholm. He says he has been to Stockholm on an exchange program and loved it - beautiful women!

I ask him if things have gotten better in America after more than five years of economic growth and he responds: I don't think so. Perhaps a little bit better but costs are high and people work hard to make ends meet. He says fewer people are sleeping rough and that would be a sign of some improvement. I say it was terrible with this unarmed guy, Amadou Diallo, who opened his door for the police and then got shot 41 times. The driver thought that was totally shocking - shot by police like an animal and the officers involved are not even suspended.

And then he refers to another murder the night before, a twenty-seven year old girl from mid-west, Amy Watkins, working in a support centre for battered women. On her way home from work she was stabbed in the back with a kitchen knife by someone who stole her handbag. She screamed twice, fell down surrounded by her groceries and died with the kitchen knife in her back. The driver says: Here was someone who obviously needed help, killing someone who had devoted her life to helping others. What a tragedy! Killing a living angel! I ask the driver if he has any children. He says: I have one, a little daughter. She has been going to a church school and has done really well but now she is starting real school. The driver says he and his wife have visited two private schools but found them terribly expensive. When the principal told us the price my reaction was - I only want you to educate her - not to feed her or clothe her or buy her!. But the principal said that that was the cost of education these days. And my wife says we will need to try and earn some more money.

I say that I thought schooling was free in the US and he responds that the public schools are, but they are so unsafe in New York that he wouldn't risk sending his daughter to one. He says that the other day a six year old kid brought a gun to school in his lunch box just to show the other kids. So now the driver tells me he has this job working for the Post Office at night and as a driver during the day. His wife is also working. I ask him when he sleeps and he says a few hours in the afternoon after picking up his girl from school. She is a fantastic girl, she likes to read to me after school! I ask what her name is and he says Amanda.

What a beautiful name, it means *the beloved* in Latin. Oh does it, I didn't know that! As I sense he is a devote Christian I ask him if he goes to church regularly. Oh yes, he says. So I tell him that I just read the bible from cover to cover. You mean the whole thing? From cover to cover? Yes, I say, there are sixty-six books, over 1300 fine printed pages. What made you do that? I tell him I visited Jerusalem last year and in order to enrich the experience I decided to read the bible. Jerusalem must have been interesting? Yes, very. The place is so charged with religion and history it is totally amazing. He says he wants to take his mother there at some stage. He asks what other places I saw there so I mention Hebron, Bethlehem, Jericho, the Mount of

Olives, Gethsemane and also the Dead Sea and Jordan. My wife had arranged to have her 50th birthday in Jordan and a number of our friends travelled in from near and afar for the celebration. He asks if there was much security in Jordan and I said no - much more in Israel.

What do you do? I am a banker. I just can't believe you read the whole Bible - more people should do that. I say that I have also made some notes - in fact forty seven pages with extracts from each book and then I summarized that down to six pages, added nine pages of comments of my own and made a little booklet of it all. The two-hour bible! That's amazing he says. As I read the Bible I had a pencil and anything I thought inspirational, enthusing and uplifting and speaking to modern man I marked and then subsequently typed those marked pieces out. I took me one hundred and twenty hours to read it and thirty hours to type it. If you give me your address I will send you a copy when I get back. Oh I'd love that!

And now that I've read it and typed it and summarized it and proof read it and read my notes a couple of times I feel I know where everything is and how it all fits together. And I am using the notes and quotes in my work in communication with staff and customers, and I have found it a great tool for building trust and relationships. I say I have also read a bit about other religions, Greek and Roman and other philosophy as well as many modern management books, and a lot of it comes back to the bible. Themes like thrift, love, humility and generosity are common in most of this writing. And of course key building blocks for a happy life. For example in Matthew it says; "Who of you by worrying can add a single hour to your life" and this is so true. Too many people worry too much. Ninety five percent of all worries are totally unfounded.

And about generosity - when you think about it, it is so obvious that generosity pays: as you sow, so you shall reap and you shall reap many fold more than you sow. Proverbs is the most obviously useful book for espousing values and Ecclesiastes is equally fascinating. By basing our business on values, it is flourishing, staff enjoy work life, our customers are happy, and I love every day of it. He gave me a card with his address: James Maxwell from Bronx.

Man, he says, you should lead the company, this company, your company or any company. I wish I met you a few days earlier so I could have introduced you to my pastor. I explain to James that my notes are not designed to promote religion as such but more to make easily available some of the wonderful positive messages about ethical living in the bible. Many people are over awed by religion and turn away from anything religious - but then they may miss out on Christian ethics and other still highly relevant wisdom of the bible. My notes are only about sixty pages of quotes of the bible, all highly motivational and uplifting.

I tell James I had just been to a three days conference where one of the lecturers showed a pie chart of what goes on in the head of a chief financial officer. It was all work - 25% servicing the CEO, 20% finance, etc, but nothing on personal reflections, interests like sports or culture, family, friends, etc. When I suggested that people also are persons and individuals who from time to time reflect on issues like - Why am I doing this? What do I want to do with my life going forward? How can I make my wife and kids happier? How can I lead a happier life? What is it that really interests me? etc. - I was told that the CFO has no time for such thoughts; there is only time for commuting and thinking about sex and money. First I thought it was a joke but when I came back to the issue he repeated his response. What a pathetic approach to life! He is going to wake up some day and find that he hasn't really lived, that he has wasted his time. And how uninspiring!

Most people, I believe, spend some time thinking about things that concern them, other than work. And most people appreciate a discussion and perhaps some ideas on how to progress these thoughts. I am convinced that a happier person is a better employee, a better parent and a better provider of service to any company. He or she generates energy and motivation. I believe it is good business to try to address people's concerns, whatever they may be.

And if you can demonstrate a strong commitment to honesty, ethics and values you are building that trust which is so important for a good relationship be it business or private. If your customers know that there is no way you are going to not deliver good value to the best of your ability, that builds relationships. So many sales people are totally plastic, soulless and robot like that you neither want to buy from them, nor listen to their gobble de gobble.

And then I say: Look, I have a set of the notes in my briefcase and I can give you that set right now. I have given out about one hundred to customers and friends already. He asks how I came to talk about the bible and I say I was impressed by your love and devotion to your little daughter, going through such effort to get her good schooling. Love and generosity are two very strong and recurring themes of the bible. Thus I thought you might be interested.

Now we arrive at the terminal. American Airlines. He stops the car and I get out. He asks for the LA check-in and is directed a bit further. He asks me to please get in the car again but I say I am just going to fish out a bible for you from the booth. It is not a bible, he said? No, it is not, - it is my notes on the bible. I'll just sign it and then give it to you. Sign it to James, he says, and I do.

We drive up a little bit further and he carries my luggage all the long way in to the check-in counter. He says: I am so grateful - I just feel God meant for us to meet today. When we get to the counter I shake his hand and say: It was great to talk to you and good luck with Amanda and her education. Please take my card and write me a note about your thoughts on the bible summary. He smiled, said he would definitely do that, went to his black limousine and disappeared into the New York traffic.

10 March 1999

2. *The Grandpa Clock*

(Moraklockan.)

I looked at it again. The grandpa clock we bought twenty years ago in Falun, Sweden. Falun – gong? No hands and a small hole in the middle of the face and the numbers one to twelve in black on a white emerald surface. The insides have been taken to a craftsman for service and greasing before another move across the equator – it's fourth. Why would anyone want to move a clock across the equator four times in twenty years? The simple reason is that as part of our household goods, it loyally moves with the household. When it's time to break up it doesn't argue.

Can a clock without hands and insides strike? If it can't really speak to you, it certainly can strike you with amazement and wonder. Looking at the unusual and empty face of the clock it inevitably raises the question; is time an illusion, does time matter? After all, day and night are not normally detected by looking at a clock but by experiencing daylight or the waning of it. Why would you want to subdivide either day or night into smaller components? Does it have any relevance to be able to determine whether it is 2.45 or 3.15. Whether it is AM or PM is usually obvious by looking out the window. And if there are no windows but eternal darkness? Well, then establishment of the precise hour wouldn't seem to make much difference.

Looking at the mute clock repeatedly reminds me how accustomed I am to frequently check on the time. This empty handless face thus keeps repeating "look at me as much as you like – I am still not going to tell you anything!" Perhaps this is a more profound and useful message than the one that the clock was designed to convey. Measuring the exact time becomes a distraction suggesting that we move on from one task to another at certain intervals. But surely this can be done anyway and more naturally when tasks are finished rather than when the allotted time has come too an end.

But how about efficiency? Efficiency is based on production per unit of time, so without measuring time there is no way of establishing how efficient a certain process is. So what? Is there not a natural ambition by he who undertakes things to try to finish them? All human activity is initiated either by a desire to accomplish some defined task, or to merely provide joy and pleasure. None of these two are really dependent on time being measured for their successful execution. In fact, pleasure and time measurement are mutually exclusive. Happiness is timeless.

Perhaps there is a business idea here. What if we started to make clocks and watches with no indicators of time. Everything as normal except no hands to put the stress on us. These hands actually lead to premature death for a great number of people. Every functioning timepiece is a ticking bomb, setting out what is left of your life. So the handless watch should be able to be promoted on the basis that it helps you, not only to live longer, but also better. It would help remind the bearer of what is important in life and what is futile. And of course he would find that most of the things and thoughts he has experienced on a daily basis are quite futile, devoid of any deeper meaning.

How backward it really is to contract forty hours of time per week to employers, the way we are so used to. This is totally void of any quality measure. Americans work 2,100 hrs per year and Germans work 1,700. What does that tell us? That Americans are smarter? That they are more committed? That Germans are happier? That Germany is heading for disaster and America for success? In fact it tells us nothing of the kind. It is completely irrelevant! For it is what you do and the amount of quality, heart and love that you put into your work that makes the difference, not the number of hours. Who has the lowest number of worked hours of all western economies? Who has the highest wage cost? Who is the most successful exporter of the biggest by value and most sophisticated internationally traded goods in the world, i.e. motor vehicles? The answer is Germany.

Please note that I am not suggesting Germans are happier than other peoples. All I am observing is that focusing on quality rather than time seems to make a lot of sense. It is not the number of hours worked that are important but how we apply ourselves during the time worked that is key. In fact, overly focusing on quantum of time implicitly suggests that quality doesn't matter or is of secondary importance. Thinking about it, anything really worthwhile in life is inefficient – children, music, caring, generosity and love.

I look at the clock again and wonder how I could get so many strange thoughts in my head from just looking at a clock. On the right side of the clock there is a large picture window with a lustrously green pear tree epitomizing early summer and life at its fullest. On the other side of the clock is a glass veranda door through which I see some beautiful summer rain clouds, a magnificent palm tree and between some other trees, a glimpse of the blue surface of the South Pacific in the Auckland Harbour. A sight for gods – where all I saw before was the passing of time.

Yes, we will have the clock restored. But in future I shall look past it and only listen to the ding-dong it makes every hour. And on hearing that familiar sound I shall not count the hours but rather ponder the beauty of nature and count the blessings of life.

28th November, 1999

3. Africa?

It is good when things go on time. SQ 986 at 2.15 P.M. 15th of March 1999. Not really sure whether I want to be on this plane but here I am in seat 47K by the window. The plane is already moving, so it is too late to do anything other than sit back and enjoy it. I offered Linda to cancel the trip and support her as she was going in for a major medical examination, but she insisted I go. I told the office that Linda was in for minor surgery and that I would be away for two days. Both statements were true but one didn't lead to the other the way the sentence might imply.

But it did provide a convenient story, as I didn't want to be too specific as to what I was up to. Linda really is worried about her ailment but I try to tell her not to discount any bad news. There is still a better than 50: 50 chance that all will turn out fine.

Very annoying phone call I got just before I left the office from my colleague in New York. Two weeks earlier I was asked to say a few words of thanks to the dinner speaker at a company internal conference, which I was happy to do. I thanked the speaker who was from IBM and underscored to my colleagues that there was not one slide shown by this speaker that didn't contain the word customer. I suggested we needed to very much take this at heart as bankers too often focus mainly on returns rather than the provision of added value to our good relationships. The customer is our *raison d'etre* it is he/she who pays our salaries rather than the CEO or the bean counters. Vision and customer care must be in the front seat and bean counters should be in the back seat providing advice but not doing the steering.

Now, that was all I was asked to do – extract and repeat key messages and thank the speaker. However my approach to life is to always deliver a bit more than minimum. Thus I continued to relate a few jokes causing a lot of laughter and then handed out song sheets with six chosen songs on them. Jolly nice evening!

Two weeks later I get this phone call, which says that one of the women took offense at the jokes. I couldn't believe it!! I had tried hard to find inoffensive stories so my thoughts progressed along two lines: Firstly, how could anyone be so petty as to be offended by anything so innocuous and secondly, how could I be so stupid as to even operate anywhere near the border line for the acceptable. This is America where views are very diverse and anything is possible. The only positive way of looking at it is to see it as an opportunity for learning. Even if it is a closed group, and after a dinner with lots of fine wines, you can never be sure that not one person will take offense at something said in jest. As being offended is entirely subjective, the mere fact that someone is offended makes whatever caused it offensive. You cannot win. So skip the jokes - be a predictable bore. I certainly won't make that mistake again.

I thought my sponsor would get me business class but here I am stuck like a sardine in monkey class. Particularly when the seats are reclined, the room to move is zilch. This made me consider not going on the flight at all, but then that would be a bit of an anticlimax. So I forget about all that and dive into my book, 'Intellectual Capital,' which I finish in a couple of hours. Lots of wisdom that I must share with my colleagues and customers!

I drink very cautiously because between the aisle and me is an older couple from England blocking my access to the lavatories during the nine hour-long trip. Very nice lady, she is, the person sitting next to me, but everything is a bit close and tight for comfort. You drop something on the floor and can forget about being able to pick it up until the end of the flight when it may have moved several rows back or forth.

Huge country Australia – more than half the trip is over this vast land mass. We land in Singapore on schedule at 8.00 P.M. which is midnight where I started from. Changi airport is as efficient as ever and with hand luggage only and am in a cab fifteen minutes after landing.

They have booked Intercontinental Hotel for me – very elegant and comfortable. I don't feel much like going out as it is now nearly one o'clock my time, so I take a nice hot bath, watch a little bit if TV and then lights off. I wake up at 6.30A.M. very grateful for a good eight hours sleep. I give Linda a call and she sounds OK – there really isn't much you can do until you have a proper diagnosis. Hers will take two weeks and she feels some relief that the process at least now is underway. With results available after two weeks only that means that we can go to Queensland as planned over Easter with Andre'. Yes, she says, that's fine.

Then Heather, my colleague and office manager calls me as agreed - she is the only one I have told what I am up to. She says all is going to be fine and no one is looking for me. One of our secretaries got a call from Singapore yesterday from a woman saying she was fine for the lunch appointment in Singapore. The secretary, thinking there must be some misunderstanding here, calls my home and when she asks for me my son says I am in Singapore. So Heather has to explain the story to her as well. Fortunately I have wonderful colleagues who really like and support each other. Other than that little incident all is fine in the office and no-one needs to talk to me, See you tomorrow around noon.

I go and do thirty laps in the pool and then try to set up appointments with my four ex colleagues from working in Singapore (in 1987 as MD for Pkbanken South East Asia), all of Chinese extraction. I manage to agree meetings with three of them, but the fourth, Molly Lim, my ex secretary is on leave so I call her at home and talk to her on the phone for a little while instead.

Shorts, a short sleeve shirt and I'm away for breakfast. Lots of wonderful fruits and fruit juices and a ham omelette made to order plus a cup of tea. After breakfast I took a Taxi to Orchard Road for a short stroll before my first meeting at 10.30 A.M. Not much is open yet but I manage to buy a Discman for my son's upcoming 13[Th] birthday. And four small jars of Tiger Balm – it smells nice and they are good giveaways. Much to my surprise I ran into a banking friend from Auckland having a morning stroll on Orchard Road. We stop for a brief chat and agree it is a small world. I arrive at the Tangelin Club – perhaps the most prestigious club in Singapore – at 10.20 A.M. about fifteen minutes before my friend Ronald arrives.

Long time no see!! I called the bank where I thought you were working but they said you weren't there anymore. No, I got retrenched when the bank got taken over. My counter party at the other bank was more senior, had been there for 21 years as against my four, so I was asked to leave with six months pay. Now looking for something new again but the market is quite recessionary and difficult. Asset prices have fallen significantly but we bought our house many years ago for four hundred thousand and it should be worth 1.3 million today. Good with a fall back piece of equity like that. Annie is doing very well as the Singapore General Manager for a Hong Kong developer. Annie also loves her painting and has a real talent for it. She takes a class every week. And I take guitar lessons. I heard this South American guy on the radio and called him up and asked if he would teach me and he is terrific. I am learning Spanish as a side benefit.

He says his boys are grown up now – one is in Washington D.C. studying law and the other at University of Indiana studying engineering. Is that for a year then? No, for the full four years – to complete a tertiary degree! That must be expensive? It cost about a quarter million dollars for each. That is an amazing commitment! We each have a café latte and an orange juice. And then we talk about Africa and he says you would have to be crazy to give up what you have in New Zealand and go to work in Africa. We also cover my family and what has happened to our mutual friends in Singapore and Sweden. I give him a copy of my book 'Carpe Diem,' and some bone carvings from New Zealand.

He signs for the drinks and drives me back to the hotel in his SAAB which is half Swedish and half General Motors these days. And Volvo is now Ford! Why did they do that? I guess they always felt Volvo was too small to cope with R&D for the future. The expense in bringing forth new models is enormous and you need scale to cope with it, which Volvo didn't have.

I say I am impressed with what you are doing for your kids – a quarter of a million is a lot of money. He says Singapore is a small and competitive, and to open up the opportunities an American educations should be very useful. I say my sons' education is costing me about ten thousand a year each and I thought *I* was generous.

He takes the car into the little courtyard of The Intercontinental, off Middle Road, and we both get out of the car, shake hands and say we must stay in touch. He disappears around the corner and I go up to my hotel room. A quick shower, shirt and tie and dark suit, gather my things and then down to check out. Three hundred dollars for a five star hotel room isn't too bad. I go and sit in the lobby and prepare a package for my lunch date, Whee Cheng, the brilliant stockbroker. She arrives five minutes late apologizing, saying the trading lasts until 12.30 P.M. and it took a while to get here. No problem. She has booked the Chinese restaurant at the hotel.

We get a nice chambre separe' – she asks me if there is anything I don't eat? No, as long as it isn't too spicy. She orders in Mandarin and says we will have a nice multi course meal. I ask her about her family and she says she has three kids. The first, a daughter, had heart problems and left them when she was three and a half years old. At first I thought this was difficult, but then she is with God and is better off than we are. Who looks after your children? Their grandmother who lives nearby. When I ask her if she is having any more children she says no, grandmother can't cope. Her husband is some kind of freelance stockbroker and I get the impression that she is the breadwinner. She asks me if I am a true believer and I say I have come a long way in twenty years recognizing spirituality and the many miracles like trees, birds, butterflies, childbirth etc but in terms of pure faith I am not quite there yet. She says she will include me in her prayers. Her family's strong faith provides positive guidance for all situations and tremendous comfort.

Her stock broking is entirely commission based – she takes 40% of the earnings and the firm takes the rest. This works well and she is grateful to God for doing OK during the current recession and that her good clients have stuck with her in spite of disappointing asset depreciation. She deals mainly with Singapore and Malay stocks but can execute orders for London and New York as well. She doesn't read much other than the daily reading of the Bible and many financial journals she needs to cover.

She wants to take her family and visit New Zealand but their little boy must grow a bit older. I tell him you are old enough to wear shoes, you are old enough to walk; but he insists on being carried by his father. Perhaps in two years time when he can walk, we can come and visit you in New Zealand.

Africa? Why would you want to go to Africa when you are doing so well and have so many friends in New Zealand? I understand you have a sea view from your house in Auckland? Yes. How big is your house? About 2,500 sq feet. My house is 4,000 sq feet. It was worth S$ 2,7 million at the peak two years ago but now probably S$ 1.7 million. A lot of values have halved. I said we have spent about NZ $ 850 K and would probably be lucky to get that. Clearly you get a lot for your money in New Zealand. She says there are swings and roundabouts in life and key for survival is to avoid much leverage. Many people who borrowed to buy assets in Hong Kong, Indonesia, Malaysia and Thailand got completely wiped out.

And then she says she feels that the big speculators and hedge funds were a major cause of the current demise of the area. When I ask her if she thinks the accused minister is guilty she says yes, of course, of corruption. But aren't all other ministers also corrupt? She smiles but doesn't answer. Malaysia is her biggest market, her husband is from Malaysia and Malaysia is the major trading partner with Singapore and provides the little thriving Island state with life giving water.

I ask her why New York fell yesterday – is it the Serbia air strikes decision? Partly that but partly that there is a Fed meeting in New York two weeks out and if the index is too high, there is a risk of an unwanted interest rate hike. Higher interest rates are bad for the share markets and to prevent a rate increase, the bigger players try to cool things down for a while. At these high levels it is almost a relief when it corrects down a bit.

She looks at her watch, I say thank you for a fantastic lunch and we walk out together. I hand her an envelop with a New Zealand bone carving and a few literary notes I think she will appreciate. She says thanks; I say it was good to catch up with you again. She is away in a taxi and I go for a walk. Pretty soon I get overheated in my dark suit and the tie doesn't help much either.

I walk past Raffles Hotel and Raffles City and a bit further to the Suntec City shopping center. (I had no premonition then that I would be working from an office in Suntec City later that same year) I don't really need anything and I have no room for anything in my carry on luggage, but still I manage to buy three ties and a pair of dress Italian shoes priced at abut 30 % of what I paid for something similar in New York three weeks earlier. Was I conned? Probably, but who cares. Now I have some great shoes that should last me a lifetime. I think of Imelda Marcos.

I return to the hotel, go through my papers and write down a few questions I want to ask the headhunter, dividing the questions into the job, the country and the contract. Someone is playing the harp in the large lobby and it sounds absolutely divine – it somehow brings your thoughts back to essentials, puts things in perspective. Anything else really pales into insignificance next to perceived beauty. This is beautiful. Twenty minutes to five – time to go.

I arrive a couple of minutes early and am ushered into a meeting room. Five minutes later we are underway. I want you to tell me the basics of your education and run through the CV. US High School 65, College in Sweden 67, military training, appointed captain 72, completed law school 72, and several courses at overseas universities since then. How was the market when you finished law School? Difficult! I got accepted as a graduate trainee in the City of Stockholm and pretty soon got promoted to be a secretary to the Finance Committee. What did that job involve? It really was like a project assessor – not too different from a credit assessment. The task was to assess proposals from the various City departments to invest or spend the City's money and the analysis I provided focused on; does this have to be done at all? And if so, can it be done in a more cost effective way or smarter? Very interesting job really, given the diversity and size of the City's operation – fifty thousand employees in thirty independently run departments including energy and water, construction and roads and schools.

So how did you get into banking and finance? After the oil price shock of 1974 the City was directed to overseas markets for its long term funding and because of my interest for anything international and my fluency in English I was asked to run with it. A few years later I was appointed City Treasurer and head of the whole finance activity including all borrowing, asset management and cash management. I got significant personal exposure to domestic and overseas banks. During this period I received several offers to go and work for banks in Stockholm and London. In 1982 after I had completed an executive finance program at Harvard Business School, I received an offer from PKBanken in Stockholm, which I accepted.

How did you find banking? Challenging, particularly to quickly build the necessary networks and relationships! Having changed jobs a few times my experience is that you always feel a bit exposed at the beginning but after three to six months, things start to fall in place.

And after three months in the bank I was fully operative and started to gain the appreciation of customers, colleagues and superiors. They kept adding more and more to my responsibilities until I was head of domestic and international new debt and equity issues as well as looking after the long term funding of the bank and also running a portfolio of ten blue chip customers. I was appointed to two boards, the Swedish Export Credit and the bank's joint venture vehicle in London.

What were your key contributions? I was positive, enthusiastic and optimistic and that colored all I did and also rubbed off on my staff and contributed to very strong customer rapport. People around the organisation could see that the unit was humming, revenue grew and staff were happy and gave it all they had. When people think Monday is the best day of the week you know you are onto something good.

What made you go and work in Africa when you were so appreciated in the bank? One of my customers was the Kingdom of Sweden through the National Debt Office and the director general and I got quite friendly and he asked if I would like a three years stint in Kenya working for the World Bank. It suited our family situation as we had a third child underway and Sweden is pretty demanding when you are two professionals and it is very difficult to get domestic help. This plus a sense of adventure made us quite enthusiastic about the idea. The World Bank salaries are tax-free and PKBanken gave me leave of absence so there really was no downside risk to the venture.

I was also offered several other jobs with Salomon Brothers, First Chicago, ABN and many of the Swedish institutions but I was a bit hesitant about job contents and wanted to make sure I did something I could get enthusiastic about. American banks are also known to go hot and cold – quite short term in outlook and unreliable as employers.

In Kenya I found that I didn't really report to anybody so I started a routine of writing monthly comprehensive reports of what I had achieved spurring myself to be as ambitious as possible. Unlike many other advisers, I knew this was not going to be my last job, so I was very keen to stay busy and agile at all times. I spread the report to those who might have an interest in what I was doing and I believe I made quite an impact –particularly by having no fear and nurturing my integrity at all times. I was instrumental in the first bond issue in Kenya, I started a seminar series of financial products and ran a number of two-hour sessions for the ministry, the Central Bank and the World Bank. I analyzed and made suggestions for how to rationalize the debt portfolio and save cost. However, I soon found that there was very little interest to progress any of the ideas and increased efficiency was not high on the agenda. Part of the reason for this general disinterest in progress may be that they were in a kind of welfare trap. With a large chunk of their revenue being grants, any improvement in efficiency could well lead to lower grants. High unemployment also makes it harder to see the benefits of more efficiency.

So when approached, I said to my friends at PKBanken that I would be interested in a new posting and was offered Managing Director of PKBanken South East Asia in Singapore. What were the challenges there? It was rather easy, as it was a well-established little bank with some good staff. My focus was to build rapport quickly with our ca one hundred customers and of course bring cohesion and team spirit to staff. My relationship with board was easy since they were my old friends from PKBanken in Stockholm. However I did contribute considerably by building staff morale and raising the bank's profile seeing customers seven days a week and looking after them well. I also downsized by twenty percent and even this was done without any dent in the team spirit.

After six months in the role I got a phone call from a head hunter in Stockholm who offered me to be the CEO of another Swedish subsidiary bank, SEBanken's London Branch. SEBanken was at that time the leading corporate bank in Sweden and London was a bigger job than Singapore, so after conferring with my family I decided to accept. As a measure of the standing I had with PKBanken they allowed me to continue to run the Singapore bank for another three to four months in accordance with my personal preference. The business in London progressed much better than expected and already in the second year it was quite profitable – in fact the most profitable overseas branch of SEBanken.

Can you tell me of any major set backs in your career or challenges and how you dealt with them? Well, in London I had a run in with one of my senior staff who was undermining my position and that became quite a thorn in the side. However I tried to deal professionally with it, until after two years when I said to head office in Stockholm that the problem is not going away and some action is needed. At that time my manager and mentor had his tax returns aggressively challenged by the Swedish press so he had to resign (although later cleared in court of any wrong doing). That meant my support thinned out so I started to consider my options. This is when I saw an advertisement in The Economist for General Manager Corporate Finance for a major New Zealand bank. So I faxed my CV across and a few weeks later I was interviewed in London and subsequently asked to come to New Zealand for interviews. I was offered the job and both my family and I were thrilled.

What were their reasons for choosing you? After a deep crisis in the Bank of New Zealand in 89/90 the new MD needed to build a new management team and bring in some fresh blood. So a handful of others and I were brought in form the outside. I think they liked my track record and also my positive and enthusiastic approach. With the bank nearly on its knees, there weren't too many enthusiastic people around at that time – all worrying about their jobs. However, I had a contract and no downside, so I had every reason to be enthusiastic and try to build again, similarly to what I had done in previous jobs.

I found it quite challenging to build networks with staff and customers since I didn't know a soul but after about a year all started to harmonize and we could see real progress. Initially we were rated fourth of four banks in the market but in my second year we were rated first in corporate banking. After four years I moved to the more dynamic Auckland market and have run a very successful business there being rated first for each of the last four years by an independent customer surveyor.

Thanks Frank. That's all I need to know. Here is an information memorandum about the bank and the job. I will try to progress this as fast as possible and come up with a short list and then there will probably be interviews of those short listed by the Aga Kahn Foundation, the major shareholder of Diamond Trust Bank of Kenya limited.

Down to the street level to look for a taxi. Join the taxi queue. Two places behind me is Hermann Rockefeller, CFO of Brierley's and my tennis partner from Wellington. I say hi to Hermann, and he introduces me to his colleague Stephen Templeton. The same day the papers have announced that Singapore Airlines are likely to buy 50 % of Ansett, the Australian domestic carrier, to create a joint venture with Air New Zealand who owns the other half. Brierley is a major shareholder of Air New Zealand. Fifteen minutes later I am in a taxi on my way to Changi airport for check in and my last meeting.

At the check in counter my former colleague, Edward Chong, comes up to me and we find a café' where he gets us two coffees. He has also recently been made redundant by the same bank that my first appointment of the day had just left. However, he now works as a debt collector on a contract basis for another bank. I ask him if it is negative and depressing to collect debt? No, not really. Like anything else in life, you have to build rapport with your counter party and try to see the mutual benefit or you wont get the co-operation needed. Debt collection skills are likely to be very useful for a while. Edward has been with several banks that have disappeared over the last ten years but because of his energy and his enthusiasm he has always landed on his feet. I thank him for the book he sent me – The Lee Kuan Yew Story – and he says he appreciate the book I sent him.

He tells me about his family and the property he bought in Perth, only five hours by air away from Singapore. I think Singaporeans feel a bit exposed in their small country and many are outwardly looking, trying to keep their options open. I give him an envelop with some written material and the fish hook bone carving from New Zealand. Thank you for making the effort to come out to the airport to see me. When I first talked to him in the morning he offered to take half a day off to be able to see me in the after noon, but I suggested that a brief meeting at the airport would mean less trouble. He said thanks for the call, safe trip and let's stay in touch.

I go directly to E 11 for the SQ 285 and another nine and a half hours flight in a full plane.

Africa? Does it really make sense?

25th March 1999.

A few months later the National Australia Bank who owns Bank of New Zealand offered me the job as Regional Manager South Asia responsible for offices in India, Thailand, Malaysia, Indonesia and Singapore. So it was to be Asia and Singapore rather than Africa this time

4. My new bicycle.

Sunday morning. A few fruits and a cup of tea and a small butter bun. Take Pixie out for a walk after feeding her some canned ham from China. She loves that ham and a 99c can lasts for a whole week, good value! Nice and sunny, a bit hot at 30 degrees. For someone who grew up in an 'icebox' the sun just feels so therapeutic and liberating, particularly in light of all the rain and cold weather in Northern Europe this summer. I have wondered whether some frequently used analogies make any sense in this environment. A warm person – here it may well bring associations to someone who has had too much sunshine and who is very uncomfortable to self and others. And a lovely day is definitely rather one with overcast and lower temperatures than one with open skies and scorching heat. Just as in New Zealand a southerly wind is freezing and a house facing north comes at a premium. It is all relative to where we are and what outlook we have.

Dog seemed quite upbeat this morning – not the normal negotiations of which way to go, in which process the dog is likely to lose out, given its mass of 7 kilos compared to my 82. Its only bargaining chips are the velvet black eyes, the miserable yelps it can produce and the higher specie's reluctance to use brute force to get his way. So Pixie wins sometimes. Back at the apartment I park the dog and get my new 21-gear bicycle out to have my first run on the streets of Singapore. This is probably the fourth one I have owned, not the most expensive but certainly the one with the most gears. I take my backpack and put in a towel and a book – Selected Writings by John Ruskin, the third book by him that I have read in quick succession. He is arguing things that are dear to my heart, i.e. work needs to be pleasurable for people to apply their ingenuities and genius and if it isn't pleasurable it is in fact exploitation. And you need to invite all to the dance of life, i.e. to make use of all their human faculties, as each and every human being is a walking miracle with immense potential. This is not so much charity as decency and common sense and even self-interest by any right thinking human.

I adjust the saddle of my Peugeot bike to allow me to use the length of my legs. I also try to understand how the gears work. Only after a few minutes do I discover that there are two levers for each of the macro and micro gears, one which you use to gear up and one which you use to gear down. I am away. A piece of cake. The steer is a bit low so I am more folded up than I would like to be, but I don't have the wrench required to raise the steer. Besides, if the pros can ride all doubled up, so can I. I know I have to be careful, because there is not much extra room on the Singapore streets and the cabbies and the buses have little understanding of anyone who gets in their way and uses transport for pleasure rather than utility. I ride down Orchard Road and onto Bras Basah towards the Padang. All going sweet and easy. I realize I have no clue what is happening behind me as there are no rear mirrors. It just means I need to be ultra careful when changing lanes. Which incidentally is true even when driving a car in this city. The greatest dangers are in moving sideways. If you stay on track and observe traffic lights its pretty safe.

When I get to Nicoll Highway I decide to go off road into the War Memorial Park and then across to Esplanade Park. There is a huge temporarily constructed amphi theatre on my right side at the Padang, with possibly a thousand seats, all for the 9th of August celebration of Singapore's 35th birthday. It is no doubt going to be a major event with thousands and thousands parading, performing and celebrating. I read recently that patriotism is a virtue in an oppressed or emerging nation, but as soon as it has entered into the club of established nations, it becomes a vice. As this year the 9th of August falls on a Wednesday it breaks the week up in two short halves which I am sure is seen as a plus by most people. It has been scientifically demonstrated that most people prefer to work rather than idle, however, the pursuit of the perfect balance between work and idleness will probably continue to the end of time.

Towards the two bridges over the river there are a lot of Japanese tourists taking pictures of the Merlion, the lion at the river entrance – so many pictures of a stone lion – occasionally it would seem wiser if we focused less on taking pictures and more on the vision and the experience. I pass the Singapore Cricket Club and cycle over the renovated no cars Cavenagh Bridge in search for a nice place by the river to sit and read my book. Soon enough I find a black marble stone seat so I park my bike and take my towel to wipe my face – this is the tropics - and then get my book by John Ruskin. It is a quiet morning. There is the odd tourist boat going up and down the river – a bit like in Paris, only on a smaller scale. Five young rather smart looking European girls are looking at a map and discussing intensely. Should I go and try and help? I decide against it. Part of the excitement of the unknown is the pleasure of finding things out for yourself. The sun is glitering beautifully in the ripples on the water surface. I feel pretty happy with life and with my new bicycle. Without it I wouldn't have been here this morning enjoying these little sights of delight.

After finishing the chapter I pack the book and continue on my bike along Boat Quay with all the restaurants, which are slowly getting ready for their Sunday trade. I am now seeking out a little Indian street café, specializing in Indian breads, on Circular Road, one block in from the river. Soon enough I find it and a table right at curb-side is free, which suits me perfectly. My new elegant bike doesn't have a lock so I don't want to part from it more than a couple of feet. I take up my book and read a few more pages and then order two onion and egg Nan breads and a lime juice. The food is just beautiful, Indian bread being probably the most tasty bread of anywhere in the world.

As I eat my bread, a taxi stops a little way out in front and a beautiful young Chinese girl comes my way. She walks up to the Indian waiter, places her order and sits down at a table next to mine. A few minutes later she is enjoying her café latte and her prata bread. I get a sense that this is one of these good value places where locals come to have their breakfast. I signal to the waiter that I wish to pay and he does the arithmetic and asks for S$ 3.80. I cant believe how cheap my lovely breakfast is and I give him four dollars with a smile.

On my bike again, now heading via Neil Road to Chinatown where I just go up and down a few streets to capture the atmosphere and then take a right on Cantonment Road and proceed to the Tiong Bahru market. At this market there is a song contest for birds each Sunday and in one of the little restaurants there are ca 50 nice bird cages, each with one or two birds singing away. Otherwise the market offers a food court, fish, meat and fruits and vegetables and many other things at low cost. Virtually all are local Singaporeans which indicates that there is value for money. I go there each Sunday to buy three Mangoes and three Papaya, which is my breakfast for the following week. A cup of coffee and some tropical fruits after my regular early morning swim sets me right for the whole day. The market is busy as ever and I struggle to bring my bike to my regular fruit stall but I get there. My fruits cost ten dollars and the lovely lady who obviously recognizes me gives me a bunch of extra little fruits of unfamiliar description.

What a lovely gesture, I think. I also decide to refer to it when I talk to all my staff at the bank this week, suggesting for all of us to always try to do a little bit extra over and above expectations, whether dealing with staff or customers or anyone else. Thus we build relationships and friendships and we might have a customer or a friend for life, rather than a one off sale. Pretty obvious logic really, but how often forgotten? Leaving the market on my bike I see Diana, my colleague's wife, crossing the road. I come to a very abrupt stop with my efficient hand brakes, we exchange a kiss and wish each other well, and I am away on my bike again.

With almost ten kilos of fruit in my backpack I am now heading straight back home past the Blue Cow bar. The Blue Cow is closed, but when I pass it at night it looks like a really cool place, giving an impression of not having changed much for the last fifty years. This makes it a rare species in Singapore. Outside the pub there is a sign saying free flow of beer for $ 25, which I take to mean that you can have as many refills as you like for that price. Interesting, but The Blue Cow is likely to remain an untapped image. From there it is only another five minutes to go, and two hours after embarking on this neighborhood adventure I arrive safely back to our apartment building off Orchard Boulevard. I get the velocipede into the workman's lift and press eight for our apartment.

At this juncture I am soaking wet and need a shower, some dry cloths and a drink. Once this is completed, I again feel quite grateful and contented over the experiences on offer by acquiring a $ 199 twenty one gear French bicycle and moving around this world City in the slow lane. What a wonderful world.

6th August 2000

5. From Singapore to Tokyo, 4/5 August 2001.

First day of Japan

Saturday 4th of August I woke up at 6.38 AM as per my digital clock radio and realised that the quality of my sleep had been impaired by last night's meal at the Grill at Raffles Hotel. Raffles Hotel looked prettier last night than ever, with illumination both on the land mark buildings and the tropical palms and vegetation in-between its many wings. Things, and people, have a tendency to look particularly attractive when you are about to lose them. A kind colleague banker, Doug Wright of Bank of Austria and his wife Carroll, had invited my houseguests from New Zealand, Errol and Jennifer and me for dinner. Doug is an Australian who heads up bank of Austria in Singapore and he has previously been with Bank of Nova Scotia – so a bit of a checkered background like my own. It was the first time I met Carroll, originally from Manchester. She looks quite happy and youthful. I offered out my hand for a greeting but she gave me a hug and a kiss, much to my delight and put me in a good mood for the evening. Doug said he was amazed I could find time to go out and eat on my last evening before my 'last' morning flight out of Singapore. A long pleasant and interesting gourmet dinner but either we ate something we shouldn't have, or we ate too late or too much of a mixture, or a combination of the aforementioned. Thus the quality of my and my guests sleep wasn't what it could have been. Not to worry – these things always find their level given time.

I jumped into my togs, put my robe on, and went down to the swimming pool and did my daily morning dose of 12 laps. This had been my ritual for the 22 months I had been residing in Singapore – not many other countries you can do that in on a year around basis. Particularly when it is a bit hard to get up, having the sensation of a refreshing awakening and weightless motion through lukewarm water sets you right for the rest of the day. I always do the last two laps on my back, which sometimes adds to the sensation by sightings of the moon, some exciting clouds or the magnolia flowers on the adjacent tree or occasionally a tropical bird. Staring up into the heavens always makes me think of a quote ascribed Abraham Lincoln when he said: "I can understand that men can look upon the earth and say there is no God, but I cannot understand how anyone can look upon the stars in the heaven and say there is no God." He also allegedly said in an election campaign: "I have been accused of having two faces, but I put it to you that were that true, why would I be wearing this one?"

But back to the morning's course of events. At 7.00AM I had showered and dressed and I put the final touches to my luggage as I was about to be picked up by a taxi at 8.00AM. I packed a deck of cards, some cufflinks, a foldable bag and my current reading by Tolstoy as the last few items. I brought my four pieces of luggage to the front door and put on the kettle for a cup of tea. I also checked the PC for any hotmail, but no catch this time, so I checked the www.ft.com for the markets position at the end of the week. At 7.30 AM Jennifer showed up and took Pixie, our Sydney Silkie Terrier, for a walk. I had a cup of tea and a banana as we were out of bread. Also quickly read the local news paper which had an article on New Zealand suggesting that NZ was on it's way down the ranking list of OECD countries, having slid from second place in the fifties to 22nd of 26 now. Don Brash, the governor of the reserve bank had that very week warned against excessive and poorly targeted social spending, which inevitably reduced the country's options in other areas. But he was promptly put in place by the politicians who reminded him that he was hired to run the Reserve Bank and not the country.

I also stopped our grand pa clock, because if it runs down its weights to the floor, the ringing gets out of sync with the time and it is quite an effort to get it back into sync again. I love the clock from Sweden – it speaks to us every half-hour and it always seems to be in a good mood. One of these pieces that over time gets to be crucial for your feeling of home. The bank won't pay for moving clocks, or pianos or dogs, but in our case we think that these are necessary for us to feel at home. And given that we have been 'on the road' for over fifteen years, we don't like the idea of postponing life till tomorrow. We like to live good quality life now!

Just before eight I gave Jennifer a bear hug and a kiss and said good bye to Pixie, and Errol was kind enough to see me out and help get my luggage in the taxi. By 8.30AM I was checked in for SQ 12 to Los Angeles via Tokyo, which was my destination this first Saturday of August, anno 2001. No queuing and very efficient check in. And my checked luggage weighed only 26 kg compared to my allowance of 30kgs. My hand roller and suits however would have weighed well over ten kilos but none seemed to bother about that and it was very easy to move thanks to the smart design. I also brought my tennis racket, as I wouldn't want to run the risk of missing any early game in Tokyo. The previous Thursday night I had played three sets with my friends and they were kind enough to arrange the teams so that I won all three sets – happy day.

Once I had checked in I thought I should get some more money to ensure I would get by for a week or two. So I went to the DBS ATM machine and tried to get $ 2,000 but it had a $ 1,000 limit so I had to make do with that and got another Yen 70,000 from the OUB currency exchange. I was going to set up a City bank account but needed enough to see me through that process and transferring money from Singapore to Tokyo.

Then through the passport control and up to the lounge. I looked for the week-end Financial Times, but they only had yesterdays so I had some apple juice and a muffin instead. The lounge was quite full, as airport lounges tend to be these days, so quite often you are better off in the public area, at least at Changi, the best airport in the world. I read a few pages in my Tolstoy book and then decided to buy one or two bottles to bring to Tokyo. On my own I never drink other than perhaps a beer before bed, but when Linda is there we sometimes like to have a GT together at the end of a long day. Special offer was two 'Bombay Sapphire' blue Gin for $ 40.50 and a back pack for anyone who buys two. Now there was a deal I couldn't walk away from. I knew bargains would be far and few between in Tokyo. When the attendant looked in her drawers for my complimentary back pack, they were out of stock, but I said I am happy to take the one on the display. So I stuffed my two bottles of blue gin in my backpack, put it over my shoulder and mover on towards gate D12. I still could move quite swiftly which was good because the gate was at the very end of all the long corridors. When I arrived at the gate there were no other passengers there so I could walk straight onto the plane – very easy and comfortable.

The Singapore Girl took my suits and my silk jacket I was wearing and I got the rest of my gear in the overhead locker after taking out some papers on Japan, the Economist and my book. I asked for the weekend FT but again was told they didn't have it, so I settled for the Wall Street Journal. I started the day with a glass of Perrier and dived into the newspaper and magazine, sucking in anything Japanese. The last three months I had read everything I could find on Japan to improve my understanding of current issues before my arrival. The Economist had Koizumi, the new Japanese Prime Minister, on the front page in recognition of his recent landslide election victory. His popularity is unprecedented partly due to his personal style and partly due to his commitment to improve on and change established practices to get the country going again. In terms of growth there has been virtually none in Japan for about ten years. However one must remember that Japan is still the second biggest economy in the world with amongst the highest personal incomes. More than 60 % of Asia's total GDP is generated by Japan –quite a staggering number. Will he be able to get things moving again? We will see. There are quite a few difficult issues including a very high level of non-performing loans in the banking system and significant government indebtedness. But over time one would have to believe that the Japanese work ethic, the high level of education and the cohesive nature of the country must bring further prosperity and success.

Reading The Economist of the 4th August 2001 I found quite an interesting article on 'The Truth About the Environment'. It suggested that: energy and other natural resources have become more abundant, not less; more food is now produced per head of the world's population than at any time in history and fewer people are starving. Although species are becoming extinct, only about 0.7 % of them are expected to disappear in the next 50 years or so – not 25 – 50 % as has been predicted. The price of solar energy has fallen by half in every decade for the last thirty years, and appears likely to do so in future. The economist index of prices of industrial raw materials has dropped some 80 % in inflation adjusted terms since 1845. Agricultural production in the developing world has increased by 52 % per person since 1961. The daily food intake in poor countries has increased from 1932 calories, barely enough for survival, in 1961 to 2650 calories in 1998. The proportion of people in developing countries who are starving has dropped from 45 % in 1949 to 18 % today, and is expected to decline even further to 12 % in 2010 and just 6 % in 2030. Since 1800 food prices have decreased by more than 90% and in 2000, according to the World Bank, prices were lower than ever before. The growth rate of the human population reached its peak, of more than 2 % per year, in the early 1960's. The rate of increase has been declining ever since. It is now 1.26 % and expected to decline to 0.46 % in 2050. Pollution diminishes when a society becomes rich enough to be able to afford to be concerned about the environment. For London, the city for which the best data are available, air pollution peaked around 1890. Today the air is cleaner than it has been since 1585. The world's single most pressing health problem is providing universal access to clean drinking water and sanitation, but that aside, there is a danger that we are all driven by too pessimistic scenarios painted by the media, because that is what people like to read.

That was a bit of a lengthy sidetrack, but that is, I believe, how minds work, at least mine. You are on to something new – you get a strong impulse – and you go off the main path to see what more you can learn.

The guy sitting next to me, an American in his thirties, seemed quite a seasoned traveler. He had ordered vegetarian, but when delivered he didn't want it. He only took water and tea during the whole trip and fished out his own bowl of foods out of his brief case and he was very short on the verge of being unfriendly to the attendants.

After the papers I dived into my Tolstoy – he being my most admired author this year after reading 'The Kingdom of God is Within You' recommended by Gandhi as his favorite. I was served scallops and shrimps together with gnocki in a nice sauce and I had one or two glasses of California white with it. Quite comfortable and enjoyable even if the quality of food rarely measures up to a good meal on the ground. Then I slept for half an hour and realised we were almost there – after six hours and twenty minutes in the air. With one hour time difference it was now 5.20 PM. I collated all my gear including my 'Bombay Sapphire' and tennis racket and proceeded towards immigration. It was quite hot around 30 degrees – not dissimilar to Singapore – but less efficient air conditioning.

I didn't know how much booze I was allowed to bring but no one seemed to mind my two bottles. My checked luggage came through fast, I got through customs and immediately saw the driver with the Frank Olsson, National Australia Bank sign. He took over my cart, led me to his President limousine, and we were away to Tokyo. Big comfortable car with a fold out stool to rest your feet on and lots of high tech panels that I didn't touch. The driver who was wearing white gloves drove 140 km / hr and I checked for the seat belt but couldn't find the two pieces – never mind. I finished my Tolstoy short story and then just looked around, as it was getting a bit dark for reading. The ride in is at first quite green and then through residential areas and quite uninteresting. We passed at least two road tolls. At 7.15 PM after 75 minutes we arrived to Oakwood Apartments in Akasaka and I had a very friendly and efficient check-in.

Up to twelfth floor to our unit 1201. Very nice looking with wooden floors only to be trodden by bare feet or in sox. Two bedrooms, nice bathroom and kitchen and everything driven by panels on the wall. Bath is by electronic display, toilet quite sophisticated with full rear shower, nice balcony and views and Internet connection – everything was there. The hotel had put some necessities in the fridge and my relocation firm had added some fruits so I would be fine for several days. Very kind, considerate and service oriented. I unpacked and then decided to go for a walk. It was dark already at 7.00PM but then it got light at 5.00 AM in the morning. Obviously it would be beneficial with daylight savings time and I was told that Japan is now considering this.

After less than an hour's walk finding many small shops and restaurants in the neighbourhood, I went back to the hotel with some eggs, sodas and some beers. I again ran through all the bank papers I had on Japan, read a little and fell asleep. The next day my mission was to find the Bank office. Since I had never been there before I wanted to make sure I knew where it was before my starting date on Monday.

In the morning I had a bath and a good breakfast of egg, fruits, cereal and tea with toast – and thought of the saying 'Breakfast like a king, lunch as a prince and dinner as a pauper' for good health. I put some maps and writing paper together with my glasses and my Tolstoy, my red Malaysian hat for sun protection, and an umbrella, all in my Sapphire backpack – what would I do without it? – and went down with the lift. There was a girl there attending the front desk and I asked her for the fare on the Ginza line to Nihonbashi. She typed in something on her computer and said Y 160, 3.7 km and 13 minutes ride. I showed her my business card and said I was the new general manager and now I was looking for my bank. She then photocopied the general area where it was located and I thought I was rather well equipped to find it. And I must admit that she gave me a lot more help and direction that I had expected. She marked an area right next to Takishimaya Department store and said it should be in that area.

The entrance to the underground – the Tameike-Sanno station, was only 100 yards from the Hotel. I paid my fare got on the train and saw daylight again in Nihonbashi. (There were four lines at my station to choose from so of eight different options I managed to pick the right one.) I walked around the blocks she had indicated a few times – knowing that the bank was located at street level I thought I would soon stumble on the Banks logo and name. After half an hour I started to ask people I met showing them the address as written on my new business card and the map I was holding. Four different people sent me around in circles until I met a guy who said I was in the wrong area altogether and needed to go five ten minutes in another direction. Now was this guy right and all the others wrong? What he said did in fact make sense so I did as he said and felt I got closer. Outside the Mitsui building I again asked a guy and he indicated a side street. I went in there and looked and walked on and suddenly I stood before the sign I was looking for 'National Australia Bank'– happy day!! Took me only 90 minutes and as a side benefit I now know my way around the area really well. I should have gone one more stop with the sub way to Mitsukoshimae, which of course was valuable intelligence for the next day. And its funny how the human brain works – I was sure I would never forget how to find it as long as I live. I was also wondering if we perhaps shouldn't write on our cards 'behind Mitsui Building' but that is probably too unorthodox to ever happen. Our proud bank wouldn't want to recognise that it is behind anything. Perhaps a better option is to say in front of Bank of Japan, which is on the other side.

Given that the train ride was 3.7 km it seemed like a good idea to walk back to the hotel as it couldn't really take more than an hour. I started my walk and headed for the Emperor's Palace as Akasaka is just a little bit west of the vast park area and the office is a bit east of it. Weather was lovely with a thin veil covering the sun and temperatures in the high twenties now at noon. Approaching the Palace there were so many people walking and cycling and running and the adjacent street was closed off for car traffic. I walked along the moat and looked at all the trees and the green grass and well kept paths and the many people taking pictures and enjoying their Sunday. I stopped in at the public toilet there and as everything else around the Palace, it was immaculate. In spite of the many years of economic stagnation people looked very happy and thriving. I sat down on a curb stone to write down a few notes and couldn't but feel quite warm and happy. What a great opportunity for me and my family. After one hour of writing some notes I had to move another 100 yards just to get the blood flowing in my rear again and then I sat down for a few final observations. At the end of the big park grounds there were some nice sofas/benches so I sat down again to further enjoy all the people, the nice weather and brought out my Tolstoy book to finish my short story. I read the final three four pages of the story and as usual got quite moved by his fine writing and touching stories.

This particular story "Two Old men" written in 1885 was about two pilgrims who have saved for a long time to go on their trip of a life time to Jerusalem. One of them stops in at a small hut to ask for some water and finds a family dying for lack of food and prospects and he says to his companion to continue without him, as he will catch up once he has given some help to the family. He gives them some food and help and then is on his way – but he turns back – realising that unless he gives more thorough assistance they are not going to make it. So he spends almost all his travel budget on the family and returns home without money. This is an extract from the last two pages relating how the first Pilgrim who gets to Jerusalem on his way back happens to stop in with the same family:

'Efim thanked the woman and praised her for her kindness to a pilgrim. The woman shook her head. "We have good reason to be good to pilgrims," she said. "It was a pilgrim who showed us what life is. We were living forgetful of God, and God punished us almost to death. We reached such a pass last summer that we all lay ill, helpless with nothing to eat. And we should have died, but that God sent an old man to help us – just such a one as you. He came in one day to ask for a drink of water, saw the state we were in, took pity on us, and remained with us. He gave us food and drink, and set us on our feet again; and he redeemed our land, and brought a cart and horse and gave them to us. "

Here the old woman entering the hut, interrupted her and said: "We don't know if it was a man, or an angel from God. He loved us all, pitied us all, and went away without telling us his name, so that we don't even know whom to pray for. I can see it all before me now! There I lay waiting for death, when in comes a bald-headed man. He was not anything much to look at and he asked for a drink of water. I, sinner that I am, thought to myself: 'What does he come prowling about here for?' And just think what he did! As soon as he saw us he let down his bag, on this very spot and untied it. Had he not come we should all have died in our sins. We were dying in despair, murmuring against God and man. But he set us on our feet again; and through him we learned to know God, and to believe that there is good in man. May the lord bless him! We used to live like animals; he made human beings of us." And Efim thought: God may or may not have accepted my pilgrimage, but he certainly accepted his!'

When I finished the story I walked out of the Palace Grounds towards the Diet (parliament) building and up Roppongi Dori until I came to the Akasaka neighborhood where my hotel was. The time was now 3.30PM and I had a meal of rice, meat, miso soup and vegetables, all for Y 480, in one of many little Japanese restaurants. Then back to the nearby hotel, checked the CNN for news and thought how uninteresting and time consuming these news programs are. One is much better off skimming the Internet or a newspaper where one is not pry to their choice of news and also not forced to spend time on boring advertisement. In Singapore I never watched TV, which allowed a lot of time for quality reading and other more important things. I took a short nap, read through all my Tokyo strategy papers once again and went out for a walk to Roppongi at 6.00PM. There I found another Supermarket and stocked up on a few more things we would need - olive oil, salad, wine, and detergent, softener and some dish washing liquid. Most of it fitted in my Sapphire bag. On my way back I got a take-out hamburger and had that with some salad and a beer at my place before checking the news, reading a bit and retiring from my first day in Tokyo thinking about the many adventures lying ahead.

5th August 2001.

6. *Akihabara*

Saturday15th September I woke up in Yoyogi-Uehara one of the suburbs of Tokyo less than ten km from the Imperial Palace. We had just been through our first night in our new home when I at 7.00AM decided to take Pixie out. Pixie, our Sydney Silkie Terrier, arrived the day before from Singapore where she had been in a dog pension for three weeks awaiting clearance for Tokyo. If this dog was pretty ordinary when we bought her as a pup she is now quite valuable if we add up all the investment in her body and tours of the world. Having broken her leg once and then been moved from Auckland to Singapore and now from Singapore to Tokyo she owes us ca NZ$ 10,000 – and growing. Will she ever pay it back? If you ask Linda she already has, many times over. If I wasn't so ignorant I would understand that it falls under this rather new concept of intangible value. When it comes to family and dogs all economic theory falls flat on its face.

As much as this is written to make you smile and chuckle, there is a serious flaw in traditional economic theory. It does in fact ignore so many essentials for more obvious easy to perceive and measure cost and benefit. Both in the corporate world and among governments sub-optimal goals are pursued that may give good and regular benefits, but which over time erode value(s) and causes 'sparks' that once set in motion can reduce accumulated capital value to nil and negative in a matter of seconds. The answer to this is a much stronger commitment to values, ethics, love and tolerance – i.e. quality of life issues totally ignored by accountants, corporate managements and often governments.

This is the week of the terrible carnage among innocent American's in New York and Washington D.C. There is not a day when I don't feel a little bit sick about the death toll and suffering and it is all made extra tangible by my having visited these places – it is all so familiar – it could have been me. One of my favorite spots on Manhattan is Battery Park, now probably covered under rubble. When you hear on the radio about war on terrorism and many (though, thank God, not all) calling for massive bombing and destruction of 'them' it gets a bit scary. The biggest risk in this horrific incident is an overreaction. Wrong can never be corrected with wrong. Evil can never be corrected by evil. It is not 'the thing' you need to deal with and exterminate – it is the mother of the thing.

What is the mother of the thing? The mother of the thing is hate, prejudice, and intolerance. There is a notion that all of a certain religion are evil – this is wrong. There is a notion that some people are not like us and can be treated and mistreated at arm's length

with sophisticated remote control weapons. This is wrong. There has been a notion that that people of certain political inclination, i.e. socialists or even communists are evil and should be kept down before they do any harm. This is wrong. You cannot fight ideas and opinions with bullets. Ideas have no mass, bullets don't bite on them. Ideas need to be argued out with transparency, honesty, understanding and love. The last word is and will be the key. From hate and violence you can expect nothing but hate and violence. Paul's letter to the Corinthian's 1: 13: 13 refers: "And now these three remain: faith, hope and love. But the greatest of these is love."

I also find it impressive that the many phone calls that have been referred to from people about to die in this weeks horror attacks spoke neither of revenge nor hate – the one word that is in all the calls without fail is Love. It is now up to all of us, Americans and non-Americans, Muslims and Jews, Christians and Hindu, Asians and non Asian's to work on paying more heed to tone down greed and intolerance and imbue all and everything with empathy and Love.

American's (and others) have supported many evil persons and leaders under the common enemy theory. If someone dislikes someone I dislike, he must be worthy of my friendship and support. When put clearly like this any reader can see the madness of it. Evil and self serving leaders were supported in Vietnam because they said they were anti communist, the wrong people were supported in Japan after the war because they were against Socialism (as per the book I am currently reading: "The Yamamoto Dynasty" by Sterling Seagrave), the wrong leaders in many Latin American countries have been supported because they are 'on our side.' If you bring a lot of manifest criminals and crooks on to your side because of the 'common enemy' theory you will get widespread disbelief and discontent.

Many of the populous in the countries mentioned had little idea of political left or right – first and foremost they need water and bread and shelter to survive. Let's widen our thinking and see it how it is. I would like to believe that the world is getting better, but much remains to be done. And we must have the integrity to stand up for Love and ethics and not put people in positions of trust that do not work for the common good! This incidentally is all inclusive - industry, schools and government. There is no business, no human activity, which is not ultimately about creating Love and happiness. Deviate from these concepts and there will inevitably be negative reactions.

Back to Pixie who is now getting a bit anxious to get out. The way the world works the previous five paragraphs is just some thoughts developed over time and on a Saturday morning they can run through one's mind in less than a minute. So the dog hasn't in frustration done it on the carpet but is very keen and happy to get out. Our first walk together in the neighborhood. Outside our building I meet a neighbor lady with another little dog and after introducing ourselves I ask her what she does with the dog during trips. This can be a big headache. She informs me that one of our neighbors has a boy who is good and keen and to help out. I am pleased to hear that.

A big black crow sits and laughs on one of the many electrical wires of which Japan is so full and leaves a big dropping just behind me. Or so I think – later when I come home it transpires that some of it landed on the back of my shirt, great! Little narrow streets in a calm and quiet part of town. Quite idyllic really. Makes me think of my child hood summers. Temperatures are about 25 degrees. I am told that we need to get into October before the weather cools down to a more pleasant level. Pixie is happy – finds many poles to not only lean against. We walk a big round on little streets and come back again about half an hour later. A side benefit of this early morning walk is that I have identified three dry cleaners and a few nearby restaurants and grocery shops.

Back at the apartment I try to adjust the air conditioning system as it is a bit too cold and the windows are all dripping with moist. I make myself a cup of tea, have a quick breakfast, and attack some of our yet unpacked boxes. The unpacked ones are all books, twenty-three boxes of them. Andre,' our 15 year old, asks why would anyone want to move so many read books around the world? The answer is because we like them and many of them are for reference, i.e. different kind of dictionaries and Encyclopedia. Linda wants them all in alphabetical order by author so now begins quite a puzzle. But we have done it before and we can do it again. Around nine o'clock when the others are up I suggest we go to Akihabara to get TV, Video, VCD and a good stereo player. Andre' is a bit hesitant to joining but decides in favour after a while.

At 9.45AM we are on our way in the Bank's nice Toyota luxury car. We get to Akihabara in twenty minutes and as it is so early there are plenty of curb side parking places. I am not sure whether it is legal parking but the car is well out of the way and it all looks pretty much ok. Akihabara is almost one hundred per cent electronics, i.e. PC, TV, Radio, Communications, Home Appliances and the like. We find the recommended LAOX shop and enter one of them – there are several on either side of the street. After about half an hour there we realize we are in the wrong building as we want export models that can run on either 100 Voltage or 220. So we cross the road to the other side. Before we went into the second shop, I ran to the car to see that the parking looked ok and there were no signs of any trouble. We are told that the 6th floor has Radio and TV with accessories.

On the sixth floor there are so many TVs and Recorded music players and after looking around a bit we ask one of the attendants: Do you speak English? Some speak no English at all and others say a little, but as the Japanese generally are understated, a little often is all you need to get through to the final purchase. We see a TV with built in Video tape recorder which we like, but soon we learn that for some reason that cannot also take a VCD player. So we look at another TV and then at the accessories, i.e. the tape player and the VCD-player. We were hoping that these would come in one, but that is not possible so we have to take two pieces. Things are complicated by our desire to have all the gear adaptable to the 220 system in New Zealand and Sweden.

After about an hour of to-ing and fro-ing and having some first choices rejected for technical or compatibility reasons we have a list of items specified. In addition we needed new plugs for all the electrical things we had brought including Linda's PC with accessories. We had already changed plugs four times on all our gear on our odyssey around the world, but this time we also needed to buy transformers for our goods – a new level of challenge and sophistication. We got all those and finally I bought a little tape playing radio so I could listen to my Japanese Teacher's tape recordings. This choosing and buying process took us nearly two hours and when we walked out the salesman came running after us and said unless we chose a bigger TV the two accessories couldn't be fitted into the back of the TV and one had to be fitted in the front. So we said – lets have the bigger one then. So I had to go back up and pay once again – the 25-inch TV being Yen 19,000 more expensive than the 21 inch one. When he started to add all the twenty or so items once again I suggested that why don't I just pay 19,000 and get out of here. He said that that would not be conversant with their book keeping and delivery systems so I had to spend another 15 minutes seeing the sales man add it all up again. He was quite kind and professional, but after over two hours I was getting fed up with TVs and radios and wanted to get out.

On the street again we walked to the car and put some of the things in the boot – the majority of things would be delivered the following Monday together with setting up service by the firm. At this stage Andre' got a bit sour as he felt he had spent so many hours just waiting for us to complete our shopping. As we seemed to have a good parking space we decided to have a quick lunch in Akihabara as well. We found an Italian style spaghetti bar and had some of that with a couple of café lattes. Back at the car after lunch, Linda offered to take Andre' to a buy a computer game. It was really quite pleasurable in the early afternoon with lovely weather and hundreds of people swarming on the main street, which was at this stage cut off from traffic. While I was waiting I thought I would buy a kettle, which I did.

When I got back to the car Linda and Andre' were already there looking annoyed at what I thought was waiting for me. However, in those last few minutes we had got a parking ticket and a big yellow plastic thing attached to the grill of the car. On the ticket was written some very large and harsh looking Japanese signs and as I couldn't understand it I looked around to see if I could see the attendant or the police. And, yes across the road there was another policeman and I hurried across to ask for instructions. I gave the officer my ticket and was asked to produce my driver's license and I pulled out my Swedish license, which was my most current one. The policeman started to talk to me actively and I didn't understand a word. He also pulled his manual out and didn't find Swedish licenses among those favored by Japanese authorities. As he saw my small family across the street by the car he motioned to them to come across so that we all could move over to the police station. I realized that if not bailed out by unexpected luck I would be down several thousands of yen, but at the same time I thought it all an interesting experience.

We marched about 200 yards on to the police station and got to the third floor 'SAN KEY' and Linda and Andre sat down outside the interrogation room and I went in. I was asked if didn't have any other license and I said and wrote down on a piece of paper that in fact I had five licenses: one Swedish, one U K, one New Zealand, one Singapore and one International. They asked me to produce my international one and I said the only one I carry is the Swedish one and all others are at my home at Yoyogi Uehara. After some internal discussions between the four or so police on my case I was asked to go and get my international license, which I agreed to do. I asked if I could take the car, but – you guessed it - no, that was not possible. I would have to take the train.

At five o'clock I arrived back at the police station with all my new papers and evidence. I took the elevator to the third floor and walked into the same office for parking violations and sat down and put my international driver's license on the table together with all my other licenses. 1 – an international drivers license issued 1986, 2 – a UK drivers license, 3 – a New Zealand drivers License, 4 – a Singapore driver's license together with my Swedish license and my passport including my previous passport. They asked if I had a German or French license and I said no, but then I saw the European stars on the Swedish one and suggested this was of the European Union.

I was told that there is no such thing as the European Union License. I also was told that my international license had expired which I refuted. 1986 was the year of issue and there was no expiry date! I was told that International licenses are always valid for one year only. I pointed out that there was nothing on the document suggesting that and I thought my international license still valid. Since we couldn't really understand each other she called her male boss somewhere and he told me over the phone that the parking violation was the small offence – driving without a valid license was another matter. I repeated that I had four valid country licenses and the International one was also still valid as per its face value.

At this stage I think they were getting tired of me so the manager at the other end of the line said that in this case they would make an exception and not pursue me for driving without a license but I must get a valid license before I could drive again. That's fine I said, but what do I do with the car. "You have to call a friend with a Japanese license who takes the car away." I said I don't have a Japanese friend to call since I am new to the country. But on Monday I could ask a colleague at the Bank to come and get the car. So the wisdom was that a police officer would follow me to the car and drive the car to the police station garage and park it there and I would come back on Monday at 9.00 A.M. with a friend possessing a valid local license to pick the car up. 'KANPEKI DESU' I said which is one of the few Japanese words I have learnt which means 'perfect.'

Before I left I had to sign some paper in Japanese – totally ineligible to me – but at this stage my options looked like signing or sitting there all night. So I signed and walked out of there with all the things we had in the boot. I didn't want to keep my family from enjoying music in our new apartment just because of a parking violation. So I took the tube back with all that gear and changed lines twice. No major problem but, because of the heat and humidity, when I ultimately got home just before seven I was totally soaking wet and quite tired. Still in good spirits though, I hasten to add. The parking fee alone was Yen 50,000 and for a memorable experience like that and three hour prime parking in Akihabara, that wasn't too bad. What you cannot cure you have to endure and not allow it to eat you. It put a 20 pct premium on the gear we had bought but who cares? And I guess a high fee helps you remember that creative parking in Japan is not a good idea. On Monday I would get the car and then pursue a proper local license with urgency.

A long and interesting day. I thought of the saying – "if it wasn't for bad luck, I wouldn't have had any luck at all" but I also thought of the latest week's shocking occurrences and in that context my insignificant misfortune paled away completely. Just happy to be alive and having a fine family and a nice expensive dog and lot of wonderful friends. And true to my commitment that any day with extraordinary mood swings I will always try to record my feelings in writing hoping that it may provide interesting reading.

I thank you for your time and for being with me to the end.

16th September 2001

Epilogue

Or almost to the end:

Monday morning I talked to my kind assistant and she said I have just the person you need and by 9.00 A.M. Mr Kyuma Kanrei appeared and we took a taxi to Akihabara. He was well dressed in a dark suit, as was I. We walked into the police station towards the lifts when asked from the front desk where we were going and I said we are seeing my friends (TOMODACHI) on the third floor. Mr Kanrei said something in Japanese and we went up to the third floor. He bowed deeply down to the level of the desk three times and I tried to follow suit. I had asked him to please ask the lady to see what I signed last Saturday, which he did and explained that all there was, was a commitment not to park illegally again. He wrote something more on a piece of paper, which I signed. I then asked if I could pay the fine then and there and he said not to worry. The female police officer asked me if I had been very worried over the weekend, and I said yes. All smiles and laughs and we were escorted to the car, the clamp was taken off and we were away, courtesy of the Tokyo police department. My parting comment to the lady Police officer was DOZO YOROSHIKU O-NEGAI SHIMASU, which, according to my lovely Japanese language teacher, is used when you just have met someone (please think well of me from now on). No expulsion, no prison, no fine – just a bunch of lovely policemen, and a new great acquaintance, Kayuma Kanrei. It seemed that through divine intervention it all turned out to be a blessing in disguise. Two days later I got my Japanese license by a simple transfer without any test.

7. Anna Karenina.

Tomorrow I am going on a trip to Auckland for a few days, then to Melbourne for two days and later to Singapore for two days. I haven't been to Auckland for almost a year and it will be lovely to see my son Felix, and many other friends. Arriving 2.30 PM on the Friday I have already agreed drinks with my ex colleagues at 5.00 PM that day and then my friend and previous colleague has invited fourteen people for BBQ dinner at 7.00PM in her home. The guests include the Tablises, our Russian friends from St Petersburg. He, Mikhail, is a very distinguished musician and she is a language teacher. Another couple is John and Margaret Andrew – he an artist and painter and also very much a philosopher and she is a very accomplished person as well, working for local government. There are also the couple, Peter and Kip, where he is a prominent conductor and she is a violinist in the symphony orchestra. Then a law firm partner and his new wife, Dermot and Sheena, great people who joined us for a party in the dessert outside Petra, Jordan a couple of years ago. And then Vanessa and Antony whom we last met in Milano six months ago. And of course the hosts, Heather and Geoff, Heather being my ex-colleague and Geoff now a long time friend who we have shared fun with in New Zealand as well as in Israel, Jordan, Sweden and more recently in Singapore and Malaysia. Heather will arrange a BBQ dinner and I promised to bring the wine and bread from the shops next door to my house in Ponsonby. Felix, my son would join me for the BBQ dinner – he loves the people too. The artist John painted Felix's portrait two years ago. I had printed out song sheets for the evening as well with the old favorites like O sole mio, Cabaret, and Giggolo chosen either for nice lyrics or happy tunes or ideally for the combination.

The next day, Saturday I am looking forward to taking the car – yes we have left our old Mercedes for Felix to enjoy while we are away – to the nearby north shore, ten minutes drive over the Harbour Bridge, and spend a couple of ours in the sunrise on the beach going for a long walk, watching the ships come and go and go into the big waves a few times to enjoy the delight of peak summer swimming. A real highlight. I will also go with Felix to the local travel agent to get him a round trip to Europe for his three weeks July break. I am keen that he sees his relatives in Sweden at least once a year. This travel agent is special – when our Singapore agent couldn't manage to get our train tickets for Europe, going from Rome to Milan to Vienna to Prague to Berlin to Stockholm we contacted the little bureau on Ponsonby Road who made all the bookings and sent us the Europe ticket to Singapore. Marvelous quality kiwi service. For 12.00 noon I have arranged a lunch in Devonport, the quaintest little harbour village across from downtown Auckland. We will meet at the Evergreens bookshop – a second hand bookshop where I always stop in to get a new bag of books. The most wonderful old books on philosophy each normally cost less than ten kiwi dollars – a real bargain. In Devonport I have agreed to meet up with my old friends Ray and Mandy, he being a doctor and she a management consultant. Also absolutely wonderful people. The four of us including Felix would have a basic nourishing lunch at the nearby café, The Manuka, two minutes away from the book shop on the corner of the main street – all lined with beautiful palm trees and having a wonderful view over the blue Pacific Ocean. Really an idyllic place, particularly in the midst of summer. I am greatly looking forward to catching up and the discussion on how to spread more joy and happiness around. I think that is what brings us all together, a desire to try to put life in perspective, promote fun and laughter, and not get caught up in any mundane (self – inflicted) misery.

In the afternoon I will go back to the beach, exercising caution not to get burned, swim a little and read one of the new bought books. One I will particularly look for is Anna Karenina by Tolstoy. Having recently insatiably read all of Tolstoy I have been able to lay my hands on I am just dying to read this one as well. I think he is a fantastic writer.

By four o'clock I am taking a nap and then seeing some friends over dinner at a Ponsonby road restaurant, just around the corner. I will also go and say hello to my friend the green grocer, of Indian extraction. He always asks for investment advice and I much enjoy talking to him and my advice is always general rather than specific as I think the broader picture is ok to discuss but specific choices must be made by the investor himself or herself. We used to have reversed negotiations about price where he was trying to round down and I insisted on rounding up. Half of the time he would get his way and half of the time I would round up – quite a lovely experience. He would always go to the backroom to get me choice product. Total trust and respect. Friendship!

Sunday morning I have a game of tennis arranged for nine o'clock with my friend Paul Hargreaves. I emailed Paul and he rounded up two other friends for a morning doubles over two hours followed by a coffee with muffins and some more philosophizing in their lovely garden. I am a little bit younger than the other guys so my running for every ball compensates to an extent for my lesser skills and we play some even and very fun games.

Then back to the house and a walk to High Street to see my friends at Unity Book shop. Carolyn there has been fantastic – calling me when I worked there, saying we have this new book that you should read. I always bought what she had – she knew my interest and I trusted her judgment – quite lovely really. When I see her again, I will just ask her what she wants to sell me and I will take that and ask no questions. Once I ordered Cato and Varro on Agriculture – written 2000 years ago, and it arrived when I was on holiday. It was a very expensive book with every other page in Latin and every other page in English. When they called my office and heard I was overseas on holiday my wonderful staff bought the book and sent it to me as a present. I loved the book and more so considering how it was acquired. It was mentioned in St Augustine's writing so I reckoned it would be worthwhile and it was. If I can't find Anna Karenina in Devonport I am sure I can here.

For Sunday afternoon I will try to entice a few friends including Felix and any of his friends, to join me and go to Kare Kare, the most beautiful and stunning beach on the west coast about 45 minutes drive away. The west coast is perfect for late afternoon as the sun sets in the Tasman Sea and it becomes therapeutically warm and lovely in the sand beneath the high hills facing the ocean and the setting sun. Swimming on the west coast one needs to be careful, as the waves are very high. It is beautiful beyond belief. When I took a Swedish friend there who visited New Zealand for two weeks she said that the visit to Kare Kare alone justified the expensive fare from Sweden to New Zealand. This is the beach that the film 'The Piano' is said to have been filmed on. Spectacular.

Monday I will work all day on my project with Mary-Jane together with whom I have been asked to run a seminar in Melbourne on Diversity, i.e. making sure that all people in our organization grow and have fun and are treated with love and care. The last ten years I have been trying to understand motivation and happiness a bit better and love the idea of running a seminar on it. My wife, Linda had gathered twenty very suitable songs, and I intend to use music throughout my presentation to try to help building perspective and fun and to get the sentiments through. For lunch we will gather a handful of ex colleagues and discuss the issues and get a bit of feedback on what the real issues are.

Monday night I plan to have dinner with a few colleagues in town, walking distance from our house. On Tuesday I had intended to speak on happiness and motivation at a breakfast but the logistics didn't work out so will have to defer to next trip. Tuesday at 11.00AM I will participate in a teleconference and at that stage we should have worked out all the details around our seminar. Lunchtime we will go to the airport for our 3.00PM flight. Beautiful airport, Auckland airport, where I know the management well and where I have also invested a little money. Everyday I follow the share price of my few investments in the Financial Times and Auckland Airport has done well in spite of the challenges facing aviation since 11 September. Up, up and away. On the flight I will be checking on the seminar materials and if comfortable with that, also spend some time with Anna Karenina, with whom I am much looking forward to acquainting myself.

In Melbourne I have a dinner planned with Ken and Wendy, newly married. Ken is a doctor of accounting and spends his life with great enthusiasm trying to make sense of intangible accounting. This is a very important work. What it means is trying to assess and include the value of all these things we know are so important but get left out of traditional accounting, because they are difficult to measure. I have told him that this art holds the key to avoiding things like the 11th September shock. If we understood better the resentment that arises from ignorance, mistreatment, poverty, arrogance and misuse of power, it would become obvious even in economic terms that our conduct isn't very constructive and smart. In whatever you do you must consider what bad will or goodwill you generate. If greed takes over and care and empathy with fellow man is ignored, things are bound to ignite from time to time. Looking at the hundreds of billions of dollars cost of 11 September and its aftermath I reflect that if only a fraction of this money had been spent in trying to mitigate the causes of it, it may well have been possible to avoid altogether. On the Wednesday we will work through our program once again, have lunch with a few colleagues and discuss the issues – and I will no doubt be asked to give my impressions of Japan as well – and I will see what pans out for dinner.

I have also set up meetings with colleagues I work with in Credit, Audit and Risk Management in order to nurture friendships and networks. Here I want to emphasize the importance of courtesy and good manners, something Peter Drucker, the management guru wrote about. When we tell people no, or disappoint them in one way or another, which is inevitable from time to time, we should take the time to position the negative message to avoid a total turn off. Making anyone unhappy or disappointed has a cost because enthusiasm and energy levels fall. With just a little bit of empathy and time, these lows can be mitigated and perhaps avoided altogether. Enthusiasm and energy together with creativity are not captured by traditional accounting, but that doesn't mean that these things don't exist, and that they when aggregated have tremendous value, perhaps more than any other asset category.

Thursday I hope the seminar goes well and that we can make the participants truly amazed with the message and the music and the energy and fun. I have the idea that we sit in a circle with no desks to make more of a community. Interactive it has to be. One thing I have thought about is that it is important to be respect-less. And respectful. The fact that we are talking to senior managers, in fact our seniors by hierarchy, mustn't in any way allow messages to be inhibited. All men (and women) are created equal and part of a good working environment is to cherish reason and energy and to de-emphasize authority and organizational standing because so often they become turn-offs and put downs.

Thursday afternoon I will be off to the airport again for the six hour flight to Singapore arriving at 9.30PM. so expect to be at the Intercontinental Hotel an hour later, as Singapore is the most efficient airport and transport City in the world. Then I will go to bed with Anna, Anna Karenina that is, and enjoy her for about an hour. Friday I will start with a swim in the pool – Singapore is wonderful for that; I really like the heat after more than 35 years in chilly Sweden. By nine I will be in the offices in nearby Suntec City to have meetings with my colleagues in the bank and also to see all the good people in the branch there. After two years with them I developed some solid friendships and am keen to nurture these and to see them again. I have a lunch planned with the management team of eight or so at the Cricket Club. It is lovely there on the veranda looking over the Pandang and the Raffles City skyline at the end and the ocean to the right. This was my favorite eating place when in Singapore. Easy, casual, cheap, friendly – what else do you need. Love perhaps, but there is plenty of that too. And next door is the Victoria Theatre and behind the new beautiful Asian museum and the views across the river. The view across the river is spectacular because the old made up three-story colorful wharf sheds contrast so nicely with the skyscrapers behind. Particularly at night the sight is divine.

The afternoon I will spend in the bank, then pre dinner drinks with a friend, and dinner at 7.30 PM with Yong Wah and Christina, chairman and CFO respectively of one of our customers. The reason they come out on a Friday night is not for business. It is for friendship. They are absolutely beautiful people both of them. Chin Hua, the MD couldn't make it, as he will be on a business trip to America. Two of my good colleagues from the bank will join the dinner as well. Really looking forward to it. When I left last year, they put on a fantastic fare well dinner for me at Chimes.

Then some more of Anna Karenina and a nice night's sleep. On the Saturday I will swim and have breakfast and then walk to little India perhaps half an hour away. It is such a nice atmosphere there and I always find something to buy that I don't need. Usually little things for presents. And later in the day I have a lunch planned with Catherine Lim, the great Singapore writer, Kim Loutonen the Finnish ambassador and Maj Liss Olsson, general manager for Svenska Handelsbanken and president for the Swedish business community. That will be a nice foursome and a very friendly, warm, intellectual and charming discussion. I am hosting at the Cricket club.

For the afternoon I am trying to organize a game of tennis, doubles as singles is a bit to taxing in the heat. I will probably have chili crab for dinner with one or two of the tennis team with wives. A great finale on a week's trip to a seminar. That same night at 9.00PM I need to check in for my night flight to Tokyo where I will arrive Sunday morning at 6.30 AM and pickup life where I left it.

That's when the phone rings. Due to some reorganization the seminar has been cancelled and the trip thus postponed. This is Wednesday afternoon twenty four hours before departure. I look at my thick packet of tickets and documents and can't avoid a sense of disappointment. But then I think again and a sense of gratitude comes over me for having so many wonderful friends and so many good reasons to be thoroughly happy, so many things to genuinely look forward to. Having set up so many appointments, I now need to deal with the dis-appointments which I will do tomorrow. Now time for a nice family dinner. And Anna Karenina will be mine soon to have and enjoy through amazone.com. All my overseas friends need to remain cyber friends in the interim. Thank you for your attention. We get by with a little help from our friends.

Tokyo 2002

8. *The Game.*

Today is the 12th of June, the day of the great game. I am to meet Andre' at 10.00 A.M. outside Tokyo Station where we normally enter. That is, we have entered there a few times before, going skiing in Gala earlier in the year. I went to the office at 7.00AM to be able to clear most things and ensure that my later absence would in no way hinder our operations. I signed two employment letters, sent fifteen emails, called Wellington to sort out a New Zealand tax issue, photocopied an article 'The Recovery Myth' (suggesting that the adjustment phase is far from over) and sent the article to a few colleagues overseas. I also read the Financial Times with an interesting letter to the editor from a Japanese official arguing against the recent down rating of Japanese debt. (It would be better if Japanese officials got on with reforming the economy rather than discussing the fine points in arbitrary ratings). The Financial Times this day also says Nokia is selling fewer mobile phones but its shares go up anyway. Major bourses around the world looking lackluster. Article again on the hypocrisy with which Europe and USA treat third world countries – saying all the nice things and sending some charity aid, but refusing to allow their products free entry into Western markets, thus condemning them to continuous economic stagnation. I also talked to one temporary female staff that wants to come and talk briefly every morning. True to my commitment that staff interaction and support always gets my first priority, I talk to her a little while, in spite of having a full morning.

I gave my kind assistant a receipt from last nights petrol fill and three bills I had received at home, as I don't know what they are because the writing is all in Japanese. Also had time to ask her to please have a very small dent on the car fixed during my upcoming holiday. I had hit a power pole trying to pass a parked truck on the very narrow roads in our neighborhood. Driving the car in that morning I had listened to my favorite tune 'The Best of Times is Now' which again reminded me that life really couldn't be much better and has to be lived now. Dostoevski also reminds me that Paradise is really now, it's this, moving around, looking at people, talking to people, making new fiends, doing fun things with those you love. If we think about it, what could be nicer. I also reset my step-counter, which I had bought in Akihabara two days ago – first day 5000 steps – today, who knows? For the day I was wearing a burgundy polo shirt from New Zealand, Khaki shorts from Singapore and soft leather loafers from Kuala Lumpur. In a red backpack I also had the mandatory blue and yellow shirt for the match and also some extra clothes should we get wet through rain. The backpack also contained my Dostoevski book (The Gambler) and my mobile phone and a hat with the Swedish flag on. I told my staff I would see the match Sweden – Argentina in Sendai that day so would only be available on the mobile phone from 9.45 A.M. onwards. There was a light rain in Tokyo in the morning and skis were still quite gray.

On my way to the train station, ten minutes walk away from my office, I pass a convenience store and buy four drinks, two oranges and some chocolates, knowing that the price a little bit away from the station is half platform price. The economic man coming through. Andre' is a few minutes late, which I knew, as Linda told me over the phone that when they arrived at Yoyogi-Uehara Subway station he didn't have any money for the fare and neither did she as she was only accompanying him – so he had to rush back to get the money and was thus slightly delayed. I know we have half an hour margin so was not concerned with his delay. Only a few minutes later I see him in the distance – he is very apologetic for being late, perhaps particularly since this day is his day, and I reassure him, no worries, plenty of time - and at 10.10 A.M. we are on platform 22 for our 10.32 A.M. train. The way to find the platform is just to find one of the many uniformed Japan Rail staff, show them the ticket and ask 'Platform?' They are always friendly and helpful like the vast majority of Japanese people. Lots of people on the move as always and today some extra due to the soccer game in the 2002 Korea /Japan Soccer World Cup Championship. We see many Swedes and a few that we recognize. The Swedes are recognized on their blue and yellow shirts and sometimes facial paint.

The first train will leave 10.16 A.M. but we stick to our designed train as we will have plenty of time and as we have assigned seats on that train. The match begins at 3.30 PM. The winner of today's match will proceed, and the loser will go home. Big match – big day. Tens of millions if not hundreds of millions of television viewers around the world and as luck would have it, here we are with an opportunity to watch first hand on the spot and be part of the great stadium spirit. On the platform we found the car no 6 space for queuing up, again after asking the attendants. Our train arrived 10.20 A.M. and all the cleaners boarded and at 10.30 A.M. when doors opened, we found our seats, 11 A and B and on 11 C is a Japanese businessman in his suit among all the football fans. At 10.32 the train moves. Andre' decides to try to sleep but first he leans over and says 'thanks for doing this for me, dad' and pats me on the shoulder. I respond 'Do Itashimashite' – my pleasure. I had paid Yen 180,000 for tickets and train rides for three Sweden games, but Andre' couldn't get leave for the Kobe match against Nigeria so I recovered Yen 80,000 in selling those tickets to a friend (at just below cost.)

Our first stop was Omiya. An hour after departure we are out on the countryside dominated by green and wet rice fields. Across the aisle is a nice looking young Japanese girl in a Swedish blue and yellow shirt and we smiled to each other recognizing we have something in common today. The girl with the drinks trolley came past every half hour but as we had our own food and drink we didn't buy any this time. The second train stop which occurred at 11.30A.M. was Nasushibara. The Shinkansen fast trains look almost like dolphins when you see them coming – totally aerodynamically designed with soft round lines suggesting capability of high speed. Third stop at 11.45A.M. was Shirakawa. The landscape was at this stage getting quite hilly and forested. The stops were becoming more frequent now – Koriyama at 12.00 Noon and Fukishima at 12.15 P.M. and Yambiko at 12.30 P.M.

Looking through the window I was reminded of Dalarna in middle Sweden (where we have a country house) as the landscape looked very similar. But the houses in the villages we saw were quite gray and monotonous.

A Japan Rail officer came through the car with an information sheet on how to get from the train station to the Miyagi stadium. First we would have to walk to the local subway line and then at the end of that line take a bus to the stadium. Once at Sendai there was an army of functionaries with signs and arrows pointing the crowd in the right direction. As I judged we had plenty of time we went to a small station restaurant to eat lunch – a bowl of noodles with tempura at Yen 850 * 2. It tasted excellent. At the previous game we tried to get some food at the stadium and that was not very good – only hot dogs available. You learn as you go. The subway was about five hundred meters away and just as we reached the subway I saw a Japanese girl I recognized from behind. I went up and tapped her on the shoulder, she turned surprised and I exclaimed 'Ichihara san!' and she said 'Frank san!' We exchanged a hug and a kiss. By sheer coincidence one of my colleagues from the bank was on a few days leave and we ran into each other like that – she couldn't believe it and neither could I. She asked – what are you doing in Sendai – and I said my son and I are going to the Sweden – Argentina Game and she was visiting her mother. I introduced Andre' and she introduced her mother. And a minute later we continued each in our own direction.

At the subway entrance special counters were set up for speedy ticketing where one could buy tickets for going and coming. I bought four tickets for Yen 600 all together. We were going to Izumi Chuo, nine subway stations away. The train was full and it was a smooth uneventful trip. I asked Andre' to memorize all the names of the subway stations for my report and he said 'you're crazy dad, who cares.' A woman with a child in a pram tried to get in and did so. The little four year old struck me as looking like a (future) bank manager. 'How do you mean?' asked Andre. ' Intelligent, handsome, determined and charming of course.' If Linda had been in the conversation she may well have objected by saying: immature, gray and lacking in character, helpless without a woman and pushed around all day. There are two sides to every coin.

At Izumi Chuo we joined a huge bus queue but it moved pretty quickly and half an hour later we were on the bus. A number of boisterous Swedes in blue and yellow hats and flags made themselves heard on the bus – a bit loud but quite friendly. Many of the locals also had Swedish shirts on. The way it all was planned, all the Swedes were at one end of the stadium and all the Argentines at the other end. The two teams' supporters were totally separated and even went to different subway stations for their bussing – all to ensure good behavior, which in fact prevailed throughout the whole Championship. The bus took us through the wilderness for a twenty minutes trip to the Miyagi Stadium. Quite pretty and wild landscape really. The suspense before the great Game was building up.

We entered the stadium and I tried to hide my umbrella, as umbrellas were not allowed, and I foresaw a great hassle trying to get the umbrella back if I checked it. I couldn't get it through and Andre' thought it was silly to try. I checked it and got a ticket and thought it would be fun to try to retrieve it in the crowds after the match.

Andre' who never has had to work for money suggested 'just forget about it.' 'Donate it to the locals.'

Entering the stadium we were seeing 42,000 people and it was all full of colors and a buzz audible from a distance. The weather was looking up and there wasn't going to be any rain by the looks of it. Sweden supporters were at the one end and Argentina at the opposite end. All the players out there one hour before kick off, warming up and playing with the balls. Lots of Swedish flags and yellow colors showing through. I assessed that 80 –90 percent of the audience must be local Japanese. One huge screen on our side showed all the players and later the whole game and particularly replays of things interesting. The excitement was almost tangible. All seemed very happy.

We participated in three Mexican waves in five minutes. The Japanese are quite reserved and well behaved so it was a little bit difficult to get the Mexican waves going. Forty minutes now until the game starts.

Andre' particularly enjoyed being part of the Swedish crowd as he hasn't really lived in Sweden at all – only visited for limited periods. He quickly picked up all the slogans 'Vi är svenska fans allihopa' (we are all Swedish fans) and 'Ni där borta är ni klara?' (you over there are you ready) 'Jajamensan, fattas bara,' (yes, shame if we weren't) - Andre' had to ask me what is 'fattas bara' and I told him that it doesn't really make much sense – all it is, is a rhyme and it fires up the crowd. Other cheers were 'In med blollen' (get the ball in) shouted at corners and free kicks, and then also 'satellite' mocking the opponents every time they made a shot over the goal which happened a lot as the ball seemed very light. Quite basic, but also a lot of fun.

The advertising around the stadium were particularly by world brand names: they included Phillips, Fuji Xerox, McDonalds, Coca Cola, Yahoo, MasterCard, Hyundai, Addidas and Toshiba. The big yellow flag of Fifa was carried around and all were standing up, clapping.

It's 3.30P.M. and the game is underway. Argentina gets close to the Swedish goal but no goal this time and Sweden has a chance in the second minute. Sweden dominates the first ten minutes but after 15 minutes Argentina has a really good header, which Hedman, the Swedish goalie, just clears. Puh – close.

To be fair, Argentina had 80 pct of the chances in the first half which ended goalless.

Andre' always thought Sweden was better whatever happened on the field. This was his team. At half time I felt Sweden should be lucky with 0-0 draw, which incidentally would be enough for Sweden to progress based on previous achievements. The South Americans overwhelming possession and almost continuous assault on Sweden's goal came to naught. In the second half, Sweden played a lot better. In the 59th minute Sweden got a free kick and Anders Svensson shot the ball beautifully just in the upper corner of the goal out of reach for the Argentina goalie. But 40 minutes into the second half Argentina got a penalty and although Hedman cleared the first shot, Argentina was allowed to score on the rebound. If Argentina had scored on just one more of their many chances they would have topped the group and advanced. But it was not to be as Sweden defended heroically, harrying and hassling at every turn. In fairness Sweden also had some more good chances in the second half. "It is fantastic. We have won the group and that gives us an extra day's rest," said Lars Lagerbäck, Sweden's joint coach. The next match will be Senegal on Sunday June 16th.

At the end of the game the Swedes were jubilant and the Argentine's understandably a bit sad. They were favorites to win the whole thing and now like France they didn't even make the second round. We learned on the mobile phone that England – Nigeria ended 0-0 which meat that England would advance and Nigeria would not. Sweden – England – Argentina – Nigeria was the final ranking in the group of four rather equal teams. This clearly exceeded the expectations of the Swedes even if many gave them as good a chance to advance as anyone else. Anders Svensson, player of the day for Sweden, said that his approach was just to go out there and do his best and enjoy it as much as possible – a simple and universal formula for success.

After the game at 5.30 P.M. we hurried out and on our way back we saw our friend Vanessa Åsell and walked up to her and both Andre' and I got a nice hug. We exchanged a few words but as she was waiting for someone we moved on. I managed to find my umbrella after a few minutes search and we hurried to not be too far back in the bus queue. We were keen to have enough time for the bus ride, the transfer to the subway, the nine station subway ride (with stations that shall remain nameless) and finally make it to our 7.20P.M. train departure from Sendai. Not too much margin there. Lots of policemen ensured good order at the exit of the stadium and I never saw any turmoil at all. Very well organized and policed. The buses were loaded six at a time and we got away with the sixth round of buses, which was pretty good.

Uneventful bus trip to Izumi Chuo and there a ten minute walk to the subway car and twenty five minutes later we were again at Sendai at 7.00PM happy that our schedule worked out so we didn't have to stay over night in Sendai. We bought some kind of chocolate looking box with fish fingers which Andre' picked out. On the train, we ate our food, but Andre' decided he only wanted one of twelve fish fingers as they didn't appeal too much to him, which led to me eating more fish fingers than I really would have liked, and yet allowing us to donate some surplus fingers to Japan Rail. I read a bit more of Dostoevski, and at 9.40 P.M. we arrived again at Tokyo Station. From there we walked ten minutes to my office to pick up the car and we hit the office just over twelve hours after I left it to go to the match. We got into the car and were home at 10.30P.M. A long day. A fun day. Son and father, father and son. A day I think Andre' and I will always remember. And yes, the step counter for this 12th day of June 2002 finished on 10,296 - a new record. Having fun goes a long way.

9. Nikko

One hour with Shinkansen from Tokyo, change trains in Utsunomiya, another hour to Nikko, all the temples, a little Japanese restaurant, transport to our Onsen hotel by Lake Chuzenji, a Japanese room, hot baths, exquisite meals, a night on Tatami, a walk along the lake shore, a visit to spectacular Kegon Falls – that's when we were ready to take the bus down the incline back to Nikko. The bus will arrive in three minutes as per the schedule on the wall of the bus terminal, which also holds a large vending machine for bus tickets. From Kegan to Nikko is Yen 1100 with 550 in brackets so I ask the local next to me if 550 is one way but he responds: "no, 550 is child, 1100 is adult, both one way." Thus I put in 2200 for Linda and me and press the right button and am the lucky holder of two one way tickets with the Tobu bus to Nikko.

Just as we come out of the terminal building and join a queue of about twenty people the bus arrives but it looks pretty full. A few people step out and then we start to board. Linda says I hope we don't have to stand for an hour down the steep zig-zag roads. In between the rows of double chairs there are fold out chairs so people start to occupy these and Linda gets the last fold out in front and I get to stand, which I don't mind at all being young and healthy. Next to the front seats there is a flat surface a bit up high in the bus and with great agility I swing my bottom up there and sit nicely. This is a bit more than the driver can live with so he instructs me to come down which I obey without questioning. All on the bus are Japanese except us.

The loud speaker on the bus announces that the driver will test the brakes for safety and he does this with little discomfort to either the seated passengers or the one standing. He goes quite fast through all the little bends where a moment's distraction could end the saga of both his and his passengers' lives. But Japan somehow is quite reliable and all people take their tasks very seriously so I never worry about these things. Writing this line makes me recall an email I got today from my friend in Hong Kong which said "my uncle died peacefully in his sleep, whilst all his passengers went into hysterics." But there was none of that. The bus followed the winding road as if it was going on tracks.

Half way down the hill it stopped to pick up two more people. Where are they going to fit in I thought, but once aboard they fitted in very close to me – one young boy and an older lady – nice and cozy. At the second stop a few passengers from the innermost of the bus wanted to disembark so all the people sitting pretty in the middle had to fold their chairs and press their bodies to the side so the disembarking people could pass and get out. This of course presented me with an opportunity to get a seat, which I did on one of the foldouts. This was quite a narrow seat with a low back and just marginally more comfortable than standing up. One more bus stop with a few people leaving and a few boarding and I saw the ones leaving putting the fare in a plastic box with a small conveyor belt in it running for about a foot to allow the hawk eyed driver to assess that the right fare had been paid, wheather by coins and bills or prepaid tickets. Every bus system in every country is different. In many countries in Europe you cannot pay on the bus so you have to prepay in a kiosk or run the risk of being caught for non-payment.

With the experience of exposing us to penalty for not knowing the system in Europe we wanted to avoid this risk in Japan by proper prepayment.

Suddenly the recorded voice on the loud speaker says we are approaching the temple area and to me it is a bit unclear if these are the Nikko temples or some other temples. However Linda sees the sign saying Toshugo Shrine and then we know we are only half an hour's walk from the rail way station. So this is the place to get off and enjoy one more temple and a leisurely walk down the hill and find a nice lunch restaurant. Wishing to get out fast I quickly grab my back pack and camera bag from the shelf, trying to not be in the way of other passengers and not necessarily hold the bus up and the traffic behind as these are narrow roads with little chance of passing and there are plenty of cars out. As I walk past the driver I think 'Oh Yes I have to give him my tickets' so I feel in my pockets to identify these small things and find them and put them in his plastic covered conveyer belt thing making him look acutely unhappy. I don't know if he doesn't want the tickets there and only money but he views me very unfavorably as I jump off and he holds Linda back as he feels we haven't discharged our duties properly.

I am now outside the bus trying to tell the driver that I put my tickets in his plastic box, that I paid 2,200 as instructed for the tickets and that is that and there is no more to it. He of course doesn't understand a word I am saying and I don't understand whatever he would say, but as he knows this, he is just looking more and more upset, ostensibly getting a high pulse and, as it seems, ready to explode. Linda suggests that I think of something fast because she doesn't want to be hostage in the bus any longer next to an angry uniformed driver. So I try to ask the driver what I can do to make him happy, if he wants me to pay again perhaps? I think him quite a stubborn and rigid person not wanting to accept that I have already paid once – but perhaps whatever I paid was some other bus or other line? Who knows? So after a few minutes of arguing and staring at each other and probably making about 100 people wonder what in the world is going on I grab a few notes in my pocket to suggest that if you are not happy with my tickets, by all means I can pay again.

So I give him 2,000, which he seems happy with, he lets Linda off, the bus moves on and we go for a walk. Linda said he was so angry it wasn't funny and I said that I thought him a bit rigid and lacking in trust. If I tell him on my best English mixed with Swedish that I have already given him the tickets and paid my fare why shouldn't he believe me. Linda has already forgotten it and I try to as well – just pondering how wrong things can go with the best of intentions. It would have been easier if we could have talked to each other.

An hour later after this upsetting experience and lunch with a glass of beer I start to giggle and Linda asks what the matter. And I show her the two tickets for 2,200, which I found in my other pocket. What I put on his fine conveyer belt must have been the two tickets I bought for us to take the elevator to the ground level 100 meters down for viewing the beautiful Kegon Falls. There was also a hole in each showing they had been used. I toyed with the idea that if I go to the station and present them I might get a refund but decided that, given it was my mistake it didn't seem too unfair that I also pay for it.

7th October 2002

10. Tokoya.

This is a day I have been looking forward to. It is 11.30AM and I am stepping out of my office to go down the stairs to the banking hall, saying hello to my colleague Ms Nishimura, and as usual asking her 'Shiawase desu ka?' (Are you happy? which she as usual confirms that she is.) In the banking hall I admire our lovely Christmas tree that staff unbeknown to me have put up. I greet the staff on the inside of the counter and progress to our front doors. Dressed in a dark suit I have added a red slip over to keep the cold at bay having noticed from my windows that it is a clear day but probably a little cool. It is the third of December and some sunshine, but this is Tokyo and it is winter, so the temperature is around ten degrees. When I can, I avoid taking my overcoat because most places have no good room to hang coats. Just as I step through the bank's front door a young lady smiles in the warmest of fashions at me and I wonder what causes this nice gesture from a stranger, when I suddenly recognize her as Lisa, our contract mortgage manager. We exchange some pleasantries and she goes in where I go out into the brisk but bright and nice day. In front of our offices is Nihon Ginko (Bank of Japan) but that is not my destination for today.

Since half a year back I am equipped with a step counter (manpokei) and I check it to see how long this walk will be. After no more than twenty steps I get another smile from Haruna, the lovely young lady who runs the mobile coffee shop. She sits in this little van all day and makes the finest Italian coffee for the office workers in the neighborhood. Her work-space doesn't allow much movement and certainly doesn't allow her standing up. In spite of this confinement, and being so busy all day, she manages to smile to each customer and make him or her feel very special. We in the service industry could all learn a lot from her. She doesn't speak much English but she likes to try so we have the most strange and funny conversations when I buy coffee once a day.

Normally I don't drink coffee but this is different – it is an experience, a high, something to look forward to. It is not really coffe but liquid love. When she puts the finishing touches to the café latte she pours the whipped milk so it always ends with a heart on top of the cup. Thus I learnt from her that heart in Japanese is Kokoro! And, as we know, the world is changed one heart at a time. One month ago I bought her some flowers (hana) for being such a role model for humanity, and since then she always has flowers on her little counter, which also offers very soft music from somewhere in the van. No wonder her business is very successful. Her patrons are more like friends than customers. At this time there is quite a queue outside her little shop but that is not my destination for today.

Not far from Haruna there is another vendor with a van selling readymade trays of rice and chicken for about 500 yen. Many office workers seem quite content to buy a tray of this and bring it back to the office for lunch. I haven't tried it but I am sure that, like everything in Japan, it is a safe, hygienic and nutritious. Everything is so well thought out and so meticulous. I continue across the street towards Kanda station (eki) and quickly come up to a traffic light, which shows red so I have to wait.

This street is just north/ south so the sun casts it's blessings along the whole street this particular day and that little extra temperature boost is very therapeutic. People around me are mostly office people – well dresses, well behaved – all very safe and orderly. Traffic light changes and I am able to cross the street into the next little street that leads into the road up to Kanda station. There are many shops in this street – first a photo and electronics shop, then a golf shop, a pharmacy where I have sometimes tried to get medicine (kusuri) and sometimes failed because I am not sure the attendant understands the nature of my ailment and as I continue the road there is restaurant after restaurant.

These are mostly low price lunch restaurants where you can eat a lunch – rice and chicken, tempura, sushi, udon, wantan soup etc for between 500 and 1000 yen with a real peak patronage between twelve and one and outside that peak business slows considerably. There are also a couple of construction sites on this busy side road and they are so neatly managed so they don't seem to disturb the business around in any way at all. Before reaching Kanda station I pass a wine shop, where I recently bought 36 bottles of Australian Shiraz red wine for my staff for Christmas, a couple of massage parlors, a lottery shop, a variety store, a bakery and a kitchen shop. But none of these is my destination for today.

As I pass the second crossing with traffic lights I walk under the rail tracks at Kanda station and I am handed a mini packet of paper napkins. These are handed out for free with some advertising on the packages. I don't understand the meaning of the Japanese advertising but I do understand the value of napkins given out for free so I always accept a small pack. Since a few years ago when there was a poison scare in Tokyo all official wastebaskets have been taken out so people don't accept any advertising leaflets unless there is some obvious value attached to them, because there is nowhere to throw them. On the other side of the underpass there is the best sushi restaurant in the area, which I have visited many times, but this is not my destination today.

I continue along the road which is still the same straight road that runs immediately outside my office, continuing for a quite a long stretch past the Kanda station. The sun continues to shower the people on this road with its blessing and there are lots of colors and people looking contented and peaceful. Everything is quite idyllic really. Tokyo is amazing this way. Here are almost thirty million people assembled in perhaps the largest city in the world but still there is a feeling of smallness in the midst of this obvious size. Every little neighborhood, it seems, has a small town atmosphere and the lack of high-rises ensures that you never feel intimidated by size. I often think that it is a wonder how well this large city works with very little signs of problems or congestions. And everybody, no matter what his/ her task might be, seems enthusiastic about being able to contribute to society in whichever small way.

I get to the third traffic light, which is red and in Tokyo you wait when the light is red for two reasons. Firstly people are disciplined and follow the rules, secondly there is almost always some traffic, making it difficult to jaywalk even if you were so inclined. I walk past a stationary shop where I have shopped a couple of times, to buy among other things a paper cutter. In most Japanese shops you have to use sign language to make yourself understood, which can sometimes be very funny. One of the girls in my tennis group, Josephine, said she needed to buy medicine for her cat which had come down with hemorrhoids and she didn't want to go to the Vet and pay the premium they always charge, but tried an ordinary pharmacy. This very cute little girl from Vermont just walked in and pointed to her bottom and made ugly faces so as to convey pain and after some astonishment (and possibly amusement – we who heard the story thought it hilarious) she ultimately managed to get the message across and got something for hemorrhoids to get the cat out of its misery. Subsequently the cat died in a traffic accident but one would think she might be grateful she got to cat heaven hemorrhoids free.

I also pass the New Central Hotel, which is something like a one star hotel, which charges about Yen 10,000 a night for accommodation. It is probably clean and safe but rather basic. There are many cheaper hotels than that if you travel out a bit and accept to sleep in one of these box drawer hotels. But the Central Hotel is not my destination for the day.

Passing another traffic light where a woman has a fruit shop I know I am getting closer. That's when I see the sign with the spiraling red and white pattern to indicate that here is a.....Barber!!(Tokoya). This is my destination of today. When I was there three months ago I decided the experience was so extraordinary I would write about it next time. I get there 11.40 AM after 1000 steps, so all things related above cover no more than ten minutes of my life.

I look in through the window and see there is no customer there – I have timed it right before the lunch hour. It seems Japanese people may feel a little guilty if they start their lunch hour before twelve and if it lasts after one. So for someone foreigner (gaijin) who is not very used to feeling guilty, it is optimal to take an early or late stroll cum lunch. The man who runs the barbershop, today dressed in a blue short sleeve shirt and gray slacks, is there and greets me – I am sure he recognizes me – but there is no sign of his wife (okusan). He starts to talk to me in

Japanese – as he has seen me three of four times he probably feels that it is about time I understood the language anyway – and I pick up (I think) that he asks me what I do so I say National Austraria Ginko and he nods and then he asks (I think) how long I have been in Japan and I say a year and a half (ichi nen han) and he nods at that too. Have I had my lunch? 'Nai desu, ato de'. 'No I will eat after' I try to tell him and he smiles as if he understands.

At this stage he realizes that the conversation is not going to take on any deeper meaning so he quietens down. I think he asks me how I want it done and I say sukoshi, meaning a little, and I also untidy my hair and show how it covers my ears to suggest he would please uncover them. This seems clear enough and anyway, I have been here before so it shouldn't be too hard.

Since I am 50 % bald I don't have to visit the barbershop very often but now my hair is getting a bit unwieldy around my ears and I particularly like this one barbershop where I am taken very seriously and catered for a full half hour in spite of my lack of hair. He sweeps me into three covers to protect my suit from getting hairy and puts a little towel around my neck for comfort. As I hold a piece of paper and a pen in my hands he asks if I am writing a letter and I say 'short story' but he looks as if he thinks I am mad and doesn't seem to think it natural that people go to barbershops and write short stories. From there on he doesn't say anything, but I jot down a word or two on what I see and experience as it all unfolds.

All things in the shop are quite tidy. There are three chairs with mirrors and washbasins and these basins fold into the wall so they look more like dishwashers. I am not looking for my hair to be washed since there isn't much of it and I always wash it every morning anyway. He warps a pink hot and wet towel around my scalp and it feels very nice and good. I look like a funny Arab in the mirror but who cares? He takes the pink towel off and start to cut gently. His wife is still not to be seen. I note that there is a large TV turned off in the shop and a radio somewhere, which speaks Japanese. At the cash register (reji) there is a large stand with free customer cigarettes, which is a bit different.

After cutting for about ten minutes he changes comb and scissors and goes at it again. I am enjoying it because in most other places they disrobe me after five minutes and suggest that's it. But not this shop – here they tend to my receding hairline with due respect. Then he goes away to his heater to heat another towel and start to brush my hair and shoulders. This is the end of act one. After that he takes a third set of scissors and a new comb and again has a go at my hair, now fine-tuning to get perfection. He gets a new towel and put on my neck and then arranges a small pot with hot water and some shaving cream, which he applies around my hairline with a brush. Then he takes out the razor and starts to shave off any remaining hair on my neck and around the ears and the whiskers. This is all done slowly, nicely, gently and meticulously. Whatever he shaves off he deposits in another little towel so just counting the number of towels I know I am in for the real thing – a premium Japanese hair cut.

Then the wife arrives from the street entrance and he hands her the washbasin used for the shaving exercise, which she goes away and cleans. I think that being handed something to clean seems to be the wife's lot in many cultures but she doesn't seem to mind – this is obviously a partnership. As she enters she says something to me, which clearly is a greeting cum recognition. It goes without saying that as long as I stay in Japan and as long as I have any hair left these are my designated barbers. I even prefer when she cuts me, but that preference is marginal, this also isn't bad. Now he takes a little powder thing and dots on to my hairline and I feel like a prince – so pampered.

Then he takes a new set of scissors and cuts a little further, just making sure there is nothing irregular in my hairdo. Thereafter he takes the towel and dusts everything off and cleans my ears with his fingers through the towel and nothing here is left to chance it seems. That's it! They both say thank you (doumo arigatou) and I say the same and we bow a little. I say 'Subarashi' (wonderful) and I smile and say now I have a short story and I think they understand but probably still think this foreigner a little mad (and perhaps justifiably so). Anyway – we all laugh a little bit together. He asks for 2000 yen which is like US $ 16 and, although I have paid less for haircuts elsewhere, I feel that this is good value. This is not only a hair cut, this is medicine for the soul – a bit similar to the product delivery of Haruna Kokoro. My parting words are 'Totemo yokat-ta desu yo, mata kimasu!' meaning 'this was very good – I shall come back.'

At 12.10 P.M. after thirty minutes of being so well groomed and looked after I step out a new person, nice and tidy and with a sense of having been really well looked after for a while. Now I am ready to take on the challenges of the world. And also ready to look for some place to have lunch. As I get back to the nearest street corner I again see the lady's fruit shop and think 'why not buy some fruits?' There is no one there so I stick my head in and say hello!? And she comes out from within. I take four tomatoes, a head of broccoli, eight mandarins and eight bananas and to add that up she uses her 'soroban' but I of course don't know what she is doing, she says the price and also takes out he minicalculator and types 1,250. It seems many Japanese still prefer to calculate on the old abacus like things rather than the modern electronic calculators and then these latter are used just to display the relevant numbers to the customer. The lady is very kind and nice. She puts all the things in a bag; I pay the money and move on across the street to continue my return walk.

When I get to the stationery store I go in to try to get some sticky clay like stuff to be able to put some posters on my walls without making any marks. I walk up to the counter and say I want some sticky stuff to put around the wall and try to demonstrate by molding this imaginary thing with my fingers and sticking it in four corners of the wall to hold my poster. She walks over to the little spikes and I say no, not spikes, and try again. I think she knows what I mean but indicates they don't have it but gives me something else; two side glue tape that looks like it comes off without leaving any mark, so I take that instead and say thank you for your good efforts.

A few more steps along the road is the premium sushi bar. I look at my watch, 12.15PM, and think it may well be full by now. But as luck would have it there are a few seats left and I hang my bag on some available hangers and order an A lunch which is number one of four choices A – D. A costs 1000 yen and consists of 12 pieces of sushi including some rice rolls with cucumber, some salmon, (Sake), tuna (Maguro), scallops, (Hotategai) shrimps, (Ebi) white fish (Tai) and some omelet look-alike. The first thing I am served is a nice large cup of Japanese tea (Ocha). There are twenty-two places around the counter and four cooks (Itamae) and people probably stay on average fifteen or twenty minutes. The cook puts out a banana leaf on the counter before me and I put some ginger (Gari) on it and poor some soy sauce in my little saucer and am ready to receive the fish over the counter.

After a minute or two my banana leaf is full of these delicacies and I start eating. Many of the pieces are quite large and you cannot cut them so they do fill up your mouth. Fortunately all are on a counter facing the same way so no one sits across to see you chew with your whole face, which may look a bit untidy. These cooks work entirely with their hands but as with everything in Japan, hygiene is such a sacred thing so you never worry one second that any food would be bad or contaminated. On each piece of sushi there is also wasabi and once or twice it really hits my sinuses – nice – makes you feel alive! The design of the restaurant is very simple – blond wood and glass and stools around the counter. And the cooks work right in front of you so you can follow the production process as you sit and eat. A little bit later I get up and am handed my tab, which I take to the cash register and pay the 1050 Yen including 5 % tax. Again I think I have been well looked after and received good value for my money. Stepping out of the restaurant, there is a lot of noise as all staff scream goodbye and thank you.

From there on I just follow the road back to the office and find that all in all I have walked 2000 steps, I have enjoyed some winter sunshine and I have been treated like a king time and again by sincere and caring people who deliver good value. It makes me feel quite happy with my lot including the opportunity to experience living in Japan. In March, God willing, I will be back for another treat by the barber on the other side of Kanda station in Nihonbashi. Just a short lunch walk a few blocks in Tokyo can be quite a delightful adventure. A line from Robert Louis Stevenson comes to mind: 'The world is so full of wonderful things, I'm sure we should all be as happy as kings.'

3rd December 2002

11. Sumida Gawa.

Woke up at five am, looked at my watch, and realized it was just a little bit too early to rise so kept tossing and turning until some rays of sun made me realize I had slept for nearly another two hours. Thank you God! I think sound sleep and relaxation are key foundations for an active and happy life. So am I happy? Believing strongly that happiness comes from within, that, like love, it is an attitude of optimism, wonder, and the expectation that interesting and nice things will continue to come across my path, I think I am happy. It is something to do with the virtuous circle. You see what you want to see, and to an extent you find that which you are looking for. But how can I be happy when other people are not? I wish all could be happy and perhaps I believe I am more likely to influence other people positively to a sense of happiness if I am happy myself.

I pull the shades in my bedroom and this bright light fills the entire room – this is the land of the rising sun – and I have always liked mornings more than evenings – one holds out promise and expectation, the other more likely to be focused on contemplation and regression. In my small apartment on the Sumida River (Sumida Gawa) in the heart of Tokyo I have this spectacular east facing view over the river. I go out on the long balcony and take in the full impression of this view. In front of our building the river widens to a lake with a three km circumference – perfect for a morning jogging round. As I wear only a kimono and socks I feel the cold a bit – it is only about five degrees at this hour in the middle of December. There is quite a noise level from the waking city. Already early Sunday morning there is a steady flow of traffic over the Eitai Bashi, i.e. the bridge that carries Eitai Dori Street across the river.

The bridge – a beautiful steel bridge - is illuminated at night, as are all the bridges across the Sumida, this particular bridge with blue light – which makes for wonderful night walks along the river. Quite recently, the way it looks, the walks along the river have been prepared for miles and miles on either side allowing people to run, jog, walk, cycle, take their dogs out, fish, sit and read, enjoy the boats and hold hands with a dear one along the river side – and all these things are daily occurrences. For every one person you would meet strolling in Stockholm or Auckland you are apt to meet thirty in Tokyo. Those are the proportions.

Yesterday, in the winter sunshine, I took my bike to see if I could find my way to Asakusa upstream along the river. I didn't know quite how far it was but I estimated it to about five kilometers. As long as I could follow the river it would be easy to find my way there and back. Otherwise in Tokyo it can be quite a struggle to keep your bearings – many, many parts look pretty much the same and except for a few reference points like the Emperors Palace, the Tokyo Tower and the Sumida River, Tokyo is vast and difficult to overview. It is easy to get lost. As we just moved into this little apartment a month ago, having sent our home back to New Zealand, my wife was calling me on the phone a few weeks ago and said she had a lot to carry and she was lost. She had come out of the subway and walked and walked in what she thought was the right direction but now she was lost.

So I said if you can't tell me where you are, I can't come and pick you up, can I? She was nearly crying unable to find the right way and also disinclined to take a cab, not being sure of her ability to describe her destination to the cab driver. At least she had the mobile phone. I suggested that she take a cab to my office which address I knew she could convey to a cab driver, and then I would drive her home. My colleague at work had an even better idea – to stop a taxi, call the office on the cell phone and then my colleague would tell the driver how to take her home. When I called her again to convey this new scheme she said she had just stumbled on our building. In empathy, I also told her that both Andre', our son, and I went the wrong way from the subway the first day because all directions looked so terribly alike. Trial and error guides us such that the second time we know.

Anyway, after cycling upriver, I soon had to leave the riverside at a bridge to get around the bridge footing to the other side. As I was carrying my bike down the steps on the other side to get to the river walk again, I asked a lady with a little Poodle 'Is this the way to Asakusa?' and she said I wouldn't get through along the river – it is better to go on the streets a bit in from the river. She didn't speak many words of English but I made out that this is what she said. I suggested that surely I could cycle along the river and just carry my bike around any further obstacle? No!, she was so adamant that I not continue, so I felt I frankly would have insulted this kind woman if I hadn't taken her advice. (How could she know that cycling along the river was as much my objective of the day as getting to Asakusa?) Thus I went back and continued on the back streets. Often in Tokyo, like London, streets aren't quite straight and I was very cautious to move along the same direction as the river or I may also loose my bearings.

Along the road there were quite a few shops, particularly in one district there were like ten toyshops and many shops selling cheap clothing. After asking for confirmation a few times 'is this the way to Asakusa?' I got there after about half an hour of cycling. I moved around the area for an hour buying presents for xmas, and our New Zealand friends, filling up my red back pack. I also had lunch in Asakusa and then returned on the same back streets being a bit more venturesome in terms of taking little streets and alleys that looked interesting, thinking that going home should be easier. The sun was now rather higher on the sky and provided a guiding star for direction as well. Mondai – nai – desu. No problems.

So much for the Eitai Bashi which is the northern point of my vista from the apartment window. Every five or ten minutes a boat or ship comes by just beneath my window – like living art – fascinating and beautiful, both daytime and night time. Some are fishing vessels, some are small tankers, some are police boats, and some, particularly nighttime, carry tourists up and down the river. It just makes it nice and interesting to look out the windows – the scene is changing all the time – never a dull moment.

As I move my sight a bit from North towards East I see a multitude of buildings on the other side of the river behind the very neatly laid out river walk. These buildings are not really pretty – in fact it is a bit like a dogs breakfast – high and low buildings and no particular style. But when things are completely random some kind of accidental pattern seems to develop anyway and it somehow depicts life (and the starry skies) – enigmatic and unfathomable – and in spite of this lack of pattern, it all comes together quite beautifully, particularly at dawn and dusk. On the near side just below my 8th story window I see eleven different fishermen with their rods over the iron fence trying their luck for some river fish. It is nice that this can happen in the middle of the world's largest city. I have seen them catch some little fish, but I guess their activity is more a way to enjoy nature and solitude perhaps, rather than expecting any economic return on the time allocated to this activity.

Right now there is a group of perhaps fifty people going by in bright jackets in something that looks like an organized power walk. A tourist boat similar to those I have seen on the Saine in Paris passes by and the gold from the reflected sun spreads all over the river through the waves of the boat.

There are sea gulls and ducks moving up and down in the waves. I can't believe my luck in finding this place on walking distance from my office. Further along on the other side there are two open dam doors. This part of Tokyo is full of little rivers and canals and they all have steel doors. I guess that if the sea is coming in high for some reason, the doors can be closed to protect all the low-lying residential areas next to the waterways. The ones I see are painted blue and numbered one and two. Outside the 'locks' there are a few barges with cranes and steel, probably for some construction work.

Looking further towards the south, there are some residential high rises built on what looks like a man made island in the middle of the river. These are really high sixty story buildings and rather uncharacteristic as most of Tokyo is low rise. And on either side of this large island there are bridges, one quite ordinary looking and one spectacular with a high tower in the centre from which the bridge hangs in many wires making it look very artistic – beauty and function combined in a most aesthetic way.

My own rooms are sparsely furnished and on the walls there are some maps of the world and Japan and a calendar for 2003 and a poster. None of the things are mine since our things left with the family a few weeks ago. But in my line of sight there are eight pot flowers from our previous abode, one a cactus blooming as I have never seen it before – pink beautiful flowers absolutely everywhere. One of them is an orchid, which I, as instructed, soak in water in the kitchen basin once a week. And on the coffee table there are five Christmas cards, which have found their way to this new riverside address.

Having taken all these sights in, I realize it is high time to have some breakfast. I make a pot of tea, and on a small tray I put a yogurt, two mandarins, half an apple – the size of apples in Japan allows you to feed a family on one apple; pricey yes, but also very good – two thin slices of toast and a little milk and sugar. This is Sunday, I have a good book, I have a bicycle and I have many friends if I want company, I have a trip planned to New Zealand to be with family and friends over the holidays, I have a job which I much enjoy and where I am appreciated. Breakfast tastes good. The view is lovely. I am listening to 'Winter' by Vivaldi. I am happy.

15th December 2002

12. Losing it.

I will just get my keys I thought before I go out to a café with Ellie. They must be in my Bermuda's. Not there? I walk around the house to the few rooms I have visited after coming back from the gym and look at the obvious places. Not there either? I know I was bringing my keys to the gym a few hours earlier. I wasn't bringing any bag and I wasn't wearing a jacket. So nowhere to keep the keys but in my Bermuda pockets. And it was only a few hours ago. Irritating! Three items on my key ring. My fancy fold out Audi car key, my ordinary door key and my new touch key for the tennis club. It must be at the gym then. Last week at the gym I lost a number of coins out of my pocket at the rowing machine. I thought I'd pick them up after completing my rowing but forgot at that stage. So I made someone a dollar seventy-five richer just like that. No big deal. But the keys would be quite annoying to lose.

Doorbell rings and there is Ellie. Hi Frank. Hi Ellie. A hug. A kiss. I can't find my door keys? Just look once more and you'll find them. I don't think so. I have already looked. Well I'll make a cup of coffee anyway says Ellie and walks into the kitchen. I will call Les Mills gym and ask if they have found any keys. After listening to a dumb answering machine I finally press zero in order to talk to someone, as there are no pre-recorded options for lost keys. Wait a minute and we will check! No. No lost car keys today! They must be there I think. Ellie, do you mind if I just drive down there to check myself. I don't mind at all but if it is only a couple of keys you could always get new ones. And if you just take them out of your mind for a while they will most likely turn up.

I get into the car with my son's car key and drive the one kilometre to the gym. At the reception I ask for found keys? Are you the one that just called? Yes. Well, I am sorry but we haven't found any. Do you mind if I go in and have a look? Not at all. They must be here somewhere? I go to the cycling machine where it would be unlikely to find them anyway as my pocket on that machine is in no position to lose the keys. I proceed to the rowing machine and there are two people rowing on the six machines available. Next to a frenetically rowing girl there are some keys looking like mine and she is a bit puzzled that I stare a bit at her. I tell her I lost my car keys and she stops her intense rowing and says sympathetically that these keys are hers. I apologize to her for interrupting her rowing and move on to the next room where I did some work out on about thirty different machines.

I walked slowly around – wearing my blazer and nice slacks – all dressed up for the café visit with Ellie – drawing people's attention a bit as everyone else in the gym is half naked, particularly the girls. So in my café outfit I walk around and look at and under all the machines, especially those where I would have been upside down or almost upside down. But no luck. No keys. I think that I must have lost them there and someone must have picked them up. But if so, why wouldn't that someone have given them in to the reception? Why am I so annoyed over losing a few keys anyway?

The door key will cost me two dollars to replace. The car key probably 75 dollars, as it is a bit fancy. And car companies make little profit when they sell a car, but they really hit you when you come back with some problem. Someone said that if you build a car with spare parts priced as per catalogue, the price would be ten times the normal car making even a Volkswagen cost as much as a Ferrari. Crazy. But the real pain is the new electronic tennis key. That will probably cost no more than ten dollars to replace, but it will take a week and I have several tennis appointments, which I won't be able to make without the key. Embarrassing.

On my way out of the gym there is a pulpit with some forms for people to make suggestions on how to make a better gym. I stop there and write my name, date and mobile phone number, also saying that I lost my car keys in the gym. I give the note to the girls at the front desk and ask them to please ring me if they find them. That they promise to do, and I drive the short distance back to my house. I wonder if I could have lost the keys on my way to and from the gym but discard that as impossible as metal keys cannot possibly fall out of a pocket when one is upright. Very irritating.

Must get back to Ellie. She isn't alone as my son and his girlfriend, Felix and Linda, are there with her. I ask Ellie if she wants to go to a café and she says no, she has already made some coffee including a cup for me so can I please come and sit down. Stop being so Swedish about the stupid keys – who cares – you'll find them or get some new ones. I want to talk to you and not when some keys are dominating you mind. So I say sure, I will put them out of my mind, even if it is puzzling and irritating.

The café visit is not happening but we have a nice friendly conversation about Fiji, and the real estate prices, about this house on Wood Street she wants to buy, about her daughter's horse, about what I am going to do now that I am retired, about how old she is now. Forty-two. Is it only two years ago you had your fortieth birthday? No, but I stopped counting at forty-two. Well I am fifty-five and a half but I feel as young as these kids here. And I think it is interesting how I can love and feel the same age as virtually anyone these days. Whether they are twenty or eighty. Age just has lost its meaning it seems. Our pleasant small talk actually makes me forget the lost keys. Pleasant human conversation cures all ills. Makes me recall that Goethe supposedly said: Gold is the best – but better is the sun, but better still is good human conversation. We talk in circles, smile and laugh a bit. Her daughter calls and wants to be driven to a North Shore friend. Yes I can do that she says and leaves in a few minutes. We agree that we will have a proper café meal in the not too distant future. A hug. A kiss. And good-bye.

As she goes to her car I realise she is pointing in the wrong direction on a one-way street. So I step out on the veranda and shout to her – do you realise this a one-way street? Half way into her BMW she says: I was always a bit of a rebel, and rather than backing the few yards to the next street she just carries on up the hill against the arrows. The neighbour who is out gardening looks after her and shakes his head. Crazy woman.

Once Ellie is gone I look for the keys again also going into pockets of clothes I know I haven't been wearing today. Perhaps there is a small possibility I didn't even bring the keys to the gym? But no luck! I know I brought the keys with me in the morning. No phone-call on my mobile. And at six thirty I have a tennis appointment. Fortunately this time it is with another member who hopefully hasn't lost his key. After a heavy rain shower at six o'clock I doubt there will be any tennis. But it brightens up and I go there anyway. Particularly among New Zealand sportsmen, it is considered very bad taste to not show up because of bad weather.

When I get there two Japanese guys, co-members of the Pompallier Tennis Club, are already playing in the lamp light. I ask them to please open the door for me as I forgot my keys. I also ask ' Shiawase desu ka?' (Are you happy?), which they confirm. One of them says two more people will come at seven. Three plus two makes five I think, which is not an ideal number for tennis. However at my suggestion we start a one single versus one double side, first to three won games and then we will change so that all get a chance to play singles side. These two guys are less than half my age, but very keen and very friendly, and I am enjoying a bit of a winning streak. At seven o'clock two ladies arrive, one, a New Zealander, about my age and the other a Japanese girlfriend to one of the guys. I suggest we play doubles and that one rests every game taking turns. This is accepted and we continue like that for half an hour. The young Japanese girl is really good and we have some fun games together. The Japanese guys are so polite so they each volunteer to rest every time there is an end to a game but in the end we all take turns except the Japanese girl where one of the other guys insist on sacrificing himself for her that she be able to continue to play. Nice.

Knowing that my son is cooking pizza and that it has been a full day with one hour of gym and an exhausting loss of my precious keys, at seven thirty I volunteer to reduce our numbers from five to four, such that a proper doubles game can be played. The Japanese guys protest thinking this is some kind of unacceptable sacrifice, but I insist that one hour of tennis in the dark is all I need, expecting the pizza to be warm and aromatic as I return home. When I get there the pizza is being manufactured but is not yet in the oven. I make myself a gin & tonic as compensation for the tries and tribulations of the day and sit down and talk to my son and his girlfriend as they are cooking with love.

As I walk past my mobile phone on the kitchen bench I see the window says '1 message'. One message! One message! What if? Must be. No one ever calls me. I have just arrived back in this country and few have yet found their way to my mobile number. And I pray: Let it please be the gym calling about my keys. I press ok on my phone and the number comes up. I call the number AND IT IS TO LES MILLS GYM. HURRA! But all I get is the stupid answering machine saying it is out of office hours. Linda says why don't you dial 707 to see if there is a message. So I do that. AND YES, 'WE HAVE YOUR CAR KEYS AND YOU CAN COME AND PICK THEM UP AT THE FRONT DESK!!'

I ask my son Andre' to drive me there – since I have already had a gin & tonic – and when we get there it is closed?! I see a cleaner through the glass and call him over to the door. I tell him my car keys are in there and he says he doesn't have access to anything. So I throw my hands up a bit surprised they close so early. He says they open at five o'clock tomorrow morning. Great! We return to the house and I open a bottle of red wine. Here is reason for celebration. And when we all have a glass of wine waiting for the pizza to cook, I make a call on the phone and ask for Ellie. She comes to the phone and at the top of my lungs I shout to her. GUESS WHAT? I FOUND THE CAR KEYS. Where? THEY WERE AT THE GYM. I LOVE YOU. I LOVE EVERYBODY. I LOVE THE WORLD. Scilly really to make such a fuss over something as trivial as a couple of keys!

Sunday 7th September 2003

13. Life Ordinaire.

I feel I haven't written anything for a while. My vow was to sit down and scribe when my emotions had been jolted and try to capture the jolt. This has worked so far but now in a period without jolts I find myself unproductive as far as writing is concerned. I though last night about what my history teacher told me. He said that the long periods in history where there wasn't much to report because no grand things happened were the best for the majority of the people, because they could get on with life and love, uninterrupted by wars and battles. So much of history seems to be eternalizing and glorifying the horrific. When I spent three days walking around Washington DC last year I had to reflect also that most of the proud memorials are related to wars. Just wars? Unjust wars? If people are out there worried sick and being killed and maimed perhaps it doesn't matter. No wars are good wars.

Anyway, the way this line of thought relates back to where I started is that the last six months have been uneventful and lovely, great. I recall that Rousseau said in his confessions that for a long period of time he didn't write anything because he was happy. "True happiness cannot be described, it can only be felt, and felt the more the less it can be described, since it is not the result of a number of facts, but is a permanent condition."

So lately I haven't done much at all of notoriety but still thought again and again that this is as close to paradise as it gets.

Since I started my new job last November I have been walking to work which takes me twenty minutes. I sleep without an alarm clock but allow myself to wake up when I wake up and then have a good breakfast before walking to work. This means I am at work anytime between eight and eight thirty and whether it is the former or the latter doesn't matter. Usually the sun is shining in the morning and my walk past some small houses and among trees is just a wonderful way to start a day. The light down under in New Zealand is so bright because of the clean air. I meet many people on the pavements and see many who drive to work in their cars. Sometimes when there is congestion I would walk faster than the slow moving traffic.

On my walk I meet and overtake many girls and the odd one gives me a smile. I reflect that a warm smile has the ability to make a person so much more alive. A smile is part of the international language of the heart and it helps put the recipient in a good mood – contagious enthusiasm! I calculated that this basic walking makes me walk 100 miles per month or about 2,000 km a year. It is clean and healthy and requires no fossil fuels to take me to work and back. Quite marvelous really and a true privilege!

Also at night to step out of the office building and walk home is a treat. The summer half of the year it is nice and bright also for the return walk whereas in winter my walk usually is at dusk. But it is pleasant and relaxing all the same. If it rains in the morning I take my car and if it rains in the evening and I am without a car I try to get Andre,' my son, to pick me up. But I also have the options to take a taxi or a bus, neither of which is difficult or expensive given the short distance.

Between my home and the office, starting from home, there is the Cavalier Tavern offering drinks, mostly beer, and simple meals and further down there is a food supermarket which is open till midnight every day. On my way home it is very easy to stop in and buy something for dinner or to complement stock of vegetables, fruits, milk etc. Continuing from the supermarket there is the Victoria Park with the flea market open every day attracting many tourists. A bit further along is the Katmandu outdoors shop and a bit further again Glengarry's wines. On Glengarry's shop there is a big sign saying 'Life is too short to drink bad wine.' I always think that life is too short to do anything bad, particularly perhaps to not be happy and enjoy oneself. Now that I have been recruiting staff I think of the wine sign and feel that 'Life is too short to mix with boring people.' So the people I hire should all be a bit fun such as to assist those we deal with to get into a good mood.

A little bit further along is my gym which makes for easy access either from home or from work. Once a week I go to the gym on my lunch hour and I would do at least two more training sessions a week, all in addition to my regular walking. These other training sessions would normally be tennis, usually at my nearby Pompallier Tennis Club. After the gym I would get to Nelson Street which is quite busy so I normally have to wait a few minutes for green light. At that intersection between Nelson and Wellesley Street there is a massage parlor, Femme Fatal, and across the next street the Sky City Casino on the left side and St Matthews Church on the other side. My home in Ponsonby and the office in the City are quite elevated and the area in the middle is very low land which previously was sea bed. This means that the end of my walk always is uphill and a little more exhausting.

When I am at the bank building I see the City Art Gallery a bit further down, a couple of hotels and to the right the Cinema complex and The Aotea Centre for Opera, Concerts and other performances. In the bank building I take the lift to the 21st floor with great views over the blue Pacific Ocean and the City of Auckland. Some of my colleagues would already be there and we greet each other before I check my mail on the PC. Checking the PC is always a bit exciting – reminding me of my childhood's net fishing. Overnight there is bound to be something in there but how many and of what sort?

Since part of my job is to build relationships I first look for any relationship entries. Relationships come in all sorts and forms and therefore the line between what is private and business becomes a bit blurred. In terms of relationship building, one success criteria is when the other party doesn't know or doesn't care if the relationship is private or business. The best relationships are sincere friendships which don't lend themselves to any limitations such as official and private. Another criterion for friends is that they are appreciated for who they are and not for how they can benefit you. This all makes it a bit ambiguous perhaps, and requires broadmindedness in approach. The success of the relationship building comes through in business growth and customer loyalty. Getting these two right are integral to running a profitable business.

Given that my job is to try to help people finance their business and feel good about themselves and about their relationship with my team and me, I have to say that it is hard to imagine a better job. To be paid for the pleasure of trying to help others and to build long lasting friendships, what could be nicer? After more than twenty years of relationship banking I have enjoyed it all along. There are challenges and difficult patches too, but the basics of it all are quite attractive. Finding a way to align what you are interested in and the job you do is more than anything else the road to happiness.

"I know that there is nothing better for men than to be happy and do good while they live. That everyone may eat and drink, and find satisfaction in his toil - this is the gift of God." Ecclesiastes *3: 12 – 13*

The people I interact with in the bank are all very positive and co-operative, building on a great spirit the bank has been know for in the marketplace. We have as ambitious targets as anyone else but the way of the bank is to pursue goals by growing and supporting the staff rather than by using undue pressure to make people feel inadequate and stressed. Although many know what good work practices look like, many succumb to just telling people to run faster and faster and produce more and more. I have always believed that if one just slows down a bit and work out goals together such that they are truly agreed, and then provide honest and sincere support in pursuit of targets, then one is onto a sustainable winning formula. My current bank is as close to putting this approach into practice as any enterprise I have seen.

The walks to and from work sets me in a good mood going either way. It allows some relaxation and forethought as to what is next to come – in the one case work and achievement – and in the other relaxation and interaction with family and friends. And in my relationship role I find myself having lunch with interesting people at least twice a week and dinners or other after work meetings of a social nature at least twice a week as well. In the after work activities there would be something cultural, music, opera, dance, theatre, art exhibitions etc at least twice a month and there would be a daytime entertaining event also about once a month including golf, sailing, tennis and speeches and presentations on interesting subjects. I agree with the findings in the book 'Flow, The Psychology of Happiness' that people are happier at work than at leisure. In between my last two jobs I had five months off and although I enjoyed it, I enjoy the present situation better. It is particularly the interaction with people and trying in a small way to contribute to their aspirations and goals that make it fun. I do find it satisfactory to try to help people for no other reason than seeing them enthused, energized and happy.

One evening a week my tennis club, Pompallier, in a high location in St Mary's Bay with stunning City views, has a social evening. Members come and mix into doubles and teams change every twenty minutes. These are all people I know only a little and it is great to just play the game for two hours and interact with perhaps twenty people I normally don't meet. It is all very friendly and after tennis there are drinks and sometimes a BBQ. Genders and ages mix and it makes me feel happy as a child again. I have been asked to come onto the Committee for the tennis club at the next meeting. I am looking forward to it. And the best thing is that the Club is only two hundred meters away from my house.

I also have two directorships I enjoy. Firstly a charitable trust, 'The Auckland Chamber Orchestra' led by a very talented and charming New Zealander who looks after all the artistic side of things and also quite a lot of the logistics. We are a group of six trustees who try to make the Orchestra work financially and this is not easy, but once the concert night is there and the music flows to a full Town Hall music chamber it feels like it is well worth the effort we are putting in to make ends meet. For every performance I have the chance to welcome patrons and potential supporters and it is delightful to be able to quite widely invite people to come and listen to lovely music. The orchestra has up to eighty members but normally about half that number will suffice for a performance.

My other directorship is in Wallace Corporation, a meat related business, one of my previous customers. This is a bit different as it is a remunerated job requiring attendance about eight times a year, sometimes in Auckland, sometimes at the works in Waitoa or Thames. My fellow directors are very knowledgeable and also very friendly and it gives me a chance to learn and also contribute to the New Zealand export industry. It is quite a difficult business to manage as so many of the parameters are dictated by the market and hard to influence, but it is good learning and always interesting.

On week ends we usually go to one of the nearby restaurants for coffee, lunch or dinner or all of those. Just around the corner on Ponsonby Road, there are twenty restaurants and it is not expensive.

As I have the ambition to read a book a week I would find myself reading for a few hours a day as well. Our small garden is attended by an outside garden firm but it falls on my lot to water tomatoes and herbs every day. In the garden we have a fig-tree, olives, pears, lime, grapefruit and fejoas. We have now had a six week dry spell so a little watering is essential. Every week end we either go to some show, have dinner with friends or we try to do something else extraordinary.

If the weather is fine we like to walk the beaches too and of course in summer go swimming. Takapuna Beach is only ten minutes drive away so enjoying a swim there is no major undertaking. Nowadays my boys also enjoy playing tennis so we would normally play some week end tennis and, if not playing tennis, I would go to the gym. It is only a short walk away and all three of us have memberships. Felix, our middle son, lives with his girl friend in a small house on the same street. He is keen on soccer and tennis but doesn't find time for the gym. He studies at Auckland University also within walking distance. Everything we need is within walking distance and for where we need to drive we have two cars for four people so always a car available.

Linda who is a great cook makes us a nice dinner every evening. She is now doing a special University course called 'The Novel' which when completed will produce her first novel and also a masters of arts in English Literature. She always walks to the university and she regularly utilizes the gym too. At least once a year we go on a trip to Europe to enjoy a second summer and also of course to see relatives and friends. At home we all have our PCs so we network with the world. Having lived in seven countries and believing that friendships is the best currency in which to measure wealth, I and my family have a lot of friends all over the world who we stay close to through email. Every morning I read Financial Times on the net and extract articles I think may be of interest to any of my acquaintances and friends. The issue of remoteness in New Zealand is mitigated by internet and reduced cost for telephoning and travelling. This literally gives us the best of two worlds.

Nothing extraordinary, nothing fantastic, and yet so lovely! I struggle to consider how paradise would be different.

25th April 2003

14. Foot Massage in Hua Hin, Thailand.

Sunday 21st August 2005

Do you do foot massage? I see the written 'Massage' on the glass doors and also 'foot massage' 60 min at 200 Bhat. Yes, come in, she says. Inside there are four or five mattresses spaced out on the floor and a system of curtains in the ceiling to enable customers to enjoy a little privacy for possible body massage. There are no other customers there so the curtains are pulled to the side creating a large open room. There are also two comfortable black leather chairs for foot massage customers.

Earlier in the day I had a first class breakfast with plenty of tropical fruits and an omelette made to order. I also had a small salad for good health but perhaps the 'thousand island' dressing I added on top made the positive health aspect questionable. A glass of orange juice, a small croissant and some coffee made it quite a complete breakfast.

I put my alarm clock on 7.30AM as I had a tennis appointment at 9.00AM and I wanted at least one hour between the meal and the match. The night before I put two pairs of briefs and one pair of socks outside to dry after washing them. I noticed one pair of Calvin Klein under wear was missing. Someone must have seen them from the beach and jumped the low stone fence, avoiding the guards, and stolen them.

Although exciting underwear now seems to be quite an industry, the loss of a pair of mine failed to excite me. It may have been my fanciest pair but I am almost certain that whoever stole them need them more than I do. After breakfast I reported the loss to the front desk. The attendant girl said 'we will investigate'. This I thought rather meaningless approach as whoever might be wearing these second hand underwear would be rather difficult to identify.

At nine sharp I was at the tennis courts but no partner to play with was there. Ten minutes later I walked towards the front desk when a hotel staff told me the 'the tennis courts are over there'. I know, I said, but I had an appointment for 9.00AM and no-one is there? I will contact the recreation team he said and I walked back to the courts. A few minutes later my partner – the resident coach, arrived. He was a little guy with no extra kilos, half my age, and he probably hadn't just had a luxurious breakfast. And he was used to the hot climate!

The balls he brought were a bit dead but I thought it didn't matter. During the warm up I felt that I could give him a match. I suggested we play a set and said he could serve. He double faulted the first two points and I got 2 – 0 game score without losing a point. Then he improved and I was getting a bit tired. After about 30 minutes he won 6 – 4 and I was happy and he was happy. I paid 200 Bhat or 8 NZ $ for his time and the court which wouldn't even have covered the court hire in New Zealand. At the end of the hour I was soaking wet so I walked back to my bungalow. I took a shower and washed my tennis clothes and put them out to dry. I realized that this was at some slight risk but I thought the risk acceptable and probably smaller at daytime.

After the shower I put on my togs and went to the pool. There I wrote some postcards and continued to read my book on Stalin (who together with Mao and Hitler caused more death and destruction than any others in the history of mankind). I did some laps in the pool, dressed in shorts and T-shirt and went for lunch. I found a restaurant on a jetty and I was the only customer so chose a table at the front with full views of the Bay of Siam. I ordered a Singha Beer and coconut milk and lemon grass seafood soup. Good beer and great soup. Walking out of the restaurant at 1.30PM I felt a bit tired and thought I might look for a soothing foot massage.

In the massage studio there were only the masseuse and I plus her little daughter. The Thai masseuse asked me to sit down in one of the chairs and pulled up a little stool for her to sit on to work on my feet. She was dressed in a red soft top that was quite revealing when she leaned forward to massage first my left foot. She was also wearing fashion blue jeans. The little daughter wore a cute little red top with a blue shirt underneath. I saw she was wearing diapers so probably not too old. I pointed to their tops and said my favourite colour is red and also pointed to my red hat.

I was asked to put my feet in a blue plastic basin with luke-warm water and she washed my feet. She packaged up my right foot in a green towel and put it all to one side as she worked on my left foot. Sixty minute to massage two feet seems a bit rich but that is perhaps why you feel so spoilt and it feels so good. Time seems to be of no consequence. The focus is on health, relaxation and pleasure. She works every inch of the foot first without oil and then with oil. And the leg from the knee down also gets meticulously attended to.

During the process the little girl is just walking around quite contentedly making little noises and looking adorable. Early on I put my Stalin book in my lap to read during the treatment but we struck up a conversation so I decided to postpone my reading to later.

The little girl was watching TV in the ceiling with Thai boxing. The masseuse asked if I like Thai boxing and I said I didn't particularly, but once a match is started and they try their best to knock each other out it is difficult not to get caught up in it.

I ask the masseuse if it is her daughter which she confirms. She says it is her only child and that the girl is half German and half Thai. Most Thai girls look for a 'falang" man for better economic opportunity. I take it that 'falang' means foreigner.

She asks where I'm from and I say I live in New Zealand. I add that I am Swedish but have lived overseas for 20 years. She says she speaks German and Swedish because of previous boy friends. But she hasn't been to Germany or Sweden. I ask where in Sweden her boyfriend was from and she says 'Varberg' in a dialect typical for that province of Sweden. She says Swedes and Germans don't like each other much. She had to give up the Swede because he was always drunk. And now she is alone with the loveliest little daughter. She asks me if my wife is with me on this trip and I say no, this time I am travelling alone. She says it is a good wife who trusts her husband to travel alone.

I tell her I have three sons 19, 26 and 30. Wow she says! I am only 33. Do they all live in New Zealand? No, one is in New Zealand, one in London and one in Sweden. So are any of them married? Yes one of them, the middle one.

After nearly half an hour she is finished with my left foot and moves over to my right foot. The little girl comes with an empty formula bottle and looks like she wants some food. She is told 'später' i.e. German for later. I remember I have some fruit toffees in my shoulder bag, and I find them and give her one. She takes it but can't get the paper off. So I take another and remove the paper and give her that one too. She sucks on it and bites off small pieces of the pink sweet and looks happy.

The masseuse is now working on my right foot. She tells me that the German father lives in Bangkok with another Thai woman. She says she doesn't mind if he would have a temporary girl, but leaving her and their daughter made her very disappointed. She will meet with him soon to try and get a passport for the little girl and make a settlement. She says she wants nothing for herself but a little support for the girl. The offer is Euro 6,000 in three installments as a final settlement.

I ask her if she always brings the daughter to the massage studio and she says only Saturday and Sunday as there is no school then. And if she didn't she would have to pay 100 Baht per day (NZ$4) and that is too expensive. It is hard to bring up a child on your own, she says. The little one has been sick for a few days and then I haven't slept at all. Very exhausting!

I ask her if Thai men are different from 'falang' men. She says all they want to do is f**k and not pay for it. Many Thai women are looking for the security of 'falang' men. And many foreigners fall in love with a Thai girl – even if she is a prostitute, and want to marry her. They are good that way! It is so easy to fall in love. She says she has come to like older men better because they are more appreciative and caring.

On TV one of the boxers kicks the other in the groin and that is the end of that match. I ask her if she fights too. She says she used to – her father taught her – but she never hurt anyone.

I comment that Hua Hin looks quite tidy and she says this is the summer residence of the King and therefore it should be tidy. The royal family come here to enjoy the better air compared to Bangkok. I ask her if she likes the King and she says all Thais love their King. She asks where I stay and how I got there. I told her I am staying at the Central Village at Sofitel and that I got here by limousine from

Bangkok Airport. How much does that cost? The hotel room is about $ 70 US per night or 3,000 baht and the transfer cost 2,800. That is not too bad she says.

When I ask her about the economy she says not much is happening. When I say that people look pretty happy she says it is also hard. Does she like the Prime Minister Thaksin? She hesitates but shakes her head and says she doesn't like him much. "But he has done some good things like reducing the drug economy. His predecessors were unable to do that."

I ask her about 'Muslim Insurgents' and fundamentalists. She says that is only in the far south. "What is your religion?" She says 'Buddhism.' I comment that may be the nicest religion in terms of not having caused antagonism or destruction in the past. She says all religions are meant to be nice but weird people have twisted messages to suit their own ends.

When she massages my right leg calf muscles I groan a bit and she asks if it hurts. Yes a little but it also feels good. The hour is up and I feel like a new better human being with two very healthy legs and feet. I motion to get up but she says stay and disappears. That leaves me with the little girl and I give her another sweet. The mother comes back with a cup of freshly brewed tea so I sit back for a few moments and enjoy the wonderful tea she made.

I again motion to get up and she tells me to move to the little stool in front. She goes behind me and gives me a neck and shoulder massage. She puts her elbow and her body weight onto my shoulders and it hurts but it also feels therapeutic. I asked who taught her massage and she says she went to an institute to learn.

After the neck and shoulders massage I feel like a well treated prince. I ask her how much it costs and she says 200 baht. I bring out a 500 bill and tell her to please take 300. She goes to the till, deposits the 500 and takes 200 out and gives it to the little girl she now carries and tells her to give it to me. I take my change, say thank you very much, and give mother and daughter a quick kiss on the cheek. As I walk through the door I say good bye and thank you again, and she says "welcome back tomorrow for an oil massage."

21 August 2005

15. The Unplanned Boat Trip

Singapore September 17, 2006

As I sat down in the boat the intense feeling of dejavue and happiness came over me. The dark wood and the oily rope and the smell from the engine brought my subconscious to the surface! I somehow sensed some of the happiest memories of my life.

Now this boat was off the quay in Singapore and I hadn't really intended to do the river cruise again but stumbled on it on my morning walk. As the morning was a bit gray and wet, a boat tour at very little cost seemed to be quite a nice idea. There was a small group of people ahead of me in the boat queue. But I was told that they were all one group so I had to wait and when it was my turn there was only I in the boat for 20 persons. Lucky day!

Seeing and smelling the rough wood made me remember the summers of my childhood with small boats used for fishing and hunting in the Baltic Sea. I used to go to this island with my sister and parents and just loved every second of the perceived wild life living. Fishing, hunting and running around the barns with all the domestic animals and the other island children. My mother told me that I used to ask every morning when there how many days still remained for us to be on the island. At those days in the early 50's the limit of my parents' holiday was two or perhaps three weeks.

I have come to see Singapore as my third home. I might have said second home but slot number one and two are already taken by

Sweden and New Zealand. But I do feel at home in Singapore after two sojourns there in 1980's and again around the turn of the millennium. As per Lee Kuan Yew's book 'from third world to first' it is well known that Singapore has experienced miraculous growth and transformation in the second half of the 20th century.

The current look of the city state suggests that affluence levels are up considerably even in the last ten years. And in spite of all looking so efficient and shiny it is also well known that there is a (shrinking) minority of people there that are poor and experience different degrees of hardship. Many well off countries seem to face a similar challenge.

Once I had stepped onto the boat I took a seat at the very front whereas the driver was at the back holding on to the engine. I looked around me as I had the scenery explained to me by a recorded guide voice and again I was surprised over how happy I felt for some reason. I am normally pretty happy but this felt special.

I came into Singapore from five weeks of visiting Europe, most of which in Sweden but also Poland and Hungary. Poland I visited as my wife's next book will be set in Krakow, Poland, and Hungary to get a little bit of a feel for Buda Pest. I found Krakow beautiful and also contemplated the fate of the significant pre-war Jewish community there. I wondered if perhaps the many tragic deaths in nearby Auschwitz lent a special spirit or glow of sad remembrance to Krakow. Without quite knowing how and why, I felt the atmosphere there influenced by this unspeakable tragedy.

My visit to Sweden had been in the name of paying respect to my many relatives and friends, particularly my mother, and also in support of my wife's book launch there. Now in Singapore I felt the freedom of true holiday with no expectations or obligations. Just holiday mode, enjoying friends and sights and memories of the past!

The night before I had dinner with a famous Singapore author, who gave me a signed copy of her latest book. During my three days in Singapore I had three meetings a day and none of them for business purposes. Just old friends getting together to enjoy some congenial conversation over coffee, drinks, lunch or dinner! I enjoyed the three days tremendously.

Now as the boat started out up river we went under Elgin Bridge and later Coleman Bridge and at Read Bridge we turned to go with the flow of the river. After passing under the Elgin Bridge, the MITA building (ministry of information, communication and the arts) with its characteristic colorful window shutters, became visible. Just at the Coleman bridge turning point there is the restaurant 'Brewerkz' which provides a very good value lunch with home brewed beer.

Nowadays it is mostly tourist traffic on the river whereas in olden days 60 % of Singapore's trade was over the quays that are now the home of restaurants and museums or other, all colorful and well maintained. The right side of the river at Clark Quay provides this stunning contrast of the old low rise storehouses, converted to pubs and restaurants, and behind about ten or so huge sky-scrapers testifying to Singapore's miraculous economic progress. Especially at night this provides a stunning sight, if viewed from Raffles Landing Site which now holds a fine statue of Sir Stamford Raffles, the founder of Singapore.

The high rises house mostly finance industry and business related to banking. It is all bustling daytime with all the people commuting in to earn their keep and make their mark. Night time and week ends it is mostly leisure activities there like touristing and socializing. It is arguably the prettiest part of Singapore, even if there are many other nice spots as well. The river banks are adorned with fine statues by famous sculptures and it is well worth walking around the area and look at each one individually.

We get up to Cavenagh Bridge by the Asian Civilizations Museum. This is the prettiest of all the bridges and only for walking. Built in 1869 it is popular as a spot for wedding pictures. Just as we pass under this bridge there is a lovely sculpture depicting five boys jumping into the river on the right just outside the Fullerton Hotel. The plaque next to the sculpture says that Chong Fah Cheong is the creator of this magnificent piece. And the next and last of the City bridges is the Anderson Bridge from 1910 to the left of which are Victoria Theatre and the famous Cricket Club, of which I am still a member.

After Anderson Bridge we are out in the sea and there is one more bridge further out but that is the modern motorway (ECP) and is not perceived to be a bridge but rather an elevated road, oblivious of wheather there is land or sea underneath. Such a motorway scores fully for efficiency but the aesthetic value is at the opposite end of the scale. Out in the sea we passed the Merlion which is the old symbol of Singapore, 'singa' meaning lion. The Merlion is a combined lion and mermaid with a fountain of water coming out of its mouth. It is a great touristic attraction and there are people photographing it all the time every day. Sometimes I wonder what people do with all these photos but perhaps that is irrelevant, key is that they are having fun taking them. On holidays you take pictures! I must admit I have given up that and rather try to get something for the spirit than for the photo album.

At this stage the driver asks if I brought a camera and if he can help me take a picture of me with the right background. I thank him for his kind offer but tell him I didn't bring a camera. I do have a little smart digital camera which my staff in Tokyo gave me upon leaving my job there but I left it in my hotel room. After that we commence the return trip to Raffle's landing. It is still drizzling lightly and I am still in this elevated mood.

Singapore is great, I love my friends there, and I am grateful for all the things I have stumbled upon in my life – including this unplanned little boat trip. When back on land I walk around the area and study some of the sculptures more in detail. There are a couple of Salvador Dali pieces that are amazing, i.e. Horse Saddled with Aged Time! On one of the plaques the sponsor UOB bank says: *As long as we enjoy peace and optimism Singapore will do well!* I hasten back to my Sunday Brunch appointment at the Billiards bar of Raffle's hotel. This has to be the ultimate smorgasbord. Life is beautiful.

17th September 2006

16. My shoes

I have very good shoes. Walking the dog in the pouring rain I thought I have really good shoes. Something to be happy about! Not that I am generally unhappy but a set of suitable useful shoes makes a big difference. I used to think that a pair of clean sheets is perhaps the nicest physical asset imaginable. If you are lucky, that is one of your first experiences in life and often it is also tends to be your last. Clean white sheets is lovely (the spell check is prompting me: when did sheets become singular? – ok, the sheets are not singular, but sleeping in clean new white sheets is singularly delightful). But you can't wear shoes in bed and this note is about shoes. One of these old signs from an American Inn said no shoes to be worn in bed and no more than four to sleep in each bed. And in Linda's book about poverty among Jews in Poland in the early part of the 20th century, children had to stay in bed all winter because there was no money to buy shoes. On Swedish Radio I heard the story of a man who had just bought new boots and needed to travel 250 miles from Jonkoping to Stockholm in the 1800s. He walked bare foot the length of the distance carrying his boots because they were too precious to be worn on country roads. Since then many steps of progress have been taken. We sometimes forget how hard it was.

Walking Ponsonby Road this 23rd day of February with the summer rain bucketing down I look down on the rubber shoes I bought New York 1999. They are still like new, and I don't even need to wear any socks in them. They are so comfortable and totally water resistant. With a big hide hat and my dry-z-bone oil skin coat I am smiling, feeling as happy as Gene Kelly. And we all know what he is famous for. When walking the streets in New York that spring day 1999 I stopped into a shoe shop and bought three pairs of shoes. Besides these grey rubber coated ones I bought a pair of black Mephisto soft walking shoes and a fine pair of American Allen Edmonds shoes, top of the range with rubber soles. Linda has always said: don't save money when buying shoes. Good shoes will put life on a new footing. I think I spent US$ 500 on these shoes making the salesman quite happy. Eight years later in New York I bought another pair of leather soled Allen Edmonds for almost as much as the package of three eight years earlier. These shoes I got in the last millennium are as good as new after eight years of regular use. Amazing! It was on that trip eight years ago I got acquainted with Amanda. I have already written her story so won't dwell on her more here.

I was out shopping this morning. Linda had asked me to get two butter-flied lamb legs. I tied the dog at a road sign outside the butcher's shop and walked in. The two butchers looked surprised that anyone was out in the prevailing weather. I told them what I wanted and was asked how many I was feeding. About ten. I said 'beautiful weather' in my Louis Armstrong voice and they of course agreed. "There will be no Opera in the Park tonight I guess and The Chinese New Year's lantern festivities will not happen either I suppose." As they finished the de-boning of the lamb legs I said: 'lamb is not very good business now, is it?' "No, farmers are not getting much for it," they conceded. 'I said nobody wants the pelts and the strong currency erodes income from exports. I said I was a director of one of the meat companies. I suggested: 'although sheep farmers are struggling, dairy farmers are creaming it.' 'I think there are too many cows in the land. At ten million total, the environmental impact equals a human population of about 50 million. The butchers agreed and we all thought that it will self adjust at some stage with pressure coming on from environmental compliance and also availability of feed during dry periods. I reflected that the ones really happy about the deluge today would be the dairy farmers. I was asked "what do you think about the suggested mega merger between two major meat companies." I said I am not so sure about the benefits for farmers and New Zealand, but I think it is inevitable with some restructure to get viability in the industry. Capacity needs to be taken out and marketing needs to get more sophisticated. I paid $ 60 dollars for a bag full of beautiful meat. Linda says lamb is good because they feed naturally and contain less antibiotics and other bad stuff.

I pay and say thank you and return to my half drenched dog who is happy to be in motion again. I look at the few people I meet and they smile nicely, possibly because the little wet dog is so endearing. That's when I look at my shoes and feel happy. I cross the street to the 'Nest' shop to buy some thick candles. The dog gets tied at the outside again. But dogs are used to that. I find the candles, pick up the dog and when I come to Rennall Street the dog wants to go home. But I want to go to the bakery and buy two muffins to brighten up the morning. And since I outweigh the dog by a factor of 10 the bakery it is. A few minutes later we are back to Rennall Street and the dog is full leash ahead of me wanting to get indoors. The dog stops outside our gate and I catch up and open the gate. I take the dog into the laundry to try to dry her a little before letting her in. I usually grab something from the laundry from the cleaning basket for drying the dog, and all I find is Andre's blue t-shirt which will do fine. I open the garden door and let Pixi loose and she runs into the house like a rocket which is what she always does when soaking wet. She calms down and parks herself on my foot stool.

My clothes are all dripping and I take my shoes off on the entrance rug. My feet are dry. I look at the shoes again. I am so happy. I have such good shoes.

Auckland 23 Feb 2008

AUT graduation ceremony 2-30pm at the Bruce Mason Centre, Takapuna, Auckland 12th October 2007

Good afternoon, ladies and gentlemen. It gives me great pleasure to have the chance to talk to this audience of graduands and friends. Many of you have now completed your studies, even if as we all know, learning is lifelong. Confucius reminds us that when a person can more than cope with his studies he or she works and when he or she can more than cope with work, further study is the answer. In order to get the best out of study you need to have experienced some difficulties of life and that perplexity makes study more rewarding and useful. When I attended New York University one of my lecturers said: 'You may think this is simple – but wait until I explain it to you!'

Many of you now face 30 to 40 years of working life and I would like to suggest some things for you to keep in mind during this voyage. Never forget that first and foremost you are all humans and whatever skills you have acquired are useful tools but the operator of the tools is you. The skills we have obtained are only useful in as far as they serve the purpose of adding value to humanity. Thus all we do must either alleviate difficulties or pain or positively contribute to happiness for somebody. In our quest for success and personal wealth we must never compromise our commitment to ethics and fair and decent treatment of all we deal with. These are not business constraints but rather conditions of sustainable success.

The biggest asset for most profitable companies is their goodwill. The goodwill can be expressed as the difference between book value and market valuation. The average goodwill value of the 500 largest companies in America (the Fortune 500) is 2/3rds of the total. Intangible assets are worth twice as much as tangible assets. When you build goodwill for yourselves you also build goodwill for your group or company.

Recently I was working as country manager in Japan for a major bank. When I recruited young graduates I explained to them that there are two things of equal importance I want you to do. One is to manage your tasks as defined as best as you can. But that is only half of it. The other half is to be a catalyst for others to be the best they can. To contribute to a climate of help and care and where success is achieved in a spirit of co-operation! Generosity and kindness once set in motion are unstoppable and very valuable traits when setting the scene for sincere and genuine customer service. All business is about customer service.

When people ask you to do something, try to understand why. Understanding why something is desired makes it easier to come up with a better solution. When someone looks to buy a ¼ inch drill, he probably doesn't need a drill but a ¼ inch hole. We talk about satisfying customer needs. But on a higher level we can actually go beyond that and perhaps eliminate the need. In Japan I also told my recruits that I don't want you to just fit in and conform. We do many things that are not optimal and efficient. I want you to help establish what they are so we can improve together. This is challenging but continuous improvement is what life is all about. Finding a better way of doing things, freeing up time for research and also pleasure and leisure!

Another important point I would like to make is to level with people. Don't look down on anyone. Don't look up to anyone. Treat people as peers. See yourself as peer of all. That is a good way to understand that those less fortunate or gifted than you, are your fellow brothers and sisters. And perhaps to help remind those higher in station that you are keen to contribute and that you won't be inhibited in your desire to be helpful by someone's higher position on the ladder. A respectful disrespect! This is sometimes called a flat organization where everybody's ideas counts and are encouraged. Courtesy and kindness can and should still be upheld. The ultimate achievement requires the engagement and commitment of ***all***.

Schools inevitably are about grading and ranking students as part of the learning process. Once out in the business world the issue is to bring ***all*** along and to ensure that ***all*** pull to their ability and capacity. Out there in the work place it is not about being the best. It is about achieving the greatest improvement. You may be smarter and more productive than most, but you need to figure out how you can improve from year to year. In that respect the challenge is the same for all – how can we be better than last year. And your usefulness to any organisation will increase if you ensure that your quest for improvements is motivational for others to do the same. No matter how clever we are – on our own there is not all that much we can achieve.

Being kind, caring and considerate is at least as important as being useful. Looking after your teammates builds 'corp d'esprit' or corporate spirit. This spirit is a major component of good will value and brand value and without it success will be elusive. Our traditional accounting and incentives have often overlooked this part because it is difficult to measure. But to measure that which is easy to measure rather than that which is relevant is not very useful. I am a keen – and often critical – reader of Harvard Business Review. Recently it suggested that many career people would do better by trading one unit of skills for one unit of team spirit and co-operation. Please don't forget that. Making people around you feel good will always be more important than outshining all around you. By weighing these issues right you can achieve both personal excellence and team success.

If we build good will by always going out of our way to help the next person we build friendships and credit with our fellow man. This credit is perhaps the most precious asset anyone can have. It cannot be depleted by inflation, corrosion, taxation or any other ill that may erode your tangible wealth. If you have helped people ten times the likelihood is that when you need help people can't wait to assist. Every career and life has disappointments and set-backs and good will and friendships are invaluable remedies against such challenges. And even if you never need any help, the feel good factor from having made a difference for someone else is perhaps one of the finest things any human can experience.

In order that you not think this presentation too conventional I would like to tell you about my goal in life. My goal is starting a Mexican Wave of Love! My view is that in the concept of love is hidden all the hope of mankind to build a better, kinder and gentler place. Love is not necessarily what happens between two people. Love is an attitude towards life. It is waking up each day feeling a bit grateful for having been given another chance to make a difference. And trying to express that gratitude in things you do in your interaction with people and nature.

Having lived and worked in seven countries I am lucky to have lovable friends of all races and religions. We must be inclusive and understand that whether we are from Sweden, China, New Zealand or Iran, we are all pursuing the same ends – to live an enjoyable life with freedom from fear and want – and plenty of time for fun, family and friends. Aristotle taught us that it is not enough only to work well – we need to be able to idle well too. People are very similar around the world and if you look for it, there is something lovable with nearly all. Find what it is and commend that person on it and the Mexican Wave of Love is starting to build. If you can love one person, you can love another person and you can love all. Let love be your guide. Please join me in building the Wave of Love.

Travel Notes

1. India, a holiday.

With pre allocated and confirmed seats we checked in an hour before departure. No people, no problems. Where are all the people, this flight is supposed to be full? They have all checked in already! Through customs we sit down to read for a bit knowing that the gate area always gets a bit crowded. Half an hour before departure we go to our gate D12 to join the security check queue. It moves slowly. The room inside is full of people. Just before it is our turn, there is an announcement that this flight will now be departing from another gate C 42 so could all passengers please move to that gate. Last in first out. Perhaps this is a good omen for us? We arrive to our new gate among the first for another round of thorough checkups. It is a bit chaotic with so many people arriving at the same time and also a bit disorganised. No allowance for passengers of old age or families with small children. Any travel to or within India also seems to have extra security precautions, a bit like travelling to Israel. Another issue with India is that people tend to have an exorbitant amount of luggage, both checked and carry on. There are a lot of protection and high tariffs in India and that stimulates people to try to carry in as much as they can get away with.

It is now obvious that we will be departing late rather than 8.30 PM as scheduled. After all this there is finally a boarding call and we go through to bus transportation to the aircraft. It makes me wonder that if we are going to be bussed around, why did we need to change gates in the first place? Linda and I get on the first bus as the last passenger which means we will be first off. After quite a lengthy drive on the Changi tarmac we reach our plane in total darkness. It is now 9.30 PM. We are on the plane in a whisker, stowing away our two small bags and dive into our literature. Half an hour later all the lockers are choker block full and all the passengers including families and infants are in place. We wait for another half hour and the captain announces his sincere apologies for the delay and further more there is a small technical problem with one of the engines being investigated and once this is out of the way we will be airborne.

Another half hour later the captain comes on the air announcing that the problem has proved more difficult than anticipated to fix and that he is awaiting instructions as to what the best course of action might be. Another hour later we learn that a new plane has been allocated to this flight and all passengers are kindly asked to disembark and bring all their belongings. The new gate will be C 30. So we embark on the busses again, are brought to the terminal, have to find our way through the maze of Changi to the designed gate and go through the rigorous security check a third time. For us being young well rested and healthy it isn't a major problem but it is getting a bit taxing on the very old and very young and their keepers. The good news is that Singapore Airlines are providing complimentary sandwiches and drinks at the gate. Well through the security, there is a 50 meter queue to the freebies but, anything free must be taken advantage of, so I enter the line on behalf of both of us. Ten minutes later we have some bread and cakes and coffees and life seems a bit more enjoyable.

In the midst of all this a young Singapore Airline employee distributes a survey to get feed back on how the situation has been handled. To my surprise I find myself more critical than Linda, thinking that the whole set up is a bit negative so it hard to get excited. I also think that even if the handling has been correct, there has been a total lack of human touch, humor or anything like that. We can all run into unforeseen difficulties but if there is a bit of extension of heart or humor it all gets easier to bear. Linda's feed back is that the hard up passengers could have been looked after a bit better and given priority in security lines etc, but there was none of that. Hopefully the feed back will be useful.

So we board again at midnight with a myriad of hand luggage which all gets stowed in every empty space and we are finally away to our second India adventure, having had the first in North India in 1988, twelve years ago. The flight of three and a half hours is uneventful and we land about 2.00 AM in Chennai which is the new name for Madras. India is 21/2 hours behind Singapore. Linda asks me how anyone can be a half hour behind, isn't it terribly inconvenient? Although it is unusual, it doesn't really matter as for the locals it is totally irrelevant. They go on full hours as anyone else. And India with 3.2 million square kilometers and 1billion plus people is so big so they probably feel entitled to do their own thing.

Immigration is easier than we think but the luggage collection takes forever. The belt that our flight has been assigned to gets a few bags now and few bags later. After an hour the flow of bags is very thin and no sign of our two smart little roller bags. At that stage Linda goes and checks the other belts and sure enough, there are our two bags. So at 3.00AM still fresh and beautiful, we take our bags on the trolley and march out into the Indian night. We thought we might be met, but anyone intending to do so has probably given up after so many delays. Although there are a great number of people on either side of the exit, no one has our name on their sign. A toutor of taxis grabbed me and says Taxi? As I don't like the look of the guy I say no, and proceed until another guy who looks a bit nicer says Taxi? and I say yes. This causes a great disagreement between the first guy and the second guy, but I am adamant that I'd rather go with the second. Linda thinks we should go with neither, but I say that if this second guy has a vehicle that looks like an official taxi, lets go with him.

Yes, the car although a bit crummy, looks like an official taxi so I ask him for the fare to Quality Inn, Aruna and he says 525 Rupiah. I say 500 Rps and he agrees. Later I learn that right fare is 2-300 but at 3.00 AM, $20 instead of 10, who cares. At this hour, time is of the essence. We drive through the night and see a lot of activity on the road, lots of cars and people. Linda says we have no clue where this guy is taking us and I agree, but I am not going to worry about it. 25 minutes later we arrive at the hotel, check in and then try to sleep for four hours which works out well. We want to get up at eight to try to track down our onward tickets to Cochin but right after the wake up call, there is another call with a messenger delivering our tickets. It is a relief to find that some things can be efficient.

Once awake we go up although our onward flight is only at 12.30PM. A first class breakfast is included and we enjoy the fruits and all the other delicacies. After breakfast we take a short walk in Aruna just to get some first impressions. Very busy street with so many pedestrians and bicycles, lots of exhaust and quite dirty. But the feeling of life and vibrancy which we had so much been looking forward to was there. We walked about a kilometer, observed and looked, crossed a bridge with a quite smelly river. We were in India again and it felt great. It is a bit of a heaven and hell experience – good and evil, rich and poor, the ultimate beauty and the ultimate depravity, advanced and primitive, a melting pot of history and religions - which all makes it so fascinating.

We catch the Jet Air flight which works well and even serves a full Indian lunch on the one-hour flight to Cochin. It is nice with a trouble free flight. The Cochin terminal is only one year old and very neat and efficient. Our baggage is checked by some ground hostesses against our receipts which we both think is a good idea to prevent your luggage disappearing with the wrong person. Walking out of the arrival hall there is the agent meeting us and we are ushered to our car, which turns out to be a rather big mini bus. When we first planned this trip we invited 20 people to join us but gradually our numbers dwindled to Linda and myself and our son Felix with girlfriend Hanna from Auckland, New Zealand. The latter two were travelling a day later so would only catch up at our second stop.

Driver's name was Joy, which boded well for the next few days experiences. Joy is a tall good looking Indian in his 40's well dressed, all smiles and very knowledgeable. He tells us he has two children and that the government recommends one or two only in order to curb the population growth. As for religion he said he was a Christian, Syrian Orthodox. We have never heard of that before but assumed it to be near Russian and Greek Orthodox. We are told our trip to Munar, high up in the mountains, will take four hours. Munar means three rivers and it is the meeting point of three rivers. The state of Kerala has 44 rivers, three floating eastwards towards Tamil Nadu and Bay of Bengal and 41 floating westwards towards the Arabian Sea, the two seas mentioned being part of the vast and mighty Indian Ocean. The inhabitants number ca 20 million. There has been a leftist/socialist government in Kerala for a long time and the literacy rate is higher than in the rest of India. The driver points out to us Tapioka, rubber trees, cardemum, pepper, nutmeg, bananas and many other spices and trees. Roads are narrow and very busy, traffic slowly moving forward in either direction. Joy explains to us that unlike northern India in Kerala there are houses and buildings all along the road without interruption whereas up north there are villages and space in between. There is life everywhere, people walking, talking, cycling and just going about their daily tasks undistracted of traffic and all the honking of car horns.

Getting up higher we start to see more and more tea plantations, a green lustrous carpet elevated from the ground by two to three feet. We learn that the tea plant gets 80 – 120 years old and that leaves are picked every 14 days. The pickers are from Tamil Nadu which is a poorer state providing labour to the rather hard and arduous task of picking leaves on the hill sides. The scenery is getting quite spectacular and at 6.30PM we arrive at our hotel which gives us an hour before dinner. We are now 1500 meters above sea level and the air is quite cool. A cyclone over Sri Lanka is moving north and giving quite low clouds and drizzly weather also in Munar. We see the clouds below where we are and from time to time we are all swept into one of the clouds. The hotel is eight rooms only and a converted animal barn. 'The Windemere.' Very simple but clean with amenities and tastefully done in wood and clay and nice red clay squares on the floor.

Not cold but cool and very quiet and quite romantic. We talk to some of the other guests at pre dinner tea. One English couple from London, one American Finance lawyer and his antropology professor wife and an architect from Switzerland. All friendly low key people. The big surrounding mountains and the spectacular views are quite humbling and invites you to speak quietly which is sufficient as there is very little competing sound.

After a superb dinner of four courses we retire to our room as we have a bit of sleep to catch up on and after some reading we are at sleep at 9.30 PM which equates to midnight in Singapore. Thus ends the first day of our second trip to India.

Next day is the 28th of December and we have a full and nourishing breakfast at 8.00 AM and are on the way at 9.00 AM. We didn't bring any warm cloths or tracking boots which seems a bit of a pity given that this day as well is a bit cool and wet. However, I put a t-shirt under my shirt and bring an umbrella and Linda brings a long sleeve shirt and we are OK.

We drive through the township of Munar up on small dwindling roads to a national park hosting a few thousand of a very rare goat which is an endangered species. Joy explains that there is a particular little blue flower in this region that blooms only every twelve years, but then it covers the mountainsides in blue and it lasts for months. We drive higher and higher, past some water falls and ultimately to a parking place beyond which we have to continue by foot. Looking up the mountain and given the drizzle, Linda is a bit skeptical, but we move on step by step until we are as high as the road goes. The views are spectacular and we see quite a few other people, Indians, on the road. Most of them seem to be young boys in their teens and they are very friendly and talkative. We seem to be the only westerners. After about an hour's walk we look for this endangered species but it is nowhere to be seen so we start our decent again. Going down is a bit easier and again we meet a lot of 'students' who want to take our picture and ask us questions. It is school holidays and that may be why there are so many youngsters, but where are all the girls?

On our way back we stopped by a tea factory and had a cup of tea and bought one pound of tea and some strawberry reserve for ca S$ 5. The tea tasted great. The area around Munar is very green and inviting. We stopped in town so I could buy a long sleeve shirt and looked at local market. Still a little bit wet and muddy. Then back to the hotel for a light lunch and a nap. By 3.30PM we went back to town a bit hesitantly as it was still low clouds and wet, but once across the bridge the skies opened up and it was most pleasant. Just before the town there was a football match going on and it all looked quite idyllic. In town we walked around and looked up the Hindu temple which we could access by crossing a small river and climbing up a number of stairs and of course removing our foot wear. It provided a nice view over Munar. After a while we crossed back to town through the market, buying some more tea, and up to the big church.

In the church we were lucky enough to witness a priest ordination and there was happy and forceful music and singing which we tried to join into as best as possible. Linda sat next to me until she detected a gender split on different sides of the isle so she discretely moved across. It was all quite colourful and spectacular and was finished in about 15 minutes followed by a reception in an adjacent building. Several of the well dressed patrons tried to encourage us to part take in the reception, but we felt that we didn't want to intrude on such a solemn occasion so walked back to town again. There we bought four fresh Parata breads for 10 Rps and enjoyed them on the spot. This Indian bread has to be the best tasting bread in the world. Back to the hotel we had a chat to the hotel owner, a doctor from Cochin having invested in the tea plantation and now expanding the business to include a small hotel activity, set to grow a bit further next year by an extra wing. A very nice a mild mannered man as many fine Indians are. We enjoyed pre dinner tea and snacks, followed by dinner and a rather early finish again. The electricity was a bit fickle so this time we did our reading to candle light which worked quite well.

On the morning of the 29th the weather had completely cleared and the full beauty of the mountains and valleys around Munar become apparent to us. Moving out from the hotel at 7.30AM we stopped several times to take a pictures of the hills and rivers. The highest peak is 2,500 meters above sea level and this morning there was no end to how far we could see. At one place we stopped to have a close look at the plants to be able to see how cardamom and pepper really grow. Cardamom is a 10-ft plant and harvesting can be done 3-4 times per year depending on the degree of fertilizing. We drove through the driver's home village where he stopped and left a little package to someone to forward to his relatives. 'Just a few pieces of clothing they might find useful.' Every time we passed a church Joy slowed down and threw a coin in the collection area.

Towards the end of our trip we were in the lowlands and surrounded by lots of water. There are 1500 kms of inland water ways in Kerala and our next adventure was to be a two day trip on a house boat together with Felix and Hannah. When we got to Alleppey there was no houseboat there, but our two fellow travelers arrived after fifteen minutes. The prime minister of India had decided to go house boating and thus all the boats were left at another landing half an hour's drive away. We consolidated into our bus and drove off the other place, and yes, there were all the houseboats. Our luggage was carried to one of these things and we were introduced to our three staff for the excursion, two punters and one cook. So no engine but two Indian men to create the motion necessary by having a very tall bamboo stick each, one applied up front and one in the stern, to get some quiet, soothing and steady momentum.

We are out on the water around noon and it is a spectacular day. It all feels a bit like Venice with these vast inland waterways, in this case fresh water. The land looks absolutely wild and untouched with greenery and palm trees all along the shores. When close to the shore one sees that virtually all along there are little neat and pretty dwellings that totally harmonize with nature to the extent that they are invisible at over 100 meters.

So tranquil, so soft, so quiet, so nice. The boat has two bedrooms with amenities, up front a beautiful 'living area' partly covered by a roof and furthermost up front an uncovered deck. The beds are covered with mosquito nets, which always looks very inviting and dreamlike. The cook works in a small kitchen in the stern. The ship is about 10 meters long, all dark wood and kept together by tied coconut rope rather than nails. It must weigh tons. All is very tastefully done in brown and black compiled entirely of natural materials. A better place for contemplation and mending stressed and high-pitched souls is hard to imagine.

We start by crossing a large open body of water and into one of the many canals. The first impression is the women washing clothes, standing in the water with their beautifully colored clothing, beating the wet garments on stones to make them clean. Once the washing of clothes is done they wash themselves, still covered in the loosely fitted cotton sarees and when done, they elegantly slip into another dry saree. No nudity or embarrassment necessary. All very original and elegant. One gets the impression that their conduct hasn't changed much since the origin of time. The odd male is also seen bathing which is a matter of applying soap all over and then taking a dip and up again clean and refreshed. The water seems reasonably clean judging from the many fish that obviously live there, evidenced by many nets and fishermen.

Hannah tests a swim but the Swedes are bit hesitant to jump into any water with low or no visibility. And the necessary washing can be done with the fresh water on board. In all the bathrooms in Kerala there is a two-liter plastic bucket and a ten liter one, whereas the showers are sometimes not that great. I find it amazing how you in fact can wash yourself completely with only two liters of water if you are careful. The amount of wasteful consumption going on in first world countries – with the US being the worst culprit - is just unbelievable. The two and a half billion Chinese and Indians will just have to do things smarter or natural resource won't be so natural any longer. Hopefully the other half of the world's population will act in sympathy. On my return from India I learned that the water level in Beijing has dropped from 7 meters below ground to 70 meters below ground since 1990. Similar things happen elsewhere and even the US is quickly running low on water. The abundance of water in our two countries of affiliation, Sweden and New Zealand, may well prove very valuable in future. The sooner we start to price what previously has been regarded as free and endless resource at a level that prevents depletion, the better. Our current course in these matters just isn't sustainable.

Two hours into our trip we are served an excellent lunch with fish, dal, rice, bread, and various Indian vegetables. Not too hot, nutritious and delicious. The drink is water or tea.

When later on we say we would like a beer with the dinner, they say they don't have any and they cost 60 Rps each. Around six o'clock they stop the boat, and ask how many beer we want, asks for the right amount of money and one of the guys borrow a bicycle and after an hour we are equipped with four bottles of beer.

Moving along these green shores we see many small children running along the water waving and shouting ' hello, one pen', or 'how-are-you, one pen'. They are obviously used to people giving them pens and we dig out whatever we have of surplus pens, which amounts to no more than five and hand them over to the wonderful little children. We realise that we should have brought 100 cheap pens, but we didn't so we just have to say 'sorry, out of pens' after a little while. Some are also asking for an empty water bottle or even in some cases ten Rupiah. Later we buy a stack of pens to be better able to meet this encouraging demand for tools of learning from the children.

There are many small shops along the canals selling immediate necessities for those who live around. There is also quite a traffic of small canoes with men and women going hither and thither. Some canoes work as ferries taking people across waterways. There is also a regular boat service of larger boats seating probably up to 100 people that come by every other hour to take people to and from the town of Alleppey. We see another houseboat every once in a while as well, some driven by engines, whereas we are quite happy being manually propelled forward. A few more conventional tourist boats pass by as well with people sitting comfortably on the roofs of the boats and waving and smiling. I think all of our little party share the feeling that life doesn't get much better.

We wake up on Saturday the 30th and the water is still like a mirror. The roosters have been going for hours whereas I only thought they announce the daybreak. Perhaps they are confused by this half-hour system that India is on – you cannot temper with nature, it always wins in the end. Other than that that it is all quiet and quite divine. Tea with hot milk, toast and omelet is served and the others join me. We start to move on slowly again, viewing all the activity on shore. Between the water and the houses is an elevated pathway where the people all walk. Very practical and beautiful. We stop by one of the banks and go for a short walk. Felix befriends a retired English teacher who lives in one of the houses with his wife and a big disc on the roof allowing them to watch world television. We see more very colorful wash ladies going about their daily task and many floating shops in canoes selling fish, geese, rice, and there is also a tailor with a sewing machine in the middle of the canoe. Some distant local music is played somewhere on shore and lends additional quality and mystique to the atmosphere.

We are having the odd discussion inbetween viewing the environment and reading our books. A discussion about whether president elect Bush is hopeless or not ends with a conclusion that he is democratically elected and not known to be evil or sinister so perhaps things could be worse. The American constitution is a beautiful piece of work and hopefully it, together with the free press and an experienced team around the president, will provide the checks and balances necessary to prevent things going completely off rail. There are few countries in the world who have manifestly competent politicians. Perhaps Singapore is one of them. I finish reading my book 'The Bondmaid' by Catherine Lim. The main character is a woman called Han and I feel so sorry that she would have to die so tragically at the end. But then, that is inevitably how all lives end, and I remind myself of Psalms 90: 12. "Teach us to ponder how few our days are that we may live each one wisely."

We all take a snooze in the afternoon, enjoy the scenery again and have another great dinner followed by a game of cards. 'Early to bed, early to rise, makes a man healthy and wealthy and wise.' The second morning is equally beautiful and completely still. Around us we see five other houseboats in the distance. We have a fine breakfast and then start to move again. We are only an hour away from Alleppey at this moment and we get there at nine, but our car is not due until half an hour later so we stay on the boat for a little while. When the car arrives we say goodbye to the crew, pay for our drinks and give them a small gratuity. A truly wonderful experience.

Just before noon on new year's eve we arrive at our hotel 'The old Courtyard' in the fort area in Cochin. Driving into the fort area, it all looks quite historic and inviting and the hotel is a very stylish old Portuguese building and the rooms are all white with brown wooden furniture. Huge beds, again with mosquito nets, and fans in the ceiling to circulate the air. Temperatures have ranged from a low of 15 degrees in the mountains to 28 degrees daytime in the lowlands, falling to 23 – 24 degrees at night. Warm but not at all unpleasant. After checking in we go for walk in the environs.

We are only a couple of 100 meters away from the sea and we gravitate towards the shore where there are lots of people and activity. The immediate eye catcher is the Chinese fishing nets. Along the shore line there are about ten of these giant creations. A big square net, probably 15 * 15 meters is attached to a huge lever being constructed of three big long logs attached to each other. At one end is the net and at the other end is a counterweight, consisting of many big rocks hanging in ropes from the back end of the lever. Every half-hour the net is brought up by five or six men pulling at the other end, the fish caught is collected and the net is lowered again for another attempt. Quite a fascinating thing to watch and this fishing looks very ancient and original. Talking to one of the guys, he confirms that this method of fishing has gone on for perhaps six hundred years.

The shore is full of colorful people and small shops and restaurants. Several of the restaurants have a sign saying 'you buy the fish, we will cook it for you.' We walk along the shore line to get a taste of the Arabian Sea rolling in by way of nice breaking waves.

We continue to the end of the pathway and then turn inland to seek our way back to the hotel. Enroute we find a book shop ' Idiom Booksellers' and as you would expect we find a number of books we cannot pass by. Linda finds me a book 'Empires of the Monsoon, a history of the Indian Ocean and its invaders ' which appeals to my interest in history. India is such a fascinating, and in many ways refined and perhaps superior culture, so it is interesting to learn how and why more basic and less advanced people from Europe could have such an impact on her destiny.

We take lunch in an art café that seems to attract all the young westerners in the fort area. It is very good in terms of serving basic nutritious food and excellent coffees and teas. And it is only two minutes away from our hotel. After lunch I take a walk back to the shore and then back to the hotel for a short snooze and out again at 6.00PM to see the sun set for the last time this millennium. The activity on the beach is immense, well dressed people everywhere, families and children walking in the waves, the light being very soft and again a strong sense of divinity. Linda probably takes a whole film of pictures, but the greatest experience is spiritual which is difficult to capture in a two dimensional photograph. All are extremely friendly, greeting, waving and smiling.

At seven we gather for a few beers on our third story balcony. The beer we walked nearly for an hour to obtain. Alcohol is only sold in special shops and most restaurants are not licensed to sell it. At eight o'clock we moved down to the courtyard below where we had pre booked a special new year's dinner with dance show. The dance show started at eight thirty and continued for about an hour at which times we were getting quite hungry. The dancers were beautifully attired and were dancing to a small group of instrumentalists and a chanter type singer. All very nice, but ultimately people went to the buffet arrangements and the show went on. A rich variety of food, particularly vegetables and sea food and we ate and continued to watch the show. Knowing as we do that time is relative, and that our friends in New Zealand and Singapore already have passed midnight we didn't see midnight as being particularly significant, so we went to bed at about 11PM after a long day. At midnight I woke up by even more intense dancing – the show piece was still going on – and some loud bangs from fire crackers around town.

The next morning when I wrote a few postcards I realised that the date was very conspicuous – 01 01 01. After a good breakfast at the Art Café we went on a tour of Cochin starting with the Synagogue, perhaps the only one in India, and definitely the oldest from the 1500's. There were only four Jewish families left in the congregation. A beautiful Synagogue with lots of fascinating lights and 1100 blue and white Chinese tiles on the floor. As with most other 'temples' in India we had to remove our foot wear before entering. Linda who has a particularly strong interest in anything Jewish just loved it. Unfortunately the film in her camera didn't move forward this day so none of the many photos came out, much to her deep disappointment. Hopefully Felix and Hanna got a few nice pictures. Three cameras for four people. I lent mine to Hannah as her's broke down in Singapore. There was a small museum adjacent to the Synagogue as well, depicting the building of it and the hardships and occasional persecution of the Jews by invaders and not by Indians.

Around the Synagogue there were lots of curious shops and we looked around and bought a few things. The white cotton shirts are particularly attractive and cost only 100Rps or ca S$ 4. After the Synagogue we saw the Palace which was well preserved and quite impressive, full of art and artifacts including the uncomfortably looking carry chairs for the royals. The walls of the queen's bedroom was full of erotic art. The doorways were low so as to remind visitors to bow their heads upon entering. Outside the entrance there were snake charmers and fortunetellers. We then proceeded to our travel agents office and met our Internet contacts, who proved very nice and helpful, and they gave us the missing airline ticket from Trivandrum to Chennai for the 6th January. We asked them for advice of a good Indian restaurant for lunch and a good place to buy clothing and fabric. Thereafter we proceeded to a lovely little vegetarian restaurant in a garden setting.

When we arrived at one o'clock it was empty but as we ate through our courses it filled up completely. For a very modest price we had a meal of rice and dal and parata and many different vegetables.

After lunch we went to a great shop with every conceivable garment of the highest quality. We were quickly assigned an assistant who helped us find all we wanted to look at or buy. After half an hour we had collected four dresses, two of silk and two of cotton, underwear, a red shirt and a loin cloth. All of it cost the same as one fine dress in Singapore or New Zealand. This particular shop took credit cards, whereas most places didn't. When we got back to the fort a big parade was on and there was a great number of people wandering around wanting to get a glimpse of the carnival. Felix and Hanna went to look at the carnival whilst Linda and I took a rest. Later when we went for a walk the parade was still on. That night we had dinner at a nice restaurant by the sea next to the big fishing nets. Again a very good eating experience with tandori chicken but no wine or beer as this place was not licensed. There was also a small group providing musical entertainment.

The next day we started early as we were going on a six-hour drive to a place on the coast, just south of Trivandrum. We started at nine o'clock in the morning and stopped at the local post office to get twenty-five eight Rupiah stamps for the postcards we had written. The road again gave us the experience of seeing dogs, elephants, cows, goats, pedestrians, bicycles and motorcycles, tuk-tuks, cars, busses and trucks, all in a big melting pot on roads that mostly didn't have any marked dividing lines. Users had to share the roads according to custom, trying always to avoid any accident or harming animal or man. Mostly this seemed to work fine but the average speed didn't exceed 50 km per hour. After three and a half hours we stopped at a hotel in Kallam for lunch. We normally would stop at reasonably respectable hotels in order to access good toilets. The more basic places wouldn't have a decent toilet and public toilets were not to be seen. As it always was quite hot we brought a water bottle each on all the trips. This particular vehicle was equipped with air-conditioning but outside temperatures hovered around 28 degrees, i.e. quite hot but a bit cooler than Singapore.

Driving through Trivandrum, the state capital of Kerala we soon arrived in Kovalam where it took us a while to find our little hotel, Nicki's Nest. This proved to be a lovely little hotel with perhaps 15 rooms, all in small air-conditioned huts with all amenities. We later experienced that the electricity wasn't all that reliable and the small diesel driven generators they had, didn't have enough power for the air conditioning system. The place was simple, tasteful and nice and situated on a slope down to the Indian Ocean so the views between the palm trees was quite spectacular. And right next door on a cliff hanging out over the ocean is a Hindu temple with equally impressive views. We quickly slipped into swim gear and went down to the beach for our first swim. First there was a small beach for our hotel and beyond another small beach for the neighbouring hotel and beyond that, miles and miles of beach with large wooden fishing canoes as far as the eye could see. Big ocean waves were rolling in and we enjoyed the swim diving through the biggest surfs. Nice salt water at a very pleasant temperature. On the other side of the Ocean is Africa about the height of Somalia and Ethiopia, i.e. just below the Arabian Peninsula. I learnt from the book I am reading that many of the plants and spices, most notably bananas were actually brought to Africa from India. Then a bit of relaxation before dinner consisting of Roti parata, dals, tandori chicken, kofta, coconut rice, cauliflower and potatoes. And some local Kingfisher beer to go with it. All taken at an outdoor table of the small in-house restaurant with views over the endless beach below. The night is dark and balmy and the stars innumerable.

The next morning we had moved on to the third day on the new millennium and the sunrise was spectacular. We moved down to the beach at 7.30 and watched all the fishermen being very active with their boats and their tasks. Their big very original looking open boats were kept on rolls 50 meters up the beach and it took about ten men to roll them down into the surf and then great caution needed to be exercised to get the ship through the high breaking waves. We saw them both come and go. A bit down the beach we see twenty men pulling in a very long net and 100 meters further down another twenty are pulling in the other side of the net. When the net finally comes in through the surf there seems to be very little in it and the women who sit in the sand with metal basins, presumably for the catch, must turn away empty handed this time. Such is the unpredictability of nature that you never know exactly what fortunes are in store for you. Will they go hungry? I don't know, but all I see on this beach look well shaped and quite healthy.

Already at this early hour the merchants are on the beach offering visitors silk and cotton shirts, scarves and sarees, shells and carvings and fruits and coconuts. We go for another swim in the surf which is both challenging and refreshing and then get ready for breakfast. After breakfast our driver takes us to Trivandrum where we start at the railway station to try to arrange for train tickets for Felix and Hannah to go to Goa, via Mangalore and Bangalore and then return to Trivandrum later in the month for their return flight to Singapore and Auckland. Goa is almost 1000 km northwards so the trip is about 24 hrs. India is a very large country covering 3.2 million square kilometers making it the 7th biggest country in the world. This equates to six times Texas or twice Alaska, bigger than Western Europe, seven times Sweden or twelve times New Zealand. After about one hour at the railway station we get the tickets. That amount of time is not too bad for interstate travel – it could easily take that long in Europe or anywhere else. At the station there is a big sign with this message from Mahatma Gandhi.

"Honoured Customers.

A customer is the most important visitor on our premises. He is not dependent on us. We are dependent on him. He is not an interruption in our work. He is the purpose of it. He is not an outsider on our premises. He is part of it. We are not doing him a favour by serving him. He is doing us a favour by giving us an opportunity to do so. A customer is not a person to argue with. No one ever won an argument with a customer."

After stopping in a few shops we seek out a little local restaurant where we eat really well – this time with our hands – the right hand - as there is no cutlery. The total cost for the nutritious and tasty meal is S$ 10 for the four of us. We find an ATM at Hong Kong bank which willingly dispenses a number of Rupiah bills from our Singapore and Auckland accounts. Trivandrum is quite a picturesque city with perhaps half a million inhabitants. A large university and parliament buildings, the railway station and several churches and temples lend character to the city. We stop by one of the temples which at the time is closed but we find a guide who gives us the low down on what we see. By all historic buildings there are guides offering their services and as long as you agree up front what the fee is you avoid discussions and misunderstandings. Fifty to one hundred Rps, i.e. two to four Singapore dollars seemed to be the going rate depending on weather it was half hour or full hour.

Back at the hotel we slipped into beach gear and Felix and I were invited to part take in a foot ball game with the locals. We played with a basketball in our bare feet on a small field next to the beach. Felix was as usual very good and full of energy. With my weight being about twice the average of the locals I made a contribution as a stopper by the goal. A number of people came up to watch. Felix's team won by 10 – 3. The next day Felix was given weaker team mates and he was a bit exhausted so then the results were reversed. They asked for a contribution to a proper football which we were glad to acquiesce to. After another good dinner at Nikki's Nest we are ready to charge our batteries for a new day – one we have decided to spend around the Hotel just relaxing. We have given our driver the day off.

Thursday we take a long walk on the beach to watch the fishermen in the sunrise. Again, there seemed to be a lot more fishermen than fish, but the activity and nature and the boats and the waves making it all seem very ancient and eternal. As we walk passed a group of locals trying to haul a boat out of the surf they indicate to me to help out. So I grab the rope and pull to. The guy standing next to me, with teeth all red from chewing bethel, points to my gold bracelet and watch, and suggest that I share these surplus assets with him. My thoughts are 'forget it but I will help you get the boat up' and I am sure he can read my body language well enough to get the message.

Later in the day after breakfast and some reading and swimming we are again approached by beach vendors with all sorts of merchandise. I have learnt not to say 'perhaps later' to anyone unless I really mean it because they inevitably will come back and remind you of your half commitment. At noon we buy some coconuts, pineapple, and mango and they dress it and we eat our fill of what nature offers. I have been wearing a t-shirt and those that haven't are looking a bit red from all the sun. If you take your shirt and hat off for the periods you swim, that is almost as much sun as your body can take with no burns. My father always used to say that in the British navy people who got incapacitated by overexposure to the sun got put in the slammer for bad conduct and judgement.

In the afternoon the girls went for Ayrovedic massage and I went with them to have a look and to enjoy the mile long walk back. They loved the massage and Linda wanted to come back here on a second two week health holiday. It is good with India that the food is mostly vegetarian and thus very healthy and that alcohol is hard to get and finally that there doesn't seem to be much on in the evenings, the sum of which stimulates healthy living. Felix and I played football with the locals again and after half an hour Felix collided with another guy and sprained his foot – nothing too serious - so went for a dip instead before dinner.

On the Friday we started out early for a trip to Keniyakumari, lands end or Cape Comorin, the southern tip of India, where three Oceans meet. This was to take about two hours but with a few stops it was more like three. As we had to cross a state border into Tamil Nadu we had to obtain a permit and pay some entrance fee. It didn't take more than ten minutes, but I reflected on another piece of unnecessary bureaucracy. The last half-hour drive before the Cape the landscape was very open and wild with a range of high hills and mountains. It looked like a vast low vegetation of banana plantations and lots of waterways. Just before Keniyakumari we stopped at a hotel for a cup of tea and use of facilities. In India it is good to plan your visits to the bathroom as you don't want to end up in the wrong place.

At around eleven o'clock we reached the final destination and a long road leading down to the green and blue Ocean marked the Southern end of India. A fresh breeze was blowing, the temperature was about thirty degrees and lots of people and markets along the roads. Out in the sea in some distance on a little rock of an island we could see a huge statue of Thiruvalluvar and a temple looking memorial for Svami Vivekananda, born 12th Jan 1863 an a disciple of Sri Ramakrishna, on an adjacent little island. These spectacular monuments were served by a small ferry challenging the huge waves rolling in, taking perhaps a hundred people at a time for the five minutes ride to these cliffs. We walked around slowly and looked at all the merchandise in the shops – most of it cheap things of no lasting value. It all looks like a bit of

Portuguese influence rather than Indian and the whole place is a bit like a fairy tale – the mix of people, the end of a continent, the shifting colours of the sea and the many visitors looking like pilgrims. Like in all the places where there are many visitors there are many beggars, old, young and mothers with miserable looking children. Although we dished out a bit of money every day, it is of course impossible to give to all. Linda took pity on a pregnant mother with a little child, and I gave some money to two old ladies, whereas I walked passed a woman with a horrible looking elephant foot – just couldn't bear to look at it.

We were contemplating taking the boat out to the two islands but Linda didn't like the size of the waves and the number of people on each boat load. We found a bookshop for spiritual writings and found a lot of interesting little books. Felix bought a cookbook for vegetarians and I got ten thin little books on Indian spirituality. We asked the guy in the bookshop if the ferry trip was safe and he said reassuringly, 'sure'. So we proceeded to the boat departure and went for the short ride. The waves were huge and some water sprayed one side of the boat, but the hull was all welded together so I reckoned that the ship was unsinkable. We got there and back with no incident.

On the island we had to pay another few Rupiahs for entrance to the memorial. It was all well worth it. The buildings were spectacular and the views of Keniyakumari were great. We walked around without shoes and explored all the various buildings and sights. There were also some of the sayings of Swami Vivekenananda:

"Let every man and woman and child without respect of caste or birth, weakness or strength, hear and learn that behind the strong and the weak, behind the high and the low, behind everyone, there is that Infinite Soul, assuring the infinite possibility and the infinite capacity of all to become great and good."

Seeing a group of ca 30 Mongol looking people, I went up to them and asked, through their guide, where they were from. They said Manipur and I asked if that is India and they said, yes, east of Bangladesh, right next to Burma. They must have come 2,000 km to experience these sights. We couldn't say a word to them but they were very friendly and wanted Linda and I to be in on their group photos. Later on the boat back one of the ladies gave Hannah her ring and Hannah offered her necklace in exchange. Value wise Hannah would have traded down but it was an emotional spur of the moment decision. Somewhere in the depths of Manipur there is a happy old lady with a green stone necklace from Singapore. Back on land again we sought our driver and went to the large Catholic Church we had seen from the rock island. We had to drive through some narrow streets with south European looking houses and finally reached the whitish high standing church and we all went out in the heat to look for an entrance which we found on the side. A few people were sitting in worship on a very large open stone floor and we went through quite swiftly in order not to disturb the worshippers.

We had lunch at a nearby hotel and then started our return trip at around four o'clock. Arriving in the nearest town of Suchindram we were impressed with the temple there and asked the driver to make a stop. Narrow streets with bazaars led up to the temple and at the entrance there were a couple of huge temple wagons – big wooden wheeled structures full of religious carvings. They must weigh tons and be very difficult to move. We paid some money for the entry to the temple, checked our shoes and found a guide to take us through. The temple area was very large with lots of little altars and also metal pillars on which the guide played something akin to music by hitting his fist against the iron. Quite a temple and a very sacred atmosphere in the whole town. As the sun was getting lower and we had a long drive in front of us, we pushed on with our journey. We got back about seven o'clock just when it got dark. A long exhausting day but a very worthwhile trip. We had our dinner at the hotel and then turned in quite early again.

The final day in Kerala started with a new walk along the beach to the fishermen who once more were pulling their long net on the shore and again it didn't look too promising in terms of catch. We did a little bit of swimming before breakfast, packed our things and then a new dip in the ocean before finally checking out and leaving at around noon. As our flight wasn't departing until 5.15PM and the train for Felix and Hannah at 5.45PM we had lunch and went to the Trivandrum Museum for a while. The Museum is a number of attractive looking red brick buildings nicely located in a large park in the City center. The things on display didn't really excite us however. So we left Felix and Hannah at the station at 3.30PM and wished them well for two weeks and then arrived at the airport at 4.00PM. Check in and flight went very smoothly and in Chennai we went to Singapore Airlines to see if we had progressed on the waiting list for that nights flight to Singapore. The attendant said that the flight was more than full so we would have to wait to the next evening when we had confirmed bookings.

So we walked over to the international arrival hall to try to find a suitable hotel. We soon ran into an agent for Park Inn Hotel who said that the normal price is US$ 70 but at this hour he would give us a room for US$ 50 including airport transfers, breakfast and also a late check out as our flight the next day was only scheduled for 23.20. He also showed us a hotel brochure and as it all looked fine we said OK. It took about half an hour to get there in very intense and slow moving traffic but when we got there we thought we had got a pretty good deal. We enjoyed a room service dinner, I booked a car and a driver for nine o'clock the next day and we went to bed quite exhausted again.

After a luxurious breakfast with all the trimmings we went on a tour with our driver for the day. He took us to a few memorials and to two shopping centers where we bought a few things.. As Linda wanted to see a church he took us to a nice little church where there were many baptizings going on and all the families were posing in their fine cloths for photographing. Two little girls were collecting money for a school trip, which we responded to whereas some other's we didn't. In the car again the driver asked us if we wanted to go to Mahabalipuram ca an hour away to the south. We accepted and were driven along the west coast with some great views over the Ocean. Close to the place we were stopped to pay some road toll and a guide offered to show us around which we declined as we didn't really know what to see and how much there was of it.

When we later got to the ticket boot we were a bit surprised that it was 10 Rupiah for Indians and US$ 10 for non-Indians, i.e. 46 times more. However, we reluctantly paid the unexpectedly high price and walked into one of the enclosures with stone carvings and recruited a guide on the spot. At this place all the full size animals and temples were carved out of the same rock, i.e. it must have been a very large rock originally and vast amounts of discarded rock must have been transported away. The statues were all early 7th century and wonderfully well carved and done. At the exit we were attacked by some very aggressive sales people. We bought some shoes and a few carved stones but then we had to take refuge in the car to avoid the people reducing prices to make us buy goods we really didn't want.

We asked the driver to take us to the one finest remaining site as we didn't have the time or inclination to see all twelve or so. He took us to a sea side site and we enjoyed another great rock carving set against the immense blue Ocean. Again we were attacked by very keen sales men and drove off. The driver wanted us to see one more and we agreed to see a whole hillside of rock carving called 'Decent of Ganges' and it was well worth it. Hundreds of animals and people and a temple carved out of a rock side. Fifteen minutes later we were ready for our return trip which took us back to the hotel in about one and a half hour at four o'clock. We thanked the driver and gave him a tip and bought a few nice Madras short sleeve shirts in the hotel shop and tried to catch some sleep in anticipation of losing the night between India and Singapore. I don't think we slept much so at seven we had dinner at the Hotel. The dinner was a buffet and the trouble with buffets is that it is easy to over eat, which we did. The good thing with the dinner was that we could concentrate on sleep on the plane rather than have dinner at midnight Indian time and 2.30 AM Singapore time.

A very good value hotel, the Park Inn! Our transfer to the airport went twice as fast as the night before and, although there were lots of people there, we went through all the customs and controls and were on the aircraft by 11.00PM. We landed in Singapore on time at 6.00 AM and were home in the apartment at 6.40AM in time to see Andre', who arrived the night before from Auckland, off to school at 7.20AM on Monday 8th January, the first day of school in the new millennium. I unpacked, took a shower had a cup of tea and arrived at work at 8.00 AM as usual. Another day of trying to add value to staff, customers and shareholders, hoping my recent rich India experience would help me live more wisely and focus better on what really counts. 18th January 2000

2. Europe on Track.

Arrived at Fumicino Airport in Rome Sunday 17th June 2001 at 6.00A.M. after an overnight flight from Bangkok and Singapore. A nice thing with EU and the European passport is that you feel quite at home as soon as you enter the EU zone with special 'domestic' passport treatment. Luggage arrives soon after we reach the conveyor belt. As we have a 10.30 A.M. train from Stazione Termini our intent is to take the train in to Rome, check our luggage and then perhaps have a morning walk at Forum Romanum. The Express Train for Rome leaves at 7.07 so with 15 min to spare we take a Café Latte with some 'pane'. We ran into a lost girl from Illinois who was two days late for her train for Firenze and she asked us if the Rome Express would take her to a place where she could find her train. Having gone by train from Rome to Florence a few years earlier we could with some credibility confirm that - yes, that would be very easy.

It was a nice and bright morning and we felt pretty good in spite of missing out on the night. At the station we found the storeroom but felt that rather than pay 6000 lire for each of our four little pieces we would look for a store box at the station. We soon found those and got away with 8000 rather than the 24000. Happy Day! Then we sought out a taxi to go to the Palatine and the driver asked, Hotel Palatine? No, just the Palatine by Forum Romanum. In my mind I really wanted to go to the Capitoleum, behind Victor Emanuel, but I had forgotten its name. However, as we were let off just by the gate to Forum Romanum, we had both Coloseum and Capitoleum within easy walking distance. The taxi drove down Via Nationale and cost a reasonable Lt 10,000 – no meter. At this stage it was 8.30A.M. so we had about an hour for an early morning walk in the warming June sunshine. First day of a four-week holiday and everything seemed very promising and rosy.

Forum Romanum wasn't open at this hour but even from the street you get a wonderful view over this fantastic old city, which sends your mind spinning in terms of imagining all the life and commerce and colors on those old streets 2,000 years ago. Behind Forum Romanum on the hill is the Palantine, which both Linda and I love, but it is only accessible through the gate to Forum Romanum, which was closed. So we walked in the direction of Coloseo, which stands like a giant monument right in the middle of the street. That is perhaps the most fascinating thing with Rome that history and modernity are totally intermingled. In some old brick wall that looks like a ruin one may well detect a little window with live flowers in it. Someone still lives in what looks like a 2000 + years room in a ruin. We had both been in Rome many times before, but every time is quite exciting because of its historic and religious significance.

At Coloseo people already started to arrive and the little tourist shops were gradually opening up. Like others we took a few pictures trying to capture a little of the mystique and atmosphere and also some of the magnificent arc flowers. We looked at the beautiful Arc de Triumph nearby. Linda wanted to go up to the Palantine but it wasn't accessible from that side. So we decided to walk back along Forum Romanum towards Capitoleum. As we passed the gate we noticed that it must have opened at 9.00 A.M. but we didn't bother to go in as the area is quite vast and we had only another half hour before we needed to go back to the station.

All our train tickets we had bought from Harvey's Travel on Ponsonby Road in Auckland as the travel agent in Singapore proved unable to assist. Linda ordered the tickets in Auckland via Internet from Singapore, Felix, our son, who lives right next door, picked up the physical tickets and delivered to my friend and ex colleague Tracey at Bank of New Zealand on Queen Street, Auckland, who sent them to my Singapore office for use on our train trip through Europe – quite amazing really. When Max, our older son, now 26 was little, Georg, my father patted him on the head and asked if he was happy and Max responded: "No, Max is big, Felix is happy!" which wasn't bad, given that he was only four at the time. Felix is very happy – Max is very responsible, as the unfathomable grace of God would have it.

But, back to Capitoleum, which we ascended along the little winding road on the Forum Romanum side. The views over the Forum and also towards the many beautiful buildings on the other side are just formidable. We couldn't stop taking pictures of the many quaint building details, witnessing the importance of this place through the ages. We just glanced at the several museums there as well, as we wouldn't have time to go into any on this particular trip. However, Rome is the place you always want to return to, and I am sure we will in due course do that as well. We walked the many stairs down to the Piazza Venezia in front of the huge and by many observers as ugly considered Victor Emanuel monument. This monument was closed and all activity we saw there was two soldiers standing guard at the Unknown Soldier's Tomb.

So we walked across the street to the taxi stand and got in for our ride back to Stazione Termini. Linda suggested we buy some drinks and sandwiches for the train and I got into a shop quite crowded with travelers. To get the sandwiches you had to first go and pay the cashier and then bring the receipt and get the goods. Someone with a backpack bumped into me and I said sorry as if I were at fault. When I paid the cashier he gave me Lt 10,000 change too little back on Lt 50,000 and I got a little bit annoyed as he, a man in his fifties, didn't apologize and it seemed to me he may be outright dishonest. We got the stuff anyway and brought our luggage out of the lockers, found our train and soon enough we were in the car and seats numbered as on our tickets and we again thought that that is amazing precision from a small ticket office in an Auckland suburb. Some things are still marvelous in this world. We made a couple of phone calls on our mobiles to Stockholm and Milano to check that our son Andre' had arrived properly from Bangkok and that the lady who was to provide us keys in Milano would be there when we arrived. All in order.

The train started with a jerk. Next to Linda sat an Asian girl and I asked her where she was from and she said Japan - Tokyo? No Yokohama. We said we were from Singapore which she found hard to believe so we explained that our home is in Auckland, New Zealand, we live temporarily in Singapore, we are soon moving to Tokyo and we travel on Swedish pass ports. "That sounds complicated," she said. She was a Japanese travel agent, speaking several European languages, leading a group of Japanese tourists through Europe with next stop Florence. I told her I could sing some Japanese songs – Sakura and Chotto Matte Kudesai – and then I saw that another girl, possibly also Japanese sitting across the aisle smiled as she probably thought I was mad.

Anyway, as I had anticipated this course of events, I fished up a map of Tokyo out of my back pack and laid it out in front of her and asked her for advice on where to live. She said it felt a bit strange looking at a Tokyo map rushing through the Italian landscape – but she did what she could to comment on the various areas or 'kus,' and provided some good advice. Time and again she said that Tokyo is not Japan – you must go out in the countryside as much as possible. She also said that Yokohama is quite nice but a bit far away from the Tokyo offices. She had been almost everywhere and even stayed at Ice Hotel in Sweden where everything including the beds is made by ice. She said the smell of the beds was quite unappealing as they were covered by rain deer hides and it felt like sleeping with the animals. She had also been to Rovaniemi in Finland but found the temperature, minus thirty degrees a bit cold for her liking. After a comfortable and relaxing couple of hours with the Italian Campagna tranquilly rolling by outside our window, we arrived in Florence and she and her party left the train. We wished her a nice stay and said we would look out for her in Yokohama.

Linda went for a short walk and I intended to put some receipts in my wallet – then realized that it was gone. I looked in my backpack and all over but it came to me that I must have been pick-pocketed probably in Rome. A bit of a shock. Fortunately – anticipating this possibility - on the plane coming over, I had moved all my valuables – money and credit cards - to a small front pocket wallet – and passport and tickets I kept in my backpack. I still blamed myself for not having done it full out and put my wallet in my luggage. The wallet was old and worn and all that was in there were two drivers licenses and some frequent flier membership cards and a few curious bits and pieces of little value. There were also a few Singapore dollars that just wouldn't fit into my little wallet. So I decided to wash it away from my mind and not let it aggravate me, but rather try to draw something positive out of the experience and be a bit more vigil in future. Since what I lost was quite insignificant in the greater scheme of things, emotions must be managed so as to avoid negative territory, failing which you are just punishing yourself. Any set back that you can handle makes you a bit wiser. And I reflected: Another reminder to consider what is important; the best things in life – friendship, love, wisdom – cannot be stolen. What a miserable way to make a living – to steal it from other people on a daily basis and in that sense I am clearly on the luckier side of the equation.

In Japan we were told two weeks earlier that there is no petty theft, because it would be seen as demeaning. We got talking to the other girl across the aisle who was also Japanese, and she was on a two year scholarship to London and now on her way to Bologna where she were to study archeology for a couple of months. She was a bit hesitant in her use of English but clearly a delightful person. And her life and interest sounded really interesting.

We had booked lunch for 1.40 P.M. and we moved across to the train restaurant. The meal consisted of Pasta, Pollo and Dolce – a complementary glass of champagne and some Chianti rosso with aqua minerale followed by coffee. We enjoyed eating our meal slowly, again much enjoying the Italian summer landscape passing by in front of us.

A very pleasant and civilized way of travel. Linda tried it two years earlier and loved it. I remember a comment by John Ruskin in one of his books where he says that rail travel has taken the charm away from traveling as it is far too fast. So it seems every generation has its challenges. At a dinner function in the garden of Singapore Cricket Club a year earlier the prescribed dress code was Red Sea Rigg. It took me a while to figure out what it meant, but someone explained to me that when the English traveled East to the colonies before flying was common, they obviously traveled by ship and when they came to the Red Sea they didn't wear the jacket anymore because of the heat. So Red Sea Rigg is tuxedo without the jacket. It must have been fun to spend three weeks on the sea in anticipation of getting there in those days, compared to today's ten to twelve hours non stop flying, staring into the chair 12 inches in front of you.

We arrived in Milano, which has its origin about 600 BC, and started to draw our rolling cases to the exit. Some Americans asked us where the taxis are and as they were standing one level above street level I suggested looking for taxis on the street level. They heeded the advice and found their car. It reminded me of some other Americans in Queen Street, Auckland, New Zealand who wondered in which direction the ferries could be found, knowing they were supposed to be at the end of Queen Street. As Queen Street runs with quite an inclination, I suggested they try the lower end, which they did. There were about 20 people in the taxi queue and that took us no more than 15 minutes. In the car Linda again called for our apartment keys and when we arrived to the address, 7 Via C. Menotti, in central Milano, the NZ woman with the keys was there. We were going to stay two nights with our friends, Anthony and Vanessa, from Auckland, but they were only to arrive late at night after a weekend in London. Now it was 4.P.M. so we decided to take a nap before going out.

At 7.30 P.M. and some rain and thunder during our sleep, we decided to go for a walk. Pretty dead and quiet on Sunday night, about 20 degrees and a light drizzle. We looked around for somewhere to have a drink and some food and a short while later we found a small café with four people in it, the owner, his wife, his guitar-playing son and probably the daughter. We ordered a Fernet Branca for me and a glass of wine for Linda. Fernet is supposed to be good for your digestive system – it tastes terrible! Given the lack of identified options and the miserable weather we asked after a while if they had food. They seemed a bit hesitant, but the son was encouraging and we were offered pasta with tomato sauce – fine! They were also preparing a Sunday dinner for themselves and for a number of family friends. The son kept playing away at the guitar and I asked him if he knew O' Sole Mio. Did he ever! He played and we sang together – the one Italian song I know the words to " Che Bella Cosa…" - and soon enough we were part of the party. We placed new drinks order for a beer and another vino rosso. At this stage five more people arrive – their friends – one girl with a little two-year-old baby in a pram. Only them and us – they all sit down and have their salad and we ask for another couple of wines. Given that this was the only open place we feel quite fortunate to be having such a good time.

Another outside couple comes in to have a beer each and we ask for a glass of Strega to go with the coffee. As they don't have Strega I settle for an Aurum – orange liqueur - which I remember from previous visits to Italy and Linda has a Grappa. We sip our drinks and a while later settle the bill which is for Lt 51,000 or kiwi $ 50 or SEK 250 – very reasonable indeed. We find our way back to the apartment and an overwhelming fatigue invades me so at 10.15 P.M. I feel I have to go to bed whereas Linda stays up a while to see if our hosts will be arriving. When I wake up at 6.00 A.M. in broad daylight I ask Linda if she met them – no at 12.00 mid night they still hadn't arrived. Linda suggest we go for a pre breakfast walk and get some fresh bread. We sneak out as quietly as we can and walk for twenty minutes to find a small café where we order café latte and four croissants – two to bring back for our friends. This is Lt 9,800 or about ten kiwi, about the same we would pay in Ponsonby, Auckland. This registering and comparing prices seems to run in my blood, it just switches on automatically and sometimes irritates Linda who has a greater capability to lose herself in the moment.

On our way back we pass a fruit market and buy some apples and oranges. Back at the apartment I bring the bags of bread and fruit in and practice some of my rudimentary Italian in greeting our hosts with "Bon Giorno, Amici – pane fresca i tutti frutti!!" and Linda smiles! At 7.15A.M. we sit down together for a second breakfast and have plenty to talk about as we haven't met for 10 months, last in Singapore. Linda hands over two books, "Daring Italy" for Vanessa and "3Bowls" vegetarian recipes for Antony, who likes to cook. Great to see them again. In spite of progress with email and reduced phone costs, nothing beats meeting your friends in person. Linda and Vanessa are business partners since several years back, promoting the arts.

Antony leaves for his job and Vanessa accompanies us to Piazza Duomo via Piazza del Tricolore, which takes 20 minutes and we get a map and sit down for a second cup of coffee before Vanessa takes the tram to her work. Linda and I found our way to the top of the Duomo, and experience great views from the roof of the great cathedral. We also take a look inside the church, the third largest in Europe, and then proceed through Galleria Victor Emanuel to Piazza della Scala in front of the famous "Teatro alla Scala." In the center of the Piazza is a statue of Leonardo da Vinci – artist and scientist. It is early in the season so not too many tourists around and the weather this Monday is divine. We see a shop for Borsalino hats and I decide and go in to have a look, but the shop is closed on Mondays. We walk down Via Dante towards "Castello Sforzesco." We are progressing through the castle quite quickly as we are heading for a 12.45 P.M. lunch meeting at Via Paleocapa next to Stazione Cadorna. Wondering for a while if we are in the right place, we see Antony and Vanessa approaching and proceed into the restaurant. The outdoors is full so we take an indoor table and have a light but delightful Italian lunch in a wonderful environment. The two of them, and particularly Antony, with Italian ancestry, are fluent in Italian, which makes it easier. Not that I was ever stopped by lack of language skills – and Linda knows Spanish. But of course the number of options and level of experience and appreciation increases with better knowledge.

On our way back to the apartment we headed for the Armani shop at Monte Napoleone. After some searching we found it. A three story display of Armani and other things for sale. But the display and space made the experience more like visiting a fine museum. All things with only the finest design – everything beautiful. Italy is the designer country of the world and Milano is the design capital. We spent half an hour there looking at all the displays, but given the long trip ahead of us and our small and smart luggage we refrained from buying anything. We walked Via Della Spiga back – wonderful old street with so many fine little shops! After four hours of walking we were back at the apartment at 3.30 PM and took a snooze and woke up at 6.00 P.M. The weather was beautiful with sunshine and the thermometer at 28 degrees, just a bit cooler than Singapore. We waited for them to return from work for a joint dinner.

We went with taxi for about 20 minutes to a restaurant called Osteria del Binari – a very unassuming entrance from a back street but inside it was fantastic with both indoors and outdoors under a very large cover of vines. The capacity would be a couple of hundred people and it all looked very inviting and special – a place you wouldn't find unless you knew where to look for it. We had a great antipasti, tagliatelli and vitelli. And we drank some beautiful Montepulciano red wine. We had an interesting discussion on Anita Roderick of body shop and weather the downturn of her business is a failure of the market to appreciate her good efforts or weather she has simply run out of steam and ideas to grow a successful business. Who knows? But in today's marketplace with so much on offer you cannot rest on your laurels and yesterday's success isn't necessarily today's or tomorrow's. Running a small-scale operation and a large scale one also has significantly different characteristics. And as usual, the more we drank, the wiser we got. Overall we had a wonderful dinner under the vines with our good friends. It couldn't have been nicer.

The next day we were to visit Cenacolo Vinciano and see the "Last Supper" by Leonardo da Vinci. Antony had pre booked us for the11.00 o'clock showing. Admission is strictly controlled and they only take 20 people at a time. We took bus 61 to Stazione Cadorna and walked the last quarter mile. We got there in time and with our pre booking we could pass the queue of casual visitors. As per our advice we got the individual recorded English explanations to assist us in understanding the significance of this world-renowned masterpiece. It is in a building that for a long time was used as a stable and someone opened up a door through the lower part of the painting. During the Second World War the building was bombed and lost its roof. But now, after several years of renovation and careful restoration, the painting is again available for inspection and admiration. The humidity is controlled for the protection of the piece and it feels really special to be there and view it. It is absolutely beautiful, the interaction between Jesus and the disciples and the light that comes through the windows. In a book I read about the artist he says the key with any piece of art is to try to capture and speak to the soul and this painting (as well as his Mona Lisa) really is a good example of that. We also looked at the adjacent church, S. Maria delle Grazie dei Padre Dominican.

The weather continued to be beautiful and we were enjoying a therapeutic, early summer, sunshine. We walked up Corso Magenta and looked at the shops, gradually working ourselves to Vanessa's job at 13, Via Annucci. We got there in time for our one o'clock appointment with Vanessa and met all her interesting colleagues – all people who were engaged in arts and conferences, and who seemed to work as much for love as for money.

Vanessa took us to a lovely local lunch restaurant on Viale Sabotino and three of her female colleagues joined us for lunch as well. They were all working on a women-in-business conference to take place late September. We had an interesting discussion. Another low-key high quality Italian lunch – you wonder how they manage to get such a nice atmosphere in so many restaurants. We ate risotto, piedina, and verdura and I had a birra Italiano medio. The girls drank water.

After lunch we took the underground from Porta Romana back to Piazza Duomo to do a little bit of shopping. I managed to spend a million lire on myself, and Linda got an ice cream. Not that I didn't try to encourage her to buy what she wanted, but she only wanted an ice cream. I got summer and winter Borsalino hats – the real thing, beautiful – and a few shirts and ties and we got Andre' a Lazio foot ball shirt which we knew would make his day. We also found Acqua di Parma aftershave which Linda recommended me to buy. I changed US $ 100 at the Piazza, American Express and as I got a lot less than advertised on their board, I was told that their fee was 9.8 % - little short of stealing.

We walked back Via Matteotti and made another coffee stop. You see so many elegant people – old gentlemen in their 60's so well presented and the most beautiful young women and men. It becomes apparent that this is undisputedly the country with the world's best designers.

Back at the apartment we put all our things together, had a gin-and-tonic with Vanessa and then called a taxi to take us to the station. Vanessa came with us and Antony met us at the station. I also previously went to their local supermarket and got some nuts and sandwiches and a bottle of wine and water so we would survive the overnight train ride. We found our train on track 14, the right car and the right sleep compartment – it was terribly hot on the train, which must have stood out in to sunshine all day. We hugged and kissed our lovely, hospitable friends and boarded the train and waved them good-bye through the train window.

The train was away at about 8.15 P.M. and the evening was balmy and beautiful. In our first class compartment I found some water cups, which would serve well as wine glasses. I opened the wine, took out the nuts and we had our simple dinner looking at the Lombardia landscape rolling by in the sunset. On the left side we saw the Alps in the distance and on the right side the campagna. The attendant for the car came and made the beds allowing us to go to bed anytime. As usual, I went out first while Linda kept reading a bit more. I recall Hanna, our son Felix's girlfriend, saying during our recent holiday in India: Early to bed, early to rise, keeps you healthy, wealthy and wise. (There are many similar sayings in Swedish) This saying obviously sits well with my character, whereas Linda who is a night owl thinks it silly.

Perhaps the efficient types are the early ones and the artists are the other. Artistic performances tend to be at night. I often felt that to be a true artist, you mustn't feel constrained by time – time is irrelevant – whereas in corporate efficiency, time is always on one axis. In the arts any incremental improvement towards perfection is always beneficial, whereas in business it is only beneficial if the cost/ delay to achieve the extra quality is less than the cost of the time to achieve it. I have come to believe that none is de facto right or wrong, it is just different approaches to life. Secretly I guess I admire those who can fully disregard time, as even Einstein suggested that time is an illusion. But as for me, I am too much a product of our times, not to try to make the most out of every hour. I recognize that this can be a bit disruptive in seeking spiritual fulfillment.

Anyway, very soon I slept like a log. Writing this reminds me of one of my banking customers in New Zealand who owned both a hotel and a forest, and when I asked what might the synergy be between these two assets, the MD asked if I never heard the expression: "Sleep like a log." Getting such a clever answer, I had no more questions. Off and on I woke up by the train stopping, sometimes to let another train through – in which case everything goes dead quiet, until the other train arrives at full speed and there is a tremendous noise level, quite a shock really – or to stop at a station including on this trip Venice. The monotonous rail sound is quite conducive to sleeping. However, I think I woke a million times, but rather than being annoyed at this, I was grateful at falling asleep a million times. There is always the other side of every coin, isn't there? and a positive outlook makes all the difference. In fact one of the many authors I have read the last few years, A.N. Wilson in his book *The Wealth and Poverty of Nations* said: " In this world the optimists have it, not because they are always right, but because they are positive, and that is the way to achievement, correction, improvement and success. Educated, eyes-open optimism pays; pessimism can only offer the empty consolation of being right." If you wake up many times you must have slept many times. Lets stay positive!

At 6.00A.M. I woke up and realized that it was light and that I didn't really require any more sleep so I went out into the corridor and read for an hour. I had brought five books to ensure that I didn't run out of reading material – and of course in relation to Linda, this is not a problem, as she reads even more than I do. Most of the books we read she buys from the Amazon book shop, one of the best and most useful legacies of the Internet revolution. We just learned the hard way to not buy any Amazon books in Sweden as they had a way of taking all the attraction out of it by adding inertia and cost to the process. We buy 60 books every quarter and we each read 20 and the other 20 we give away. It is, I believe, hard to imagine a nicer present than one that requires the recipient to also invest some energy – a joint venture - and that sends him or her on a trip to the higher stratospheres. But do they all read them? I really don't know, but as the saying goes, you can lead a horse to water, but you can't make it drink. You also learn over time what falls in good soil and what falls on the rocks.

Through the window I saw the Tyrol landscape rolling by – lots of rivers and creeks and small and high mountains. You inevitably wonder what it would be like to live in a small house like the ones passing by in the middle of nowhere. This thought brought to my mind a passage from Mark Twain's *The Innocents Abroad* written in the late eighteen hundreds. "In the lake district of Italy we passed through the strangest, funniest, undreamt of old towns, wedded to the customs and steeped in the dreams of the older ages, and perfectly unaware that the world was round! And perfectly indifferent too, as to whether it turns around or stands still. They have nothing to do but to eat and sleep and sleep and eat, and toil a little when they can get a friend to stand by and keep them awake. They are not paid for thinking – they are not paid to fret over the world's concerns. They were not respectable people – they were not worthy people – they were not learned and wise and brilliant people – but in their breasts, all their stupid lives long, resteth a peace that passeth understanding! How can men, calling themselves men, consent to be so degraded and happy"? This was not far from Italy's lake district and I thought of Mark Twain's comments and how they are spot on in terms of demonstrating the non-existent correlation between worldly 'success' and happiness.

At 7.00 A.M. Linda woke up and we had some oranges and bananas before our first class coffee arrived. Our attendant said we would be 40 min late, which later turned out to be an hour. However we weren't going to worry about that. We looked through our Vienna books and considered our options for the two days. If we both want to do the same we do that and if Linda wants to do something different, we do that. Very democratic – in the case of equal number of votes for either side, there is no other fairer way than letting someone have the casting vote, is there? She is happy, I am happy! Very obvious really!

I also called Tokyo on my mobile to follow up on my son's school application. Not much progress but it can sometimes help to keep the pressure on. Some additional documents were needed and of course we would send those from Singapore soonest. Schools and Insurance companies seem to intentionally be out to test the stamina of parents, and the many who understandably give up – for lack of skills or endurance – never get their entitlements.

We also called our friends, Else-Marie and Claas from Sweden, who we were to meet at our hotel, and yes they had arrived. These mobile phones do make life a lot easier as long as you don't let *them* run your life. The train arrived at 9.40 A.M. and we disembarked and walked to the main hall where I changed some money to Austrian Shillings. We found a taxi and asked for Slössergasse 11, 'Pensione Andreas' which was 15 min away so we arrived there just after 10.00 A.M. The streets are very neat and tidy in Austria and our hotel looked just like a normal apartment house, but with a small sign saying Pension Andréa's 2nd floor. We met our dear friends in the lobby and we were having the rooms next to each other. I hadn't seen them for a year so it was quite emotional reunion, particularly as my friend Claas had a close encounter with death, in a very freak accident last August. And though he almost paid with his life, through tremendous will power and endless hours of training – also not discounting professional treatment and loving support - he had worked himself back very close to his normal self. When I told Rose, my Singapore secretary, how shaken I was about his horrific accident, she asked for his name to be written out in full, and then told me that he would live and recover after she had prayed for him. Thank you Rose, thank you God.

We got a map from the hotel and commenced walk towards Herengasse with the purpose of having a traditional coffee with apfelstrudel, which together with Strauss and Mozart, probably is what Vienna is most famous for. I guess it is also famous for its fantastic buildings, many from the period 1558 – 1806 when it was the seat of the Holy Roman Empire. We found the most beautiful café and got a nice taste of the world famous Vienna apfelstrudel. Claas always had cake with cream for every coffee we subsequently had, as he tried to add a bit of weight. Linda who has a special interest in anything Jewish wanted to see the Jewish museum on Doroteer Strasse, so we all did that. Quite a fine little museum, whose main focus was a Jewish entertainer and artist from the thirties – not someone I had ever heard of.

As we walked out of the museum, just across the street there was a music shop where Linda suggested I buy a tie with music scores and then on to Stephan's Platz where we bought tickets for a concert that night at Schönbrunn outside the city. The guy who sold us the tickets was all dressed up like Mozart and very friendly and strong on marketing. We also took a look inside the great church, St Stephen's Cathedral, built during the 12th century. ` However, great churches have a way of looking the same, and although often very beautiful, it really is that which is intangible and in your soul which is infinitely important and beautiful, rather than any physical building. But to be fair, sometimes the artist or architecture can be instrumental in reminding you about, and bringing to the fore, that soft inner divine nucleus that potentially resides in all human beings. Here I think of an Armenian preacher in Jerusalem who reputedly said that when God prescribed for us to love all human beings he hadn't met the Turks. When in Jerusalem a few years earlier I learned about the Armenian holocaust in Turkey 1917/18, something I was unaware of until then. It is difficult to fathom how cruel humans can be.

We continued our walk to Stuben Ring No 5 to look at the MAK (Museum for Angewandte Kunst) museum, a Jugend and Art Deco style museum, with mostly furniture. I got a bit bored, but Linda thought it was great, which made me glad. She found the chairs we have in our dining room in Singapore, which she loves. Our chairs were made in China, but clearly the model must have been the chairs we saw there at the exhibition. Claas and I sat in the middle of the large hall and waited for the ladies (I mistakenly first spelled it laidies and at first couldn't see what was wrong with it and then realized that this might be a Freudian slip) to inspect all chairs and urns from every angle. I tried a bit of singing as the hall was great and of stone, but soon realised that if I did it full on, the alarm would probably be activated and we would be thrown out. After the museum we walked to a delicatessen on Wollzeile. They also had an inner room with a small restaurant and we all thought that might be a good idea for lunch. The ladies had omelets with Chanterelles and Claas and I had some good sausages and some beers and wines to go with it. Sehr Schön. The other patrons were an overweight Swede who tried to help us with our ordering and a little lady and her lap dog. All three looked like they knew how to get the most out of life.

After lunch we continued to walk back towards our hotel and made a short stop in Volksgarten and watched all the people enjoying the sunshine. By 4.00P.M. we were back at the hotel and had a rest for a few hours and then at 7.00P.M. we took a taxi to Schönbrunn. We had a good chat to the taxi driver in German. The driver was an Indian from Heyderabad who had spent 11 years in Austria and he said he had no desire to go back. He was very friendly. We arrived a bit early so went for a pre concert drink at a nearby bierstube. The concert was in the Orangerie – a beautiful little annex to the enormous palace - and the program included Mozart's La Clamenza di Tito, Die Zauberflöte, Le Nozze di Figaro, Don Giovanni, and of course Johan Strauss' Die Fledermaus, Eine Nacht in Venedig, Die Zigeunerbaron and An Der Schönen Blauen Donau. Then I said that it would be perfect if they finished with Radetzki Marsch and that they did with all of us including the many Japanese clapping ferociously. At the end of the show when we got to the street it was raining, but as luck would have it we stepped right into a taxi. We debated if that might have been someone else's ordered taxi, but my view was that these guys know when this daily show ends and that there is plenty of business then, particularly when it rains. If it works, don't worry!

The taxi driver thought we paid a lot for our tickets. Before we reached the hotel we asked the driver to stop on Floriangasse where there was a nice looking restaurant 'Hermann Adam' only a few steps away from the hotel. We thought we would have a late supper there and get back to the hotel with ease. It looked like a typical Vienna jovial restaurant and we found a table for four, placed our orders and had a very enjoyable hour eating well and drinking some beer and wine. When we were ready to leave a middle age chap insisted we have a schnapps at his expense. It proved to be Herr Adam himself, the proprietor. Nice, friendly, warm, Austrian. Then we found our way back to the hotel after a long and eventful day.

The next day we had breakfast at the hotel at 8.30 A.M. – eggs and ham, bread and coffee with juice – just right. Then we set out for The Hundertwasser House and took the tram to Schweden Platz and had a nice walk from there. We hadn't yet figured out where to buy tram tickets so we traveled courtesy of the Viennese taxpayer. The Hundertwasser is a block of flats in so many colors and styles it looks like a giant play house, really something quite unique. Nothing repetitive or symmetrical. All crazy, and yet quite appealing. We also visited Kunsthaus Wien where there was a Tiffany and Hundertwasser ausstellung.

After these cultural treats we walked in the direction of the Belvedere Palace and gardens. At one o'clock hunger and fatigue stopped us – it was quite hot at 25 degrees and sunshine - and we went into a pizzeria to have our lunch. The quality of the lunch exceeded our expectations and we got the break we needed. We found our way to the Belvedere, a beautiful palace cum garden in the middle of Vienna, and we spent half an hour there, had an ice cream and then boarded another tram on Prinz Eugen Strasse that took us to the Rathaus in ten minutes where Claas and I went one way and Linda and Else-Marie went to look for the Jewish cemetery. After no more than a few steps we heard bras band music and walked in the direction of the music. We sat down on the steps of the Rathaus and listened to the band play three or four tunes and thought that life couldn't be much nicer. Then we proceeded on to Slösserstrasse and our little hotel.

In the evening we decided to go to Grinzing for dinner so we took tram no 28 by the University for our tram trip to the end station. This time we got proper tickets – Ats 152 for 8 single trips to and from Grinzing and we reached there by 7.00P.M. The tram was quite full to start with but gradually the number of passengers reduced, so we all could find a seat. Wien is a very neat and tidy place with some beautiful buildings more or less in every block, particularly in the older central parts. In Grinzing we walked up the hill – there were some musicians in 1700's outfits coming out of the church, presumably from a wedding, and many busses were arriving with tourists seeking a meal. We looked into two or three places before we settled on one that looked pretty nice and where we could sit outside and enjoy the young summer night. We ordered a liter of white wine and water. We asked for the menu but were instructed that it was all buffet style. So after trying the wine out we all went to find some food – salads, vegetables, hot schinken, chicken etc, etc. followed by cheeses. It didn't take long to finish the wine and order another one. The evening was just divine – light, blue, spring like, optimistic.

Two and a half hours later when it was still light we walked back to the tram station and returned to the hotel. We needed to wake up 5AM the next morning for the 6.25AM train departure. I woke up 4.30 A.M. as it was already daylight then. I had intended to pay the hotel bill the night before, but had forgotten and thought it could be a problem as no one may be there so early in the morning. However, when I met Else-Marie in the corridor, she had paid for all of us the night before. It is wonderful when you can have relationships like that, where money flows back and forth without any worries and the conviction that it all evens out in the end. Thanks, Else-Marie. When we took the taxi it was only a ten minutes trip to Sudbahnhof. The train on track one was already in – Wien – Breclav – Brno – Praha. Six chairs to each compartment but ours only contained ourselves. A group of musicians joined our car but in another compartment. Next to our car was the restaurant so perhaps we could get some coffee or meal.

After we started rolling we went to the restaurant and had an American breakfast, which was probably only half of what you would get in America, but twice what normal Europeans would eat. The four of us enjoyed the early morning breakfast with the middle of Europe rolling by outside the window. In fact, the landscape looked pretty much like Sweden. Going past the little villages I though what a nightmare it all must have been sixty years earlier with all of Europe at war. So much fear, misery, cruelty and death. One also wonders what 45 years of Soviet occupation meant for the people and their hopes and aspirations and how it might have changed in the last ten years. Perhaps we would find out. The weather was a bit mixed and it looked like rain in the distance.

I walked back to our compartment early and found three young women from Canada sitting there. They saw I was reading a book called 'Growing Within, Inner Development,' which Linda had bought from a small book shop in Little India in Singapore and we got into a discussion on spirit and soul; what brings people together and motivation – all sparked by the title of a book. We arrived in Prague at 11.00 A.M and it was now raining. We found a taxi and got to the hotel – Pension Pav - on Kremenkova by 11.30 A.M. paying the price as per the laminated price chart the taxi driver showed us. This proved to be twice the going rate. Our room was not available until 2.00 P.M. so we decided to take a guided bus tour around the City after having a taste of a Check beer.

We learnt that the City was founded in the ninth century. The Vltava river cuts a north south path through central Prague. Most of our tour was spent above the City on the west bank in the Kralowska Zahrada area in and around the Hradcany Castle. All very pretty and the views over the river and the old town were spectacular. Parts really looked like a museum and we went by the house of Franz Kafka and many little shops. I asked the guide, Hannah, a woman in her 50's how she found life and she said for many it was still very hard but at least there was hope that the children would get a better life.

We were back at our little hotel at 2.30 P.M, accessed our rooms through the staircase as there was no lift. The rooms were really a small suite, very basically furnished, but clean and ok. The bathroom also had an old look to it and among other things furnished was a condom. Neither we, nor our friends, had ever come across that before. We called our friends from London, John Watson and Haruko Momonoi, who had traveled out to meet us in Prague and agreed to meet them at our hotel at 7.00 P.M. Then it seemed quite appropriate to have a rest after the short night and long train ride. We had a good sleep and when John and Haruko arrived a bit early it was still raining so I suggested that they go to the establishment next door and wait a few minutes until we were ready to join them.

The next-door pub turned out to be a brewery and a huge restaurant with live music, and John had found a table for six so we decided to stay for the evening. The restaurant obviously consisted of many large separate rooms and we were in a full room with ca 50 people. There was an old guy with an accordion who sounded like an entire orchestra. He played popular tunes like Que Sere Sera, Santa Lucia, etc. When he heard we were Swedish he also played a Swedish tune 'Dansen den går uppå Svinsta skär.' I also asked if he knew O' sole mio, which he did, and he played and I sang full out and received some tangible appreciation. We also later asked him for Radetzkimarsh and Berliner Luft and he knew them all. There were about fourteen Japanese people in the middle of the room and for them he played Sakura, which made them all happy.

In the meantime we were served black beer brewed on the spot and some kind of schnapps. You could have anything to drink as long as you wanted black beer or yellow schnapps. The same principle applied to the menu so we all had some Goulash. It was all very good and not expensive, so we all quite enjoyed it. At the table next to ours were some locals, one of whom had emigrated to Sweden in the sixties so spoke the language well. She lived somewhere in Västergötland at a place I never heard of so couldn't really understand. Anyway, we sang, talked, ate and drank and felt quite good about life and being in the middle of Europe. I reflected on how a little bit of live music can make such a difference to the spirit and well being. After dinner we saw our London friends off at Narodni street where they took a tram just outside the National Theatre.

The next day we met up at the same spot at 9.30 A.M. for a more extensive walk trough the old town. We found it quite a challenge to walk from A to B as there were no straight streets at all. We found our way up to the Jewish quarters, but since it was Saturday, everything was closed. Linda decided she would come back the next day to see the cemetry and the museum. It was quite cold with temperatures around 15 degrees and a bit of a wind. Must be unusual for this time of the year and I had packed my gear in Singapore so didn't really have anything but short sleve shirts. There were plenty of tourists from the east and west and everywhere. Each and every other building is so well ornamented or interestingly designed so there just isn't any end to things to look at, even if we know from all the fine churches of Italy that the excess of anything tends to be a bit exhausting and the sensation gradually diminishes.

As we walked through the old town many people tried to sell us music performances in the evening and we decided on a five o'clock concert in St Martin-in-the-Wall Church. The program included Bach, Vivaldi, Mozart, and Schubert – with only three performers; an organist, a trumpeter and a soprano – two men and a lady. She sang Ave Maria and The Queen of the Night from the Magic Flute. Delightful concert all in all with about twenty in the audience. Particularly the organ player was an outstanding musician. Back at the hotel we had a short rest, then went out to find a restaurant and discarding about ten we finally found one we all agreed looked pretty nice – the Golden Duck. This was an elaborate old place where they played Glenn Miller music, much to my delight. We had a bottle of red Check wine, sparkling water and a couple of beers. The ladies had some light meal and I had wild boar, a typical local dish. Afterwards we went for a short walk and went to bed at 10.30 P.M. quite exhausted after so much walking.

The third day, Sunday, was a beautiful day with higher temperatures and we again met up at the National Theatre and decided to go accross the Legil bridge to the other side of the river. The views from the bridge were impressive – a very active river with islands in the middle and a special lane with one or two locks at the side to allow boats to go up and down. On the other side we turned north towards Charles Bridge and when we reached that we turned left to slowly work ourselves up the big hill west of the river. This meant up, up and up along little wonderful alleys and stairs to Strahovsky Klaster. Each time we turned around the views became more and more impressive. On one little street there were an another acçordion player doing 'Que sera sera' again and I helped him with the singing. At the top of the hill we saw a restaurant and we sat down to have our lunch by the park with full views over the entire city with the river and all the bridges. Nothing short of marvellous! Someone asked where John got his beautiful hat from, and I said I bought three of them at Arab Street in Singapore, one for John, one for Claas and one for me. When all three of us wore them we looked like coming from the same asylum. If you are not a little bit mad you are not normal.

After the lunch with the million dollar view we slowly walked down again and stopped by the St Nicholas Church, perhaps the most beautiful of all. There we separated because Linda wanted to see the Jewish museum and the others preferred taking a tour on the River, Moldau. Yes, I decided to join Linda, as it wasn't really on to leave her alone and also that some experiences are even greater in small groups, i.e. a group of two, her and I.

We found our way to Charles bridge, 'Karlov Most' and the sun was at her nicest and all the people were out walking enjoying the lovely summer weather after a few quite cold days. The bridge was full of people, many artists selling their wares, lots of tourists and lots of locals. We walked very slowly feeling that this is Prague, a piece of heaven. Two thirds across there was a jazz band, the Bridge Band, who played wonderful Dixieland jazz. I just love it so we stopped for a while to enjoy. After the first tune I asked if they knew 'Just a closer walk with thee' and sure enough, they played that tune next, and I sang with them. This tune reminded me of my late father, Georg, who also loved the tune. At his funeral there was a small jazz band in the church who played that tune and a few similar – the most beautiful funeral experience of my life, and I know my dad would have been so pleased. I bought their CD for 300 krona and also contributed a tip of 50 k. And then we moved on to the museum.

Soon we reached the Jewish quarters and got the tickets for all the different sights. First we entered the white hall where 60,000 Jewish names with birth and death dates were written on the wall, on a per village basis. This was the only recognition of their existence post the Nazi exterminations. 60,000 out of a total of 6,000,000 that succumbed! Totally and completely unbelievable that this could have happened less than a century ago – small children, young boys and girls, middle aged and the old. All brutally, savagely and systematically murdered. Cruel and uncompassionate conduct beyond comprehension. The museum was all very well done and touching beyond words. After that we went through the cemetry, the oldest Jewish cemetry in Europe, which hadn't been used for three hundred years so all tombs and gravestones were very old and dated. We also saw the Synagogue and the museum. Inevitably a very emotional experience. I waited half an hour for Linda at the exit and we then visited the museum shop. I bought four Kafka books, two to give to our travel friends, and we also got six beautiful replica old Jewish wine glasses. The museum shops I often find interesting, as they in fact give you a snapshot of what the museum is all about.

On our way back to the hotel we stopped and had coffee on the main square enjoying the music from a brass band playing away there. Afterwards I exchanged some money with a street vendor and got quite a good exchange rate. Only later did I discover that the money I received was worthless as it was Bulgarian – hard to tell, really. So I paid for my trusting attitude, or naivite if you wish, and I tried to understand what might be positive with the experience, being determined that in the overall scheme of things, it wasn't the end of the world and I wouldn't let it ruin my or anyone else's day. I thought that firstly I need to get a bit more critical and examining of new situations and people, particularly in a touristic melting pot like this, and secondly that when you are trusting and lose out, the cost is very easy to determine, but when you gain relationships and good will by being trusting, which must be much more frequently occurring, you cannot easily express that in monetary terms. This was the second time on this trip that I got ripped off and I vowed to be more vigil and alert to avoid a third time. Mistakes are there to learn from. Just as we reached our hotel we heard music from next door so we went there for a beer and a rest to enjoy the little brass ensemble. We listened to a couple of tunes under the big trees and then finally went to the hotel and an afternoon nap before dinner.

At seven we all met up for a joint dinner. We soon enough found a pretty basic but nice place on Narodni, patronised by many locals and we had dinner with beers. After that we had decided to go to a jazz club, which advertised that both Bill Clinton and Madeline Albright, the latter with Check ancestry, had been there enjoying themselves. It might be good enough for kings and princesses but we found it quite noisy and lacking in charm and harmony, so we stayed for little more than half an hour and then returned to the street. A bit of a disappointment, but for there to be ups, there must be the odd down as well.

The next morning we packed our things and stored them at the front desk as we would be taking the train to Berlin in the after noon. Afterwards, all of us met up at the Theatre again. John and Haruko's tram stopped there so it was quite a good place to meet. They normally live in Hampstead, London, in a great building 'The Pryors,' on East Heath Road, and in that building one of the old tenants is a Check lady who has a small flat in Prague. She had insisted that our friends live in her flat while in Prague. There are friendly little people everywhere so there should be hope for mankind after all. This last day we walked across the river on Legil bridge again and then turned south after the crossing. This area was less spectacular, but still quite interesting. We walked until we reached the post office just before the next bridge down, Jiraskuv Most.

At the post office we queued up to buy stamps and we got ca thirty stamps for our total number of postcards. The service was friendly but slow, which, to be fair, is better than just slow. We crossed the bridge back and gradually worked ourselves back to the Vaclav Platz where we intended to have coffee at Hotel Europa, a bit of a legend. It was pretty ordinary but after such a long walk it was like medicine to sit down and have a chat. Back at the hotel we checked out at 12.00 noon and then the six of us went back to next door restaurant of the first night to eat and drink and sing. The same guy was there playing and we sang with him, although at this early hour, no-one joined in the singing. We took coffee in the garden and agreed that this place was pretty good value anyway – worth coming back to. We bid John and Haruko good-bye – hugs and kisses - as they would not come with us to Berlin, but would stay one more day in Prague and then fly back to London again to prepare for a long holiday at their place near Cullen, Scotland.

At two o'clock a taxi took us to the station at half the price we paid coming in –the benefit of local familiarity showing up. Having lived in New Zealand and Singapore for the last eleven years I guess Linda and I had been underexposed to fraud and deception. At the station we learned that the train would be half an hour late, but the weather was nice and we had quite a pleasant view over some trees and a lake, so no worries. We also bought some fruits and ice cream. The chart at the station showed us where our car would be so we could wait in the right location, and at 3.30 P.M. the train arrived and we were on our way to Berlin via Dresden. Perhaps it took two hours through spectacular countryside – very steep and high hills on either side of a river valley - to reach the border and there were customs officers on either side of the border inspecting our passports. Quite calm and peaceful and they didn't make you feel uncomfortable in any way. Again I reflected how many worried and scarred people would have made this trip in the early unfortunate nineteen forties.

Of Dresden we saw very little from the train. It originated as a Slav village and used to be called the 'Florence of the north' before it was wiped out by a bomb raid by 800 aircraft on the night between 13th and 14th February 1945 killing tens of thousands of its inhabitants just before the end of the war. Through the Elbe it is connected with both Check republic and with Hamburg. And of course until ten years ago it was quite inaccessible inside the iron curtain.

The four of us enjoyed a good dinner in the diner. 'Dinner in the diner, nothing could be finer' as the text goes in Chatanoga Cho Cho. We had chicken salad and a beer to go with that and coffee to finish off. It is indeed quite a luxury to sit so comfortably and take your food whilst the scenery is changing outside – quite different from doubling up in an aircraft to take your food and drink in order to avoid the chair in front and the neighbour sitting less than an inch away from you. At 8.30 P.M. we arrived at Berlin's Zoo Station which was very close to our hotel in Charlottenburg, off Kurfurstendamm. We found a taxi and he got us to our hotel, Castell, Wielandstrasse 24, in five minutes. We checked in and decided to go for a walk. It was still light and warm and pleasant – June is my favourite month for north Europe – it has a bit of a virgin Friday feeling of it, fueling your anticipation in the knowledge that most of the much longed for summer lies ahead, thus the expression, *spring is in the air.* Walking nearly to the end of Kurfurstendamm, we sat down at a cafe and had a beer and looked at all the people out strolling. And again we had a rather early night after another day of long walks and travel and new impressions. The hotel Castell was another internet find – a clean and efficient little place on three floors in what looked like a normal multifamily house. They requested payment in advance to which we found no objection.

The next day we were up early and had a full German breakfast including a glass of sekt, i.e. sparkling wine. We walked back to the train station, stopped in at a little museum there, and then bought our one day bus pass at DM 7.60 each – a bargain to have access to all the buses and the trams. In the three cities, Milan, Vienna and Berlin, there were no regular checking of tickets but only the odd ad hoc ticket control which if you hadn't paid your fare, caused a fine of something like 60 DM. Thus threre are probably a fair amount of free loading, but perhaps the lost revenue is less than the cost of extra staff and resource required for checking every traveller. It is also quick and swift as no time is required to hassle over tickets. If you don't have a day or season ticket you need to stamp your one trip ticket inside the bus at a stamp machine. We had due fare most of the time, the only problem being when one couldn't find a ticket agent. If we looked dumb and Swedish – which shouldn't be too difficult – we might be able to convince any controller of our purity of heart and intent. Fortunately this never came to a test.

We went for bus number 100, a double decker that goes all around the city. At first we went in the wrong direction, which proved to be a blessing, because when it turned and came back we had the good seat at the front of the upper level. After twenty minutes, driving down Unter den Linden, we alighted at Slossbrucke and had a look at the Opera house and the Berliner Dom and sat down for a morning coffee at a nice outdoors place. As nothing much seemed open we rejoined the bus and went to the Volkspark and on to Branderburger Tor where we stopped for lunch on Wilhelm Strasse. After the lunch we went through the Tor, which was covered by cloth as it was under renovation, and continued to Richstags-gebäude. Here we encountered a big queue to enter and go up in the glass dome. Linda didn't feel like it so she sat down and read a book while we got in and up. Linda said she felt a bit uneasy about these imposing buildings and the wings of history over the place. The wait wasn't long and after security check and a lift ride we entered the roof level of the building. It was quite worthwhile to walk the spiral all glass walkway to the top seeing all of Berlin unfolding under our feet. In the dome there was also an interesting photo display of the history of the German parliament, which as you will know, isn't very old. It included the big fire of the building during the Nazi era. Otherwise the City which is now the capital again, dates back to the 13th century.

Checkpoint Charlie, the American checkpoint to the east, today is little but a white kiosk in the middle of the road. It looks so small and quaint so it is almost hard to believe that these square meters were among the hottest points in global security politics in the world for decades. Some sixty people were killed over the years trying to get across the infamous Wall, erected August 13th 1961. Although each death is tragic and the Wall was a symbol of oppression, the number is small compared to twenty million dead Russians during the war or the six million innocent Jews that had to pay with their lives for the Nazi malice and madness. There isn't much left of the wall. Claas and Else-Marie wanted to move around a bit further in the area and Linda just wanted to get away, so she and I took the underground on Friedrichstrasse to Rosa Luxembourg Platz.

Rosa Luxemburg, with byname Bloody Rosa, was born 1871 and was assassinated during the Spartacus Revolt 15 Jan 1919 by reactionary troops. She was born in Poland into a middle class Jewish family and moved to Zurich to escape the threat of prison in Russia. She consistently underrated nationalist aspirations and stressed Socialist internationalism. This became one of her major points of disagreement with Lenin and his theory of national self-determination. She and Karl Liebknecht exercised considerable influence on the public and were a contributing factor in a number of armed clashes in Berlin in 1918. They became founders of the German Communist party in 1918. She always remained a believer in democracy as opposed to Lenin's democratic centralism. No doubt an interesting person, obsessed with the issue of participation of the many in the fruits of progress built with their labour. This leads thoughts to contemporary demonstrations in Genua, Gothenburg, Seattle, Davos etc against perceived narrow mindedness, exploitation and lack of cause and purpose in world political and business leadership.

When we got there and saw daylight again, we stopped in a large young cafe and had a beer. A lovely cafe with tiled floors and dark wooden tables and chairs with a capacity of a few hundered people but now on a warm Tuesday afternoon virtually empty. One could just imagine the level of noice when full of young people a Friday evening in political debate in the presence of Rosa Luxembourg's spirit. Someone said that he who isn't a socialist at the age of twenty has no heart, and he who is one at the age of thirty has no brains. This is a bit harsh, but we must never let the end justify the means because we never reach the end as the end is an illusionary dream. Life is a continuum and a direction rather than a destination and thus, if the road is strewn with corpses rather than flowers, we have chosen the wrong path. In his book 'The Kingdom of God is whithin you' Leo Tolstoy makes the point that any violent overthrow of the current order always leads to more violence and deterioration. Gandhi and Jesus would vouch for the same thing. And from Francis of Assissi we learn: 'I don't ask you to be perfect, I ask you to be loving. This is not the same thing, in fact it is quite the opposite.'

We identified the direction to the Synagogue and started to walk Torstrasse in that direction. Interesting quarters in old East Berlin. A lot less flashy than the former west. However there was also something charming about these quarters with children playing and the streets a bit less commercial. On Torstrasse we stopped in at a Photo Studio as I thought I would need a few photos to get a new drivers liscence in Sweden after being pickpocketed in Rome. The shop, Foto-Ateljer Kettenbach, Torstrasse 106, was run by a heavy set jovial lady and I asked her if she had been here for long. She said she had been here since 1947. Then I asked if things are better now after the unification. She said 'I don't know – I used to pay DEM 90 per month for the whole ground floor of this building and now after liberalisation I pay DM 900 for a third of the area.' And the politicians are all the same, read or blue, they all cling to power and run their own agenda. But at least you can enjoy bananas now I suggested. That we could already before, she said. "Haben wir auch dann" (I had heard the story that when the East Berliner's streamed through the wall in November 1989 they quickly bought all the bananas in the west – perhaps that story was just a fabrication). She took my photo, and we waited a bit for it to develop. She showed us how she had been in the business since the early forties and some articles written about her with the picture of a young beautiful photographer. Now she was 72 but she didn't look it. She asked for DEM 14.70 and I gave her 15 and both Linda and I thought the discussion the highlight of the day. Simple and sincere human interaction is the ultimate joy – always has been, always will be. The conversation was all in German which we don't really speak, but where there is a will, there is a way.

We continued along Linien Strasse and Linda photographed a building riddled with bullets. This means that it mustn't have had any overhaul since the war that ended 1945.

Now we sighted in the distance the shining Cupola of the Synagogue on Oranienburger Strasse and moved in its direction. The biggest Synagogue in Eastern Europe it looked magnificent. During the Kristall nacht 1938 it was put on fire and although damage was limited thanks to a German officer who intervened and drove the SS troups away, after further sabotage and bombings, the reamains were dynamited in the 50s as what remained was too unstable. Since 1995 it was fully restored externally, but internally it remained a shell and a museum rather than a house of worship. A tribute to all the Jews in Berlin that succumbed by Nazi atrocities. About six hundered Jews remained in Berlin at the end of the war compared to a pre war population of 60,000. Now there are about ten thousand again, mostly from Eastern Europe. After this we took a tram to Karl Lieberknecht Strasse where we again found our bus 100 which took us back to the hotel. The area we travelled through adjacent to Oranienburger Strasse looked really nice and arty. At the end of the day, we pefer someting genuine and spiritual, rather than something pretencious and flashy. You want people and environments that suggest 'Here real and loving people interact and enjoy themselves, rather than We are not interested in anything other than your money.

We had dinner in the Charlottenburg area on Bleibtreustrasse, at a nice little Italian Restaurant – good meal, in a small residencial outdoors environment. All very happy we shared two bottles of Chianti after a rich and long day. In the morning we checked out of one room and retained another room for our late departure. We had a big breakfast again with all the trimmings. With all the walking we did I guess we wore the calories off. Amazing that Claas kept up with us, walking over ten kilometres a day, only a short time after it was questionable whether he would ever walk again.

For this second day we had decided to go to Potsdam to get a bit of a change of scenery. Potsdam was the host of the end of war Conference in July 1945 between the three victorious powers – US, UK and Russia represented by Harry S. Truman, Winston Churchill/ Clement Atlee and Josef Stalin. The amity and good will that had largely characterized former wartime conferences was missing at Potsdam, as each nation was concerned with its self-interests and particularly Churchill didn't trust Stalin. The war with Japan was still going but after the dropping of the atomic bombs the next couple of weeks, Japan capitulated on the 10th of August.

We took a train all the 24 km out to Potsdam seeing a lot of green trees and villas on the way. Berlin gives the impression of being a city of parks and trees and the locals seem to love to get out in the parks with a blanket and sit around and enjoy the freedom. As we stepped out of the train we were a bit lost for direction and a friendly German asked us where we wanted to go. I answered, 'We don't know, any suggestions?' and we were advised to take the tram to Schopenhauerstrasse and then walk into the Park Sansouci from there which we did. This day was clear skies and close to thirty degrees again. We got to the big gate towards the Sans Souci Palace completed 1747 and walked about one kilometre to reach the palace which was all very beautiful. It had terraces with gardens in front and a big fountain, Grosse Fontäne, and dams and quite a few tourists enjoying the sunshine and the beauty of the set up. Although you could probably spend a week in Potsdam and see new things every day, we decided to limit our ambition as our map indicated that the park grounds were just endless. As it was about one in the afternoon, we would rather turn back to Potsdam City to find somewhere to eat.

We found a nice car free street, Hegelalle, full of restaurants, and we sat down and had a great lunch out in the open, under a parasol. After a long lazy lunch we walked along all the shops, bought an ice cream, but didn't really find anything else that took our fancy so we took the tram back on Friedrich-Eberstrasse across the Havel to the train station, Potsdam Hauptbahnhof, to go back to Berlin. We did try to take a boat back which was in theory possible, only next sailing was two hours out, and that tilted our preferences in favour of the train, which we had anyway already paid for.

The train ride was nice although a bit hot. Linda and Else-Marie wanted to do something more, whereas Claas and I favoured taking a nap so we split up to meet at the hotel later. I slept like a log for 30 minutes and then went up and sat on the balcony and read for an hour before the girls returned. We all had a shower in the middle of the room so one gender had to be on the balcony, whilst the other gender showered. It all worked quite well and clean and neat we went to the very nice restaurant on the corner of our street to have dinner. This was quite a posh place so all the young beauties and the guys driving the convertible cars ate here. Sometimes I reflect that it is quite wisely arranged that your eyes are designed to look out and not in. Makes you feel as young and beautiful as whatever you are looking at.

After the meal we took a new taxi to the bahnhof and waited for our train. We had about an hour before the train was to leave. I saw a girl who tried to buy a local train ticket so I gave her my day ticket as it was valid for another few hours and I would have no further use of it. We decided to have a beer, but everything closed at 10.00 P.M. so no beer this time. Our train arrived at 10.40 P.M. and it was a sleeper only, bound for Malmö, Sweden. There was a bit of confusion with double bookings of compartments but after a while that was sorted out and we got our own little place. Some youngsters travelling on Interrail passes boarded without any sleeper ticket and they were a bit surprised and annoyed that there were no seats on the train. After a few hours ride the train would enter the ferry in Sassnitz, and perhaps there they could have some seats over night. We went to bed pretty immediately and I think I slept all the time to the docking in Sweden.

We spent about an hour in Malmö and then got on to the last leg to Stockholm where we arrived around 1.00 P.M. and took the subway out west to our suburbs. I called my 82 year old mother from the subway and she met us in her car and took us back to her place, where we also met up with Andre,' our son. Now awaited a few days in Stockholm catching up with Max and his lovely girfriend, Kristina, sending Andre' off to a language and tennis camp in Marbella, Spain, and going out to our summer place in the Baltic Sea to enjoy the Swedish summer

– doing the things we traditionally would do. Although the Nordic Summer is short, it is very precious and delightful on a nice day.

We were happy with our train journey from Rome to Stockholm. It is good to try to do something outside tradition every year to expand ones consciousness. Milano is probably the most livable City, perhaps Vienna is the most charming, Prague has the most beautiful buldings and scenery and Berlin is the fastest growing and the most intriguing. We thoroughly enjoyed all of them. We also cherished the informal and easy interaction with our New Zealand, British/Japanese and Swedish freinds. True wealth is best measured in your number of sincere friendships. I later continued my trip to Bangkok where I had dinner with my good colleague. Then I proceeded to Singapore meting people I feel very close to. I feel so lucky to have good friends in so many places. What is the meaning of such good fortune bestowed upon me? The answer eludes me, but I do feel lucky and grateful.

May I end with a line from The City of God by St Augustine:

'Let those who think I have said too little, or those that think I have said too much, forgive me; and let those who think I have said just enough join me in giving thanks to God.'

Thank you for your time.

Singapore 28th July, 2000

3. Spoleto, Umbria in the summer of 2002

First all the birds, mostly swallows, making themselves heard through the curtains. A trickle of light penetrates the green shutters, promising another beautiful summers day. Opening up the windows avails the most spectacular view of the little Umbrian town and its country side surroundings. We had a delicious meal last night with cold veal in tuna sauce, a mixed salad, some vegetables plus a bottle of Chianti with some mineral water. This was at the best of the numerous restaurants in Spoleto, the spectacular view over the rooftops, the churches and the valley adding to the culinary experience.

The girl serving us was more charming than professional – not necessarily a bad trade off. The only other guests were a group of fifteen people of mixed description sitting under a gazebo. They seemed to be a mix of Italians and Americans, between thirty and seventy years old, perhaps some returning emigrants to America celebrating with old friends. One member of their group, a middle aged male Italian, suddenly stood up and sang the Prisoners' Choir quite well and to great acclamation. After a while a couple arrived and sat down at the table next to us. They were from Melbourne and after exchanging some courtesies he said he was a long time customer of the National Australia Bank, which I have been associated with now for ten years. Very nice people they seemed to be.

Waking up this 21st day on June 2002 I feel a bit slow from the indulgences the night before but a shower and a few exercises quickly sets me right. Whilst showering I also wash yesterdays cloths, an easy way to keep current with the washing. We have learnt over the years to travel light. All the church bells start ringing to announce seven o'clock and the start of the working day. The ringing continues for at least five minutes suggesting perhaps that no one should be sleeping after seven. It is a lovely way to wake up as the sounds create a picture of the many old churches in the town and the many people from previous generations who must have lived in the environs and enjoyed the same bells.

I quietly move across the marble floor to open the window and with the view in front of me read a few lines in my book whilst I wait for Linda to rise. My current reading is 'Voices for Peace' which consists of twenty-seven separate contributions on peace, all written post the nine eleven attacks on America. I expect to finish the book today and then move on to reading a couple of books on Francis of Assisi which I bought two days before in Assisi. Voices for Peace turned out to be very interesting, the main message being that to deal effectively with hatred and frustration there is only one way and that is to understand their causes and then work on eliminating or mitigating those. Indiscriminate use of force may well deepen hate and resentment.

Today we are having breakfast at opening and then we intend to visit Orvieto about sixty km away. We will go by train but know it will take a couple of hours as we must change trains at Orte, half way, to get there. Sitting in the train and seeing the Umbrian landscape pass by is very enjoyable and will also accommodate some light conversation and some further reading. Orvieto is known for its Dome and also for its wine. These little Italian towns are all like jewels. In addition to all the historic sites there are many shops and wonderful restaurants. We have had temperatures above 35 degrees every day and it does get a bit exhausting just after lunch, particularly if one has a glass of wine or two with the meal. The civilized way is to take a nap for an hour or two during the peak of the heat, but when on excursion, that is not really an option.

Orvieto turned out to be everything we hoped it would. Linda found two dresses and just after I discovered the most delightful restaurant, which was a combined furniture shop and restaurant. The exquisite furniture promised a good eating experience and that we did have. After lunch we looked at the most impressive Dome, but it only opened at three o'clock so we spent half an hour waiting in the heat, feeling quite lethargic. Fortunately there was a drinking fountain near the square, which allowed thirst to be quenched and also some cooling off of faces and necks. This church is amazing among Italy's many stunning churches, in itself making the trip worth its while.

When back at the funicular that takes you from the elevated town to the train station below, we saw the old well and thought we should have a look at that too before we left. It looked like an interesting little brick building, which I took to be a small museum, not too taxing after all that walking around earlier in the day. The entrance fee was three Euros, so I thought this should be good, to give value for money. Once through the ratchet type gate I realized that the building was nothing but thirty meters decline by way of a circle of 150 stairs – and then another 150 up again. This was more than I had bargained for but as there was no turning back, we just had to enjoy what was on offer. I have to admit it was quite a unique old well, but going in circles three hundred steps at the end of a long day was a bit much.

Orvieto offered many different wines for sale and also Grappa and other Italian spirits but we resisted purchases, given that we had four train changes and one change of flights ahead of us and one doesn't want to carry more than necessary in the heat. Perhaps in Milano we could pick up some Grappa and Fernet Branca to spice up our subsequent holiday in Sweden.

On arrival back at the Spoleto train station we decide to take the bus up to the old town and our hotel and in a few minutes the bus is in sight. This is almost twelve hours after we started the trip. When the bus arrives we enter quickly only to later learn that this bus goes in another direction than we want to go. Great! We get off at the first station with two options, either wait for the return bus half an hour later or walk back. No taxis in sight. And no nearby bars to enjoy a beer during the wait. Linda is tired and scolding me for the wrong choice of bus. She says she is not walking and not waiting. I find the rejection of both these options a bit puzzling but reflect that time will provide a solution, one way or the other. Twenty five minutes later we are at the hotel by way of foot, quite exhausted after a long day. But it has been a good and interesting day. Personally I quite enjoy walking in the warm evening sun.

As I finish these notes on our balcony overlooking Spoleto, I reflect that life is pretty agreeable. Travel helps expanding the basic understanding that we are all one big family of human beings and our pursuit of progress must be inclusive to its nature so as to promote participation by all in a good quality life.

Our route to Spoleto was via Milano. We arrived in there on the 15th of June and found our hotel just next to the railway station. The next morning we went for a short walk to the station and bought all the train tickets we needed. First we were going to Ancona on the east coast for one over night. I bought second-class tickets and this I later regretted, because the price difference isn't much and it was overcrowded on the first trip such as there were no seats available. We ultimately did ok anyway, but with luggage and very hot weather it gets a bit uncomfortable to be disorganised.

Ancona is quite a nice little town and the point of departure/arrival for all the ferries to Yugoslavia and Greece. We walked around and found a restaurant open on the Sunday afternoon and had a nice lunch while some world soccer championship game was going on the TV in the next room. We were served by the most beautiful black woman from Cameroun. Italy these days is quite a diverse society. After lunch we choose to take a nap and later went out for another longer walk and found this wonderful square with a church and theatre stage and two restaurants so we dined there. To sit outdoors in Italy and absorb the atmosphere from centuries old facades and cobblestones and eat and drink well for very little money really is delightful.

In the morning we walked up to some old fort with spectacular view over the sea and saw the ferries come and go and then later left for the train station to go to Spoleto. All our hotel bookings were done over the Internet and that worked very well. We paid on average one hundred and forty Euros for our accommodation so reasonably up market places - up market for tourists that is, about three star palaces. I prefer anyway to avoid the business hotels as they seldom have much atmosphere and are designed for corporate expense accounts.

In Spoleto we took a taxi at the station and arrived at this most beautiful hotel in a five hundred years old building. We were a bit ahead of the season so the occupancy was very light and we got the top room in the place. Delicate furniture and the best thing was the stunning views over all the old houses and churches and in the distance the mountains and the fields and meadows. The room had a hand painted ceiling and an old but clean and efficient bathroom, also with this million-dollar view. The hotel provided a full breakfast at from eight o'clock in the morning with frutta, pane, latte and all the other trimmings. We were always there at opening time as we tend to be up early and not have too late nights.

In Spoleto (in Umbria) there are about 25,000 people and the old town is within walls and it takes only an hour and a half to walk around the whole place. But it is full of buildings and squares and churches so there is a lot to see and experience. Also many lovely restaurants and shops. I bought a pair of read linen Armano trousers, a red linen jacket and few shirts and ties - all very nice. My favorite colour is red as you know. (The colour of love). At the top of the hill of Spoleto there is a great castle to protect the inhabitants from invasions. On the backside of this hill there is a most fantastic bridge also five hundred years old over a big ravine. The next day we bought bread and cheese and ham, some water and wine and went across the bridge and through the woods for a four hours walk. Very nice and picturesque but quite hot.

Before dinner we would go to one of the bars and have a drink and look at all the people. I normally drank Fernet Branca, which tastes a bit bitter but is supposed to be like medicine for your stomach. A typical dinner would be a tomato salad (pomodore), some risotto and perhaps a bit of meat after that and wine and water. After dinner I don't take coffee but enjoy a Grappa, which is the non-sweet liqueur based on grapes. Italians eat really late often starting at 9.00 PM. We would normally be a bit earlier than that whereas we normally eat at 7.00PM and in Sweden even earlier.

One day we made an excursion to Assisi - I have been fascinated by St Francis of Assisi who I think must have been a wonderful person - perhaps a bit too ascetic for my taste - but a person truly committed to non-violence, love and tolerance - concepts we all should try to live and embrace. For the rail trip they have very smart ticket machines so you buy your own tickets all over Italy from these machines. To Assisi it was only forty-two km and the cost was four Euros for about an hour's ride. Assisi is absolutely beautiful, also on a hill, the hill being full of churches and old houses and many shops and restaurants and of course also offering fine views over the Italian landscape. Umbria is the only Italian province which is landlocked - i.e. no access to the sea. We looked at St Francis church and there is a big gift shop and I was hoping to find some books in English to improve my knowledge of St Francis. I was delighted to find two books and Linda picked out a CD and other little things - I often find museum gift shops quite interesting with replicas of old jewelry and glass ware etc.

It was terribly hot in Assisi but we found a nice lunch restaurant were we ran into some people from Los Angeles and San Francisco. I have a tendency to talk to people to find out where they are from and to exchange a few views and I find that most people welcome that. When we got back to the station there was another two hours wait so we walked over to a little square with a marvelous church with a little church that St Francis built, now inside the bigger church - quite something! As you know I am not religious but the love and humility and compassion and peace messages of many religions appeal to me, whereas I think particularly Christianity is too negative on sensuality. I think that area can be a tremendous source of joy as well. Body and soul - interdependent - one needs the other, neither is superior, both are precious. I also think guilt and sin as concepts should not be promoted, but I can understand that, as the rules were written and laid down for brutes two thousand five hundred years ago, they perhaps needed to be clear and harsh to be understood. But for modern times this comes across as quite nonsensical and negative.

We made another tour to Orvieto witch I described above. And the last week end our friends from Sweden joined us - they had been on a train and boat holiday in Croatia. It was good to catch up with them again and we could show them all the nice things in Spoleto and see them off to the train station as they left one day before us. In Spoleto all were busy making everything nice and shiny for the Festival that would start 28th June, just after we had left. This is an annual two weeks of theatre, music, dance and opera festival - it must be fantastic to sit under the stars and watch it all. If you go there it might be good to try to time it to catch some of the Festival events.

For our return we went to Milano and had dinner with my sister's son Patrick, who works there, at another really nice restaurant, walking distance from Piazza de Domo. Before that we went for a walk and bought two bottles of Fernet Branca and Grappa to later share with our friends in Sweden. Milano must be one of the nicest cities in Europe to live in - a unique combination of modern and old and beauty both in the city and the surrounding landscape. Near Milano you have the nice lakes and the alps for skiing and in Milano there is all the fashion industry – and the beautiful people.

So to Stockholm where the weather had been quite bad for some weeks. We had a dinner with my son Max and his girlfriend Kristina. They had arranged a BBQ for us to meet her parents. She is one year away from a doctorate in Micro Biology and she is very nice and good-looking too so he is lucky. It rained but they had a marquis so we were ok anyway. The next day we went out with my mother to our Island in the Baltic Sea, where Andre', the youngest son had been since his arrival from Tokyo 15th June. It is just beautiful out there but it rained a bit every day. I did run every morning, which is a nice way to start the day. At the furtherest point of my run I would sit down and just look at the sea and all the little islands. From the spot where I would rest for ten minutes I could count to thirty five little islands. One run would give me 4200 marks on my step counter so it was about 3.2 km, each step being about 0.8 meter. This step counter is quite fun.

We made a number of boat trips to the various islands, one to our relatives on an adjacent island where we watched the World Cup Final game between Germany and Brazil and also had dinner with song and music. It makes such a difference wherever you are to also have access to some good friends.

For the weekend we flew to Paris where an old friend of ours was getting married - second marriage. Unfortunately I don't speak much French but the whole week-end was lovely. He was the mayor of Suresnes, a small city adjacent to Paris. About two hundred people attended the wedding in the City Hall and afterwards we were all treated to a great dinner on a floating restaurant on the Seine. Between them they had five daughters, all in their 20's and very pretty and attending. We also had a chance to walk the streets of Paris - Quartier

Latin and Mont Martre. First day we had lunch on Ille St Louis in the Seine and the second day we had dinner just down from Sacreceure, the impressive church with the fantastic views.

Then flying back and out to the island and now the weather had improved and was beautiful. The last day we took a boat trip to the outermost islands and enjoyed a full day on the soft polished rocks out there. All rocks in Sweden have been shaped by the inland ice which was over one km thick making them very smooth and soft and lovely to lie on summertime because they are warm and nice - very therapeutic.

Back to Stockholm on the Wednesday and on Thursday we had lunch at the Östermalmshallen food market with an old friend and the later dinner on the lake with sons and mother before going to the airport for the flight back to Tokyo on Friday. Even in Stockholm I ran each day to try to stay fit and healthy and collect more step points. Stockholm is absolutely spectacular in summer when the weather is nice - it is built on over fifty islands and the sea is all around you. Couldn't be nicer really - but food, history and culture is richer in Italy and weather, prices and taxes are better in New Zealand. Each place has its attraction and the contrasts make life richer.

July 2002

4. The Second Lease

Leaving Japan

So many things happening that I am just overwhelmed experiencing it all. Yesterday I worked my last day in Tokyo, my last day in Asia, my last day with the bank I had been with for 13 years, and the last day of a continuous 30 years' finance career. Many lasts to build up to some exciting firsts, I hope. The Emirates' Airlines had run an advertisement on my Japanese TV asking "When was the last time you did something for the first time?" and this was it. Not being employed would be a big first for me since I started my working life in November 1972. Now I am entering a stage of being self-unemployed. Perhaps that is the best and most natural state of affairs. I am not quite sure if I am sad or happy or maybe a little bit of both, possibly a bit melancholy. My intellect and heart always suggests that I am happy but I also sense that quite strong emotions are at play. I have always felt I am lucky to be alive and amongst living I cannot but feel that I am very privileged.

I have just sat down at a seafood restaurant off Waikiki beach in Honolulu. It is only 20 % busy. It may be a bit early at 7.00 PM but I also understand from talking to shop assistants that after the nine eleven horrors two years ago, tourism to Hawaii hasn't fully come back to what it was. In addition, the SARS flu epidemic has taken out all traffic from Taiwan and Hong Kong. My 'Sweet and Sour Pork' has just arrived and it is looking great. Good tasting food with all the nutrients and energy I need.

I left Tokyo on Saturday May 31st at 8.30 PM to arrive 8.55 AM the same day in Hawaii after nine hours flight. This gave me another Saturday, which is nice given how the one just completed in Tokyo was so full of chores and packing. The night before I had attended a concert at Suntory Hall, listening to the Tokyo Philharmonic Orchestra, directed by a beautiful young lady, Ms Anu Tali, from Estonia also featuring Jan-Erik Gustafsson on cello. Two of my friends, Tom Tsui (Chinese American who grew up in Japan – he claimed to be able to speak all the languages spoken in heaven) from the World Bank and Tracy Whiriskey (a young lawyer from Sydney on a two years stint in Tokyo) from one of the law firms, joined me for the concert. After a fantastic performance we took a taxi to Roppongi and had dinner at a very Japanese place, The Inakaya. Restaurant patrons were all sitting in a semicircle and all the food was laid out on ice in the middle. To order, one just had to point out whatever one wanted to eat and a young man would cook it on a charcoal grill in front of you. The staff shouted melodiously all the time to each other in a very Japanese way to increase the experience and give a sense of entertainment.

That last day of work, Friday May 30th, started out with a brilliant sunrise. When the sun woke me up I felt a strong need for a shower and a cup of tea in light of the dinner and singing at the Mitsui Club the night before. This morning of my last working day I took it easy and left a bit later than normal. At 8.30 AM I went down to the Sumida River to read the newspaper and watch all the traffic on the river. In the morning the river would glow like gold and the motion on the water made by the many vessels made the gold glitter beautifully. I spent nearly half an hour there, reading the Daily Yomiuri, one of the best newspapers we ever have come across. The reason it is so good is that it prints articles from many overseas newspapers and the editor chooses the articles with great skill. When I had finished my reading I walked 'Etai Dori' from 'Etai Bridge' to 'Nihonbashi' and my office just across from Nihon Ginko, the Bank of Japan. This is about 2,200 steps according to my step counter, i.e. just less than two km as each step is about eighty centimetres. All the way along Etai Dori the sun was shedding its generous warmth on all the people along the road. In the morning the foot traffic is so intense so cars trying to get out on to the main road from the little side streets have an almost impossible time finding a gap to get through, unless there is a traffic light. I had considered myself very lucky to live on a beautiful river within walking distance to my office in this City of thirty million people. The average commuting time for those working in Tokyo is probably close to an hour one way, quite often in crowded train cars. Particularly summertime when temperatures often exceed 30 degrees the commute can be quite uncomfortable.

Once in the office I greeted my staff that would get in between 7.30 AM and 8.30 AM. More often than not I would be the first to arrive, not so much out of a great sense of duty, but rather to reflect my body clock that signals to me to get up with up with the sun and activate myself. In Japan they haven't been able to agree on daylight savings time so daylight begins before 6.00 AM and dusk sets in about twelve hours later. I signed a few letters and also wrote a few letters, I serviced my email and finished packing three boxes to be sent to my home in New Zealand. These contained mostly my notes and office materials. This filled my day until noon when my colleague and friend, Kimie Ichino was taking me to a Sukiyaki lunch. She had asked me for my favourite eating for this our last meal and she found a great restaurant one stop away with the JR line from Shinbashi. The lunch with finest meat and vegetables was cooked in a coal-fired bowl in the middle of the table. We sat in a separate room with Shoji sliding doors and a little garden in the corner. An expert middle-aged Japanese lady cooked the meal for us with skill and love. And we talked about work and life. I suggested to Kimie that some of the challenges she was experiencing after about one year into her role were perfectly natural and I gave her a few tips on how to ease tension and achieve cohesion amongst her staff.

Once the lunch was over she guided me through the underground maze to Citibank, Otemachi branch, which I needed to see to close all my accounts and transfer any balance overseas. This took me about an hour involving three people, as nothing is ever easy in Japan. Walking back from the bank in Otemachi I thought this is the last time I walk these nice little streets. I stopped in and got half an hour's massage to try to get the last days tension out of my system and it was good. Writing these last words reminds me of St Augustine's 'City of God' where he points out that God did this on the first day...and it was good, and that on the second day, and it was good, and after seven days the scripture said what God had done was *very* good, which St Augustine takes to mean that God says that the whole is greater than the sum of the parts. 'All things taken together is better than superior things by themselves.'

Back in the bank I processed a few emails. My work routine the last ten years had changed to always make me first clear emails. I feel the same excitement about emails as when I had nets in the sea overnight and approached them with great excitement in the morning to see what the catch might be. Perhaps ten percent of my incoming mail tended to be 'semi private' spicing it all up. Thirty percent of mails were just copies of other people's traffic and those attracted least excitement. One of my colleagues had found a way to put such copied mail to the side. I also signed some loan documents.

My previous colleague Kikuchi san, who left the bank five months earlier, had asked to come in to say good-bye too. He arrived and said he hadn't found any job yet but wasn't panicking about it and in the mean time he enjoyed his leisure by photographing birds every morning. I always found him very cheerful and positive even if he wasn't always as expedient as he might have been. Anyway, his leaving the bank had been under the most amicable circumstances. I think parting on good terms is very important for many reasons, not least for the spirit and confidence of those who remain. In the long term we will all be excitants and it is important for good team spirit that people see that dignity, care and respect reigns. Kikuchi san gave me a few fantastic samples of bird photos he had taken. He also said he had seen many things he hadn't noticed before, i.e. he had got to know his neighbours in the last few months. I asked him if his wife worked and he said she was working part time. He asked me what I was going to do and I told him I would take three months off and then perhaps look for some directorships in New Zealand and also try to get on the lecturing and speaking circuit.

I asked him if he wanted a cup of coffee so we both went out to the little coffee van outside the building. I brought a compilation of short stories to give to the coffee girl. We got there and she gave me a red folded paper heart in which she had written the following:

Dear Mr Olsson, Thank you everyday. I can't speak English very well; I am not good at English. But I enjoy talk to you. I'm sorry that I couldn't see you. I forget you. We forget kokoro (then a drawn heart and a cup of coffee where the steam above the cup forms a heart – kokoro in Japanese) (and signed) *Juasumi Yukitake.* Her English was always enthusiastically spoken but not quite perfect and I took her last lines as intended to read *'won't forget'* rather than the way it was written. All the same I was delighted and quite touched to receive her little note and gave her my short stories. I also shook her hand as warmly as I could, wanting to give her a hug of love, but her confined space in the van made that not possible. Kikuchi left and we wished each other good luck. At this stage I went to our newly formed securities company in response to a kind invitation to a small farewell function there. Watanabe san, the manager of the securities company gave a nice little speech and I was given a card and a little paper lantern with my name printed on it in kanji. A very nice and positive farewell from the small professional team I had been supporting in getting its operating license at the beginning of the year.

As I went back to my room my colleague Akiyama said the girl from the department store next door was there to see me. What girl, I thought? asking that she please be shown in. To my surprise the girl from Mistsukoshi department store 6th floor watch department came in. I had had my watches repaired by the professional watch (not witch) doctors there and as they spoke little English she, Kumi Mihara, an ex air hostess for PIA, now selling fancy watches, volunteered to translate our discussions. In appreciation for her kind assistance I had given her some notes of mine, particularly my 'Tokoya' (barber) story, which she had renamed 'two thousand steps of happiness'. She came to say good-bye and give me a small present and I asked her how in the world she had picked up that I was leaving. She said that the day before she had asked the girl in the coffee van if she knew Mr Olsson and she had said yes, very well, and that I was leaving the next day in completion of my Japan posting. She said she had liked the happy and positive outlook on life that I had expressed in Tokoya. I thought it exceptionally nice and friendly that she would come with a card and a little gift for my departure. We had a short chat, I gave her some writings from my file, and we hugged and said good-bye and that we would try to keep in touch.

Now it was almost five o'clock and time for our staff function to begin. This would be the last send off after similar good bye sessions, individually with many of my Japanese and non Japanese friends and collectively with the Australia and New Zealand and Swedish chambers of commerce in Japan as well as my Australian tennis club and Swedish wine tasting club. A Japanese staff party is normally a pretty ordinary affair where food and drink, mostly non-alcoholic, is consumed pretty quickly and then the party fades away. Just after five we were all gathered in the banking hall and Shigematsu san, head of corporate banking, gave a short farewell speech. I was given a wonderfully framed collage of staff comments and photos and other little things. I responded by thanking them all profusely for the fantastic piece of art they had prepared for me – said it would adorn my walls in Auckland for a long time - and also gave a short speech. I said if there is one thing I want to be remembered by it is that I am an apostle for happiness. We owe it to ourselves, our families, colleagues and customers to try to find happiness within and try to act in such a way that happiness be promoted. I asked them to please remember my daily question to staff: Mina sanwa shiawase desu ka? Is everybody happy? By asking thus I display my ambition that all be happy and raise any issue with me immediately standing between them and happiness, and also showing my sincere concern that life in the bank be part of each staff member's pursuit of happiness. Life is wonderful and we must all try to recognise that. I told them about my experience during the day and said my posting in Tokyo had been some of the best days of my life. I had also typed two songs on a sheet of paper, which I distributed to all – The Moon Belongs to Everyone, the best tings in life are free..... and Three little words, oh what I'd give for that wonderful phrase.....I Love You!! We sang these songs together at no surprise to staff as we had sung at each previous function too. After that I was given another present of a very slim and smart digital camera, which I also thanked them for. In less than an hour the function was over as staff wanted to finish their day's work to be able to go home. When I returned to my room, four of the back office girls came to my room with a camera and each of them was photographed next to me. One of the girls said working life had improved a great deal during my tenure. I had interviewed all staff twice and I had tried to address all their concerns.

At 6.00 PM all the cleaning staff in their blue and yellow over alls – an outside contractor did all the cleaning in the branch – came into my room and formed a semicircle and the senior cleaner said some words in Japanese and they all bowed. I took it to mean that they were paying their respect and wishing me good luck in future and I felt very touched again. I bowed deeply too and expressed my sincere appreciation in English. I left the office a little later taking the Ginza line six stops to Tameiki Sanno to make my 6.45 PM meeting time for the Concert at Suntory Hall. Once gathered we met with Kate Cowan (a musician from Glasgow, now living in Tokyo) who works as a project manager for the Tokyo Philharmonic Orchestra. She gave us three premium tickets possibly hoping for some future corporate support. I had met her a couple of weeks earlier and explained to her that my wife and I supported an orchestra in Auckland and that we might be able to learn from each other. From there on events for the evening unfolded as described above. I was back in bed by midnight after eight stops on Hibiya Line from Roppongi to Kyabacho.

Early next morning I was back at the bank for the final closing touches. I spent just over three hours in the office before returning to my apartment for a meeting with my Swedish friend Anders Asell who wanted to pick up a few things for his daughter Vanessa who would continue to live in Tokyo on her own after their imminent move back to Sweden. We had a glass of beer together and he took some things including a fancy vacuum cleaner, iron and ironing board etc. After he left I cooked an omelette with ham, onions and tomatoes to get some energy. The agreement I had with my assistant at work, Okikawa san, was that I just leave things in the apartment and she and a cleaning lady would fix it all up for my colleague who would come up from Singapore to look after the Tokyo Branch. Very convenient for me and I told her I was grateful for the arrangements.

At four o'clock, after I had time to write a few letters, and get my luggage organised, my friend Mark Crawford, partner of KPMG Tokyo, came to pick up a few things and also to take me to Narita airport. Mark and his wife Hine, both from New Zeeland, had been terrific friends during our stay in Tokyo. At this stage it was raining and the rain was intensifying as a typhoon was coming in from the south. My flight for the day was ANA 1052 with departure time 8.30 PM for Honolulu. When I got to the check in I was told that the counter opens at 5.30 PM, which I found a little bit strange as they were all there just waiting for the right time to begin. I went for a short stroll with my cart and when back the bell tolled 5.30 PM, all the staff, about 20 people, lined up ceremoniously, bowed deeply in the direction of the gate and the passengers and the check in could begin. I thought it all quite amazing and something very Japanese. Being among the first to check in, I was served by a nice and helpful girl. I had two check in bags weighing about 25 kgs and three pieces of hand luggage – a bag, two tennis rackets and a suit bag. A bit much perhaps but then this was my final move so I had to bring everything I didn't want to leave behind. I asked the girl to put airmiles to Singapore Airlines, which she did. After check in I exchanged most of my yen to pounds and Swiss francs, which I would be needing later on my trip. The bank officers counted the money at least five times, which is very typically Japanese. At the security check I was asked if I had a knife in my bag, which I denied. Then I realised I had tucked my little backpack in my bag and there was a Swiss army knife. Fortunately they had a system for checking prohibited things so I got a baggage tag for a box in which my knife was put. Good service I thought, thanking them for their helpfulness and continued through.

As I had plenty of time, I brought out my Financial Times and went to a Sashimi place for a light meal realising that dinner was at least three hours away. Then I went through customs, giving up my alien registration card as I would not return to Japan as a resident again. I found some chairs and sat down to go through some of the papers I had brought and also to unpack my new camera and get rid of any surplus packaging. I was wearing my Borsalino panama hat from Milano and my red jacket from Wellington mostly because I didn't have anywhere else to put them. To that I wore a short sleeve shirt, Levi's jeans from Shibuya and black leather shoes, which I bought 1999 in Singapore. Attached to my brown leather belt was my 'Manpoke', the step counter I had been wearing the last year. 'Man' means ten thousand in Japanese and the idea is that one achieves at least 10,000 steps a day for longevity and good health. As each step is about 0.8 meters the target is to walk about eight km or five miles a day. I was bringing ten of these 'Manpokes' as I think they make good presents at a moderate cost of yen 1000 or eight US dollars. . I got them from 'Laox' in Akihabara about fifteen minutes walk away from my office in Nihonbashi.

ENROUTE TO HONOLULU

Boarding was smooth and I got my bag, tennis rackets, suit, hat and jacket stowed away in the overhead locker, putting my book for the trip, 'The Chrysanthemum and the Fish' in the chair pocket in front. If the airplane is full it can sometimes be a challenge to stow things away but by being a little early in boarding this usually isn't a problem. It is good to get rid of the carry-ons as freedom of movement for legs and feet is important for comfort on long flights. My assigned seat was the aisle seat (always my preference) 29 B so I started to wonder who 29A might be hoping I would be lucky and get some nice company. Much to my delight it was a Japanese girl 'Patricia Shinakoda' born 20th November 1974. This information I picked up as she was filling in her landing card. Patricia was quiet at first and I was wondering if she spoke any English at all but after a while I found out that she was Canadian from Toronto and she spoke fluent English, French and good Japanese. She had a marketing degree from a university in Toronto and was now working in Yokohama as an English teacher and loving it. It struck me that most people coming into Japan to work were loving it as it is a bit of a fairy tale country and culture. We soon were involved in deep conversation about Japan, Canada, USA, about love and religion and many other things. She was one of four children and her brother was getting married in Hawaii and attending the wedding was the purpose of her trip. Her cousin from Taiwan would pick her up at the airport for a tour around the island of Oahu.

Patricia was very good company and I thought myself lucky. She said she'd never been to Hawaii and I said I was there in 1969 at Christmas time.

As we were about to cross the date line I told her that in 1969 I flew over the date line going west and in the process lost my birthday and perhaps that was the reason I looked so young. Flying in to Hawaii I wondered how many passengers think of the 7th December 1941 events. Some say Franklin D Roosevelt had good previous intelligence about the attack but chose to ignore it as he needed a pretext for entering USA in the war to prevent Europe from falling to the Nazis. After Pearl Harbour all but one member of Congress voted for entering into the war and America declared war on Germany, Italy and Japan. The rest is history. Patricia felt that the historic events would pass through the mind of most passengers on a flight from Tokyo to Honolulu. I said that I distinctly remember from visiting Pearl Harbour 32 years ago how the commemoration plaque said 'we shall never forget' rather than something more forward looking and reconciliatory. From my good friends in New Zealand I had picked up that the commemoration monument at Gallipoli where so many New Zealanders and Australians died in the early 1900's, the Turkish legend and founding father of modern Turkey, Attaturk had written 'that many a mother on both sides lost their beloved sons here and may it never happen again.' No matter what befalls us I think we should always try to be forgiving and try to build a better world for the future.

Before parting we exchanged email addresses. We also accompanied each other through the long immigration lines and a Hawaii shirt clad attendant who looked at my immigration form said I must fill in an address in Hawaii or there would be delays for me. I said I intended to book something from the airport but he looked at Patricia's form and told me to just fill in the same as hers. She said: 'But we are not staying together?' and the guy said, it doesn't matter, you just have to fill in something which I did. I was asked a number of questions by the immigration officer like why was I coming, why I was staying so short, and why I was visiting so many US cities. I answered the questions and got through. The process reminded me of flying El Al where the screening process is extremely thorough and each passenger is interviewed for at least half an hour. When I got to the conveyor belt, all bags were already off loaded so I picked my two up. A lady with a drugs detection dog asked me if I had any fruits in my bag and I said no and proceeded through customs.

I needed to find a hotel and after a couple of phone calls I got a room for $ 50 at Ocean Resort of Waikiki Beach. That is when I realised I had forgot to pick up my pocket knife. Although it felt a bit weird I told the information lady that I forgot my knife in the luggage area. She called 'Felix' on the phone and he looked but couldn't find it so she recommended I go to the ANA airline office upstairs to retrieve the knife. On the one hand I thought the little knife isn't worth too much effort and time, on the other hand I thought that time was now less of the essence in my life as I was not employed anymore. When I look back at my life I don't want to get first price for time efficiency, but rather see a wealth of experiences, friendships and love and to have my children understand the true values in life. Back to the knife – on the second floor I found the office and a kind attendant who asked me if I was Mr Olsson and gave me my knife. At this stage I needed transport to Waikiki and opted for the shuttle service at 13 dollars round trip. The obvious trade off here is slightly longer time for the transfer against a savings of 37 dollars as a Taxi was 25 dollars one way. As a side benefit I got to see most of the hotels in Waikiki, at least from the outside – happy day!

When I got to the hotel I was told that check in was 3.00 PM and that no room was available before. This was a bit surprising but I took out my back pack some shorts with swim suit underneath and a t-shirt and beach shoes together with my valuables and went to the men's' room and changed gear. The hotel was one block in from the beach and soon enough I was there enjoying the sight of the palm trees, the waves, the swimmers and the immense sea. Quite a change of scenery compared to overpopulated and business minded Tokyo. I walked along the beach and found a place where I could put my backpack and submerge myself in the waves. I kept my back pack in view all the time and never moved away more than twenty meters from it as I had a lot of cash for my trip there as well as credit cards, my gold watch, my gifted camera and all travel documents. There were plenty of showers along the beach allowing for salt and sand to be washed away when leaving the beach. After two hours of walking up and down the beach I had a light lunch and returned to the hotel for my check in. The room was fine, comfortable bed, TV, ok bathroom and a little balcony with two chairs. Good value!

I went to bed and slept for two hours. Then I went out to the beach where the sun was getting lower and casting a warm light on palm trees and people. I came across a free Hawaiian style performance with song, music and dance and sat down and enjoyed the show for a while. This show was on four nights a week and was sponsored by the City of

Honolulu for the benefit of the many visitors. As I walked away from the show there were plenty of 'stand still' performers on the side walk waiting for some money to be dropped into their bucket and they would come live and perform some ritual. Quite fascinating and well done. I bought my son Max in Sweden a Hawaii shirt as his 28th birthday was coming up soon and some fish bone monkeys – see no evil, hear no evil, say no evil – for Linda's collection, now exceeding a hundred sets. I was enticed by a Chinese man to try his seafood restaurant one flight of stairs down and had a god meal. This meal puts me back to the second paragraph of page one of these notes. Sitting down at the restaurant made me think that although I would be visiting interesting places and people, the events of the last few days in Japan also had been quite unique and memorable experiences. It is often in the rather ordinary that some of our finest moments and memories originate.

After dinner I walked the streets of Honolulu with quite an active market type commerce for about two hours before returning to my hotel where I watched TV and read a little before a long nights sleep. An uninterrupted good nights sleep is a gift from God and of course the basis for the full appreciation of what a new day has to offer. I had a full hotel breakfast with eggs, sausages and hash brown potatoes with a few pieces of toast with marmalade and coffee this Sunday morning. Then I went out to the Waikiki beach and took a left turn away from the city. I passed the war memorial and had a swim at the little beach close to the point. This looked more like a family beach and again I parked my backpack where I could see it and went for a dip in the waves. The last few years I have found swimming, whether in a pool or in the ocean, very relaxing and satisfying. Although I am not a particularly good swimmer in terms of skill and speed I nowadays much enjoy swimming and bathing. I moved on from the beach to a vast park further in where several games of baseball were underway. I sat down in the lovely sunshine at a pick nick table and made a few notes to ensure I was current. If there is too much lag in note keeping many things may be overlooked and forgotten. I am sometimes asked how I find time to write, but sitting in a park off Waikiki is less like labour and more like love, perhaps a labour of love. Waikiki may not be a fantastic beach – it is not very wide and the human structures are quite close to the beach and sea - but it is there, right next to the fine hotels, leisurely shopping, and entertainment. And outside the palm trees, the sand and the developments is the seemingly endless blue Pacific Ocean rolling in as it has been and will do eternally and giving the holidaymakers a sense of freedom unlimited. The seawater is clean and life generally seems pretty nice and bearable.

I walked back through the vast park and came upon an outdoors arts exhibition and saw some nice nature photos but my luggage overweight and multitude of hand luggage served as a break on any acquisition. I used to be a happy and keen shopper but have gradually come to think that friendships and experiences are easier and lighter to carry than physical possessions. I bought some sandwiches and a container of Guava Juice at a convenience store and brought it to a bench at the beach to have my lunch there. After lunch I wanted to go sailing – the day before I saw that the Catamarans took people out for an hour for $ 15 – so I walked along the beach and found an operator getting ready to leave. Soon enough we were away with three crew plus a dog and seven passengers. Once outside the immediate beach area we set sails and the boat flew away over the waves at great speed. When standing there on the Catamaran two tunes came strongly through my mind: 'Seaman' with the line 'Uber Rio und Shanghai, Uber Bali und Hawaii' and I reflected that I had been to all of these places except Shanghai which I had hoped to visit but SARS kept me away. The other tune was 'Oh how I want to be a country girl again' which in the Swedish translation goes 'when one loves the sea and the winds and has tired of stone and concrete – is it strange that one longs to go away.' I sang these into the wind confident that no one could hear me.

For about half an hour we sailed straight out into the Ocean and then we jived and sailed back to Waikiki. To view this fantastic world famous beach on Oahu from a point out in the sea was quite a sight. I thoroughly enjoyed the experience. The weather was perfect with a good breeze and I sensed a great feeling of happiness, thinking that perhaps I should try to sail a bit more often if it makes me this happy. Shiawase desu! After another swim in the Ocean and some reading I went back to the hotel for a quick shower and a nap. When I woke up I got some macadamia nuts and a beer and continued my reading in the warmth of the setting sun. People were still swimming at 5.00 PM and strolling along the beach and the Hawaii guitar music from some outdoors hotel restaurant added to the special atmosphere. Being current with my travel note I thought I would go and seek out some dinner. It was still a bit early but as my wake up call tomorrow would be at 4.30 AM I planned for an early finish. After an Asian meal with mango juice I again joined the outdoor song and dance show on the beach. On my way back I walked slowly on the beach, looked at the sea and stars before ending up back at the hotel.

GOING TO LOS ANGELES

On Monday 2nd June I had an early pick up to go to the airport for my 8.00AM departure. Driving through the hotel district I saw several smart looking girls walking the street and realised that this must be the tail end of Honolulu night life. In just under an hour we reached the airport and with five pieces of luggage it was a little bit of a challenge to move around even if one of my luggage is a smart little roller on top of which I could put another piece. The carts are all locked away in US airports requiring either credit cards or 2 – 3 dollars to release them. Slightly annoying and reminding me of US stamp machines which give you about twenty percent less value back than you put into them, making the USA the only country in the world where stamps are sold for more than their nominal value. Anyway, the good news this morning was that I could check my luggage through to Ontario, Ca. and would not have to worry about it in Los Angeles. Sticking to the same airline, United also makes the transfers easier as all flights are operated from the same terminal. It is yet another beautiful morning in Honolulu as I sit down and write and read a little. Hawaii is a nice place with beautiful scenery and a very high quality life style. I thought that when I visited 33 years ago and this seemed to still hold true. My seat allocation this morning is 10 A and next to me are two oversized Americans in their late 70's on their way to Chicago. I realised that this seating precluded me from getting up for the next five hours. They were friendly enough though, residents of Hawaii, going to see relatives in Chicago. The flight was uneventful, other than it was the first time that I have experienced that passengers by emergency seats are asked to be prepared to open doors in case of emergency. Those sitting by emergency seats were required to read an instruction sheet and would be reseated if not willing to take on the responsibility of assisting in the case of an emergency.

In Los Angeles I transferred to a small propeller plane which got me to Ontario on time at 6.30 PM. I understand that that twenty minutes flight would translate to at least a three to four hours drive during the Los Angeles rush hour traffic. I collected my bags and got through to Linda's aunt, Monica, with whom I would stay for a few days. Monica, now 65, born in Sweden and moved to the USA over forty years ago, lives on her own after a second divorce.

She has her three children, Linda's cousins, all living nearby in California. One is a manager of a super store and is married with two children, and the only daughter works for Home Depot as a supervisor and lives with her daughter, and the eldest has had many jobs and a bit of a chequered career and is currently unemployed. The latter is about 6ft 5 and was a very promising basketball player. Monica says he has a big collection of old cartoons and now lives off trading these on the Internet. It takes about an hour to drive from the airport to the little town of Hemet in Riverside County where Monica has her home.

When we get there her two dogs, Beagles, Maxi and Mini, greet us. Monica has prepared a Gaspacho soup with vegetables, which we enjoy together with some red wine and bread. She recently moved her mobile home her from Orange County as the ground rent here is $ 300 a month compared to $ 800 a month before and the new landlord paid the $ 7,000 moving expense. As she is now retired, $ 500 a month makes quite a difference she explains. Mobile home in this case does not mean a house on wheels but a house consisting of two halves, which can be separated and transported and then put together again. It looks pretty much like any permanent residential home. We talked about many things and I asked her what caused their divorce. She said they were just arguing/ quarrelling all the time about little meaningless things so they didn't see any point in continuing. Monica is a very positive and contented nature so she seems perfectly happy and on one level she is pleased with her independence, but she also concedes that something has been lost in terms of financial capacity, family gatherings for holidays and birthdays, playing games together and going fishing etc. Inevitably children (as well as friends) get a bit confused by divorces and one goes with this person and one with the other, which can cause mental scars and challenges. Monica was a bit sad about having almost no contact with her second son after the divorce. Rarely, it seems, is it all rosy and harmonious and often the disadvantages are greater than imagined. I had a few small things for her – a CD Linda had compiled in New Zealand and a Manpoke (step counter) from Tokyo and some bound short stories.

I finished off the evening by servicing my email and then went to bed. The next morning we had a good and healthy breakfast with cereal, juices and fruits and coffee and continued our conversation while listening to some more music. After breakfast we drove to a nearby park to walk the dogs. After a long walk she clocked up 3,300 steps and she asked me "Do I have to do this three times a day to get to my 10,000 steps?" but I calmed her and said just walking in and around the house would probably give her half the difference and the rest would require another walk or some jogging. It is a nice sunny day with temperatures around 25 degrees.

In the afternoon we drove about one hour – it seems that in California nothing is ever less than hour's drive away – to see Monica's daughter, Joanne, and her daughter Annika. Annika is a cute little twelve year old who is active in a soccer team as goal keeper. They live in a condominium with nice small-semidetached houses and a swimming pool on the grounds. We went to the pool and had a swim – no one else was there - and afterwards I got some beer and wine and pizza for us to have for dinner. I caught up with Joanne and listened to her experiences and aspirations. It is always a challenge to be a single parent but she seemed to be doing fine with a nice car and a home and access to relatives and parents. She also has a cheerful disposition like both her parents. I sang a few songs and related a few carefully chosen jokes and we talked about management, life and world events with no major disagreements.

The next day we picked up John, Monica's eldest son, to go mountain biking in a nearby state park. First we cycled seven miles uphill seeing many rabbits, squirrels and hawks. After some challenging hills we reached an open area with a picnic table where we took a pause and then started the downward run. I knew I was fit so I kept up well with them. Perhaps most surprising was that Monica at 65 kept peddling uninterruptedly for seven uphill miles.

When we started to go down, John disappeared in a daredevil ride and I went as fast as I deemed safe with Monica not far behind. There was a slight overcast, which probably made it all a bit more comfortable. The ride down took about one third of the uphill ride and we were back by the car around one o'clock. We finished off with a hamburger and a drink, said good-bye to John, and drove the one-hour required to get back to Hemet. We got there around four o'clock and as it was a lovely afternoon I went for a long walk to look at the environs. I walked in a big circle of three to four miles and saw only residential roads and houses – all green, nice but perhaps a bit monotonous, i.e. so many streets and houses looking pretty much the same. We had dinner together on chicken and vegetables with a bottle of pinot noir listening to some of the music I had brought. I also gave Monica a 130 pages paper on Religion, which was highlights from thirty books, including the Bible and the Koran. It is quite a unique material, but if she will find time and interest to read it all is another matter. My notes are designed to pick up everything positive and uplifting from all these books. My firm belief is that religion is there to help people make their life lighter and brighter and that the emphasis must be on love rather than fear.

CONTINUING TO ATLANTA

The next morning I woke up early of birdsong and after a cup of coffee we were rolling at 6.00 AM and got to the Ontario airport about one hour later. Check in was quite swift but the coffee shop was after security so my intention to invite Monica for breakfast came to nought.

At the security check they found a small mini-folding knife I had long forgotten and which got confiscated. My departure time was 8.38 AM but due to some problem with the loading bay we got twenty minutes delayed. My transfer time in Denver was only half an hour so I thought it would be touch and go as to whether I would make it or not to my final destination Atlanta on the designated flight. Fortunately I was seated on row six near the front and I had my boarding pass for the next flight so I left the airplane at 12.02 PM, Gate 16, for my 12.16 PM departure at Gate 31. When I got to the gate they had already closed it but then opened it again for me and two other passengers. My main concern now was my luggage. If I had been so quick in transfer what were the chances that my two bags would make it? The lady that boarded me said I might be lucky and have the luggage on the same flight.

After two and a half hours flight we arrived at on schedule at five o'clock in Atlanta and I walked one thousand steps to the baggage claim where I found Mike Thompson right away. I told him that I might not have any checked luggage here but he suggested I check with United's baggage attendant. I showed the attendant my receipts and he quickly confirmed that my bags were loaded on to the flight, which I thought nothing short of a miracle. Ten minutes later I had all my five pieces gathered and my panama hat on top and we were moving across to his parked Mercedes. His car was full of newspapers and magazines and he said his boot was full so he suggested I put my things in the back seat, which I did. And we were away to his mountain house in North Carolina. We worked our way through the Atlanta rush hour traffic and continued northwest towards Toxaway Lake – a two and a half hours trip. It was a nice evening with the sun setting. Mike stopped at a wine store and showed me the enormous variety on offer at different prices. He pointed out a Lindeman's Shiraz from Australia at $ 5.99 and asked how anyone can make money when wine is sold so cheap so far away from source. Later we stopped for a meal of salad, chicken and baked potato with sour crème. As United had not served any food on the flights and my transfer in Denver was so quick, this eight o'clock dinner was my first meal for the day.

When we got to his house at about nine o'clock it was dark and I couldn't really see much of the surroundings. I got to sleep downstairs with my own bathroom. After a bit of a chat we called it a day a couple of hours later. I had a good night's sleep and woke up hearing Mike's steps on the floor above. I showered and dressed and went up to greet him good morning. He was having a cup of green tea and asked if I usually had any breakfast, as he normally didn't. I said I was flexible and could wait. I told him of the saying: for good health, eat like a king for breakfast, like a prince for lunch and a pauper for dinner. He responded that that formula probably was healthy but he tended to do the opposite. After tea we walked out and had a look at his property right on the lake with only a few trees in-between. A little path led down to a nice dock or landing with space for his boat. He owned the next section as well and said he had been offered one million dollars for it but had decided to keep it for privacy. The whole area is a retreat for people from Atlanta seeking to avoid people and congestion in the big city and to enjoy the cooler weather during the long hot summer. Atlanta had grown from eight hundred thousand people in the mid sixties to nearly four million now. Michael's father had been a civil engineer doing jobs in different countries. Thus Michael was born in Colombia and had lived in Honolulu during the Japanese attack 7th December 1941.

After checking out the immediate surroundings and the beautiful Lake Toxaway – an Indian name for the Cardinal bird – we were going on a two and a half hours hike to look at nature and some rapids and waterfalls. It sounded like a big walk on just some green tea but I was comfortable that if he could do it, so could I. He drove about 15 minutes to the end of the road where a few cars were parked and we followed the path through the woods. Michael called the vegetation rain forest as he said it rained a lot up here. He told me about Carlton, an 82 years old guy whom hade made all the trails and tracks up here. Carlton who I didn't meet was said to be thin as a needle and very fit and out in the woods every day. Carlton had claimed that Eric Rudolph, who had been hiding for five years in the Appalachian woods, had come up behind him twice as he was tracking. Eric Rudolph was the prime suspect for the Atlanta Olympics bombings that killed two and wounded fifty people. The rumour was that many of the locals would help any fugitive, as they didn't much like the government up here.

We saw many trees, plants and birds and no people. Finally we reached the rapids and it was well worth the walk. Mike said the river divided a bit further up and one branch flowed to the Atlantic coast and one branch flowed to the Mexican Gulf. He also told me that during the prohibition a lot of 'Moonshine liquor' (based on corn and sugar) was made in these forests. Michael said it was so strong it went straight all the way to the toes right after you had drunk it. During the prohibition there were these two families – Hatfields and McCloy - involved in a drawn out feud in this area. The area is also known for inbreeding and poverty in certain parts. Mike also owned a farm a few hours drive away. He told me that when Chrustjev from USSR visited the USA in the sixties and was asked what he found most puzzling, the answer was that there was only one person in all the cars.

At noon we were out of the woods again and went for a sandwich lunch tasting really good. A good hunger is always the best spice. In the afternoon we took a nap and then discussed our mutual project 'the St Francis Vineyard' outside Wellington in New Zealand. We had both put in more than twice the money we originally envisaged – NZ$ 165,000 for him, having a 38 % share and NZ$ 47,000 for me having a 11% share. Both of us agreed we didn't want to put any more money in as prospects for pay back looked quite bleak. Mike had researched the wine industry both in New Zealand and also in Napa Valley, California. His conclusion was that our project would never make money. In New Zealand you need to nurture your project like a baby and make your own successful brand wine to make money and in Napa Valley any profit would normally be related to land appreciation. We agreed we were willing to give up ownership share to allow 25 % to be sold to a new party that might contribute some new funds. If required we would also accept going further down to zero percent without any compensation. Fortunately we had not allowed any debt so only our paid in equity was at stake. We each wrote a letter to our 51 % partner, on whose property the vineyard is located, and who in principle made contributions in kind rather than money. In the letters we both said we had enjoyed the trip so far but that for going forward a new source of funds would be required as we felt we had reached the end of the line. None of us had any hard feelings about the money ostensibly lost. The vineyard was what had brought Mike and I together and even if that common denominator would be lost, as Mike was a fan of New Zealand and expected to spend at least one month every year, we would no doubt meet up again.

In the evening we had a fine meal at the local quite fancy country club. Mike had been a very active golfer but now only played casually. It had started to rain about seven o'clock and it kept pouring down all night and the next day. We left around 11.00 AM and made a detour to see two small towns, Walhalla and Westminster. I explained to Mike that Walhalla is the 'home of the gods' in Nordic mythology, which was news to him. We stopped at the BBQ shed and had some nice ribs for lunch. The cost of a full lunch out here was about the same as a Starbucks coffee at the airport. Michael was treating me to all the meals and I was hoping I could do the same when he comes to New Zealand. Late in the afternoon we got to his house at 1160 Peach Tree Battle Avenue NW. Only in the USA does street numbers run into the thousands. It was a very nice brick house with at least five bedrooms. His wife Ray greeted us upon arrival. She had been active in a not-for-profit organisation, the American Garden Association, for decades. She looked very kind and fit and had an aura of efficiency and good organization around her. With Mike travelling and golfing and spending much time in their mountain house their relationship clearly involved a lot of separate spheres and living. Perhaps this is the ideal way to keep a marriage fit and healthy. She offered me to check my emails on her PC and I gladly took up her offer. I had forty new ones with the majority as always being junk emails. She cooked us a great meal with meat and vegetables and salad and ice cream and berries for dessert. We all withdrew early; I did some writing and reading and then slept well until the morning. Mike showed me the grounds around the house in the morning and took me to the Heartsfield Airport after I had said good-bye to Ray. I was at the airport at noon, thanked Mike sincerely for his great hospitality, and checked in for my flight to Washington DC.

WASHINGTON DC.

I boarded the small shuttle plane with two chairs on either side of the aisle. I had seat 6 C and on 6 B there was a guy who was busy on his mobile phone writing some information on a piece of paper. The girl having seat 6 A waited for 6 B to finish his conversation but as this didn't happen and she was blocking the aisle I suggested she take 6 D instead which she did. She was Camero from Florida on her way to spend summer outside Portland, Oregon with her old friend. Camero looked like a young lady in her prime but she told me she was only a freshman and fourteen years old. Her parents were divorced, she had one brother, she lived with her mother from Panama who was running a travel agency, and she wanted to be a dentist in a future professional life. I asked her what the issues were, if any, at school but she said life is ok and she listened to her CD music and played some word game trying to find words in a multitude of letters on a piece of paper. She offered me chocolates and a choice of three different chewing gums. I told her that in Singapore chewing gum is illegal. Why? Because it sticks to all sorts of things and can be quite annoying. She recalled once stepping on chewing gum and then into her friend's new car creating a real mess. In between conversations I read my book 'The Social Contract' by Jean-Jacque Rousseau – every page worth reading slowly and with contemplation as the book is full of wisdom. On leaving the aircraft – or 'deplaning' as flight attendants on the speaker system called it – I said good-bye to Camro and wished her well and she reciprocated.

At the baggage claim, which I reached after a long walk trying to follow arrows and directions in the ceiling, I found my friend Jim Adams with wife Jane and daughter Kim. After greeting them I put my five pieces on a cart and we went to their 4WD Toyota Jeep. They were under some serious renovation work at home and suggested I'd be better off at a hotel. He drove to their home and together we booked three nights for $ 500 at the Watergate hotel over the Internet. This was the first real expense I had encountered on my trip and I thought it nice to have a good hotel at walking distance from all the sights in Washington DC. Everything was upside down at their house but I could see it was a nice house and, post renovation, it would be great. They kindly took me to the hotel, I checked in and then we went to nearby Georgetown for dinner at Pizzeria Paradiso – pizza, salad, pane, olives, oil, Valpolicella. The restaurant and the streets outside were bustling with activity and I much enjoyed the company, the meal and the atmosphere. I suggested that Washington must be a nice place to live. I asked Jane if she enjoyed her lunch at the Alice restaurant in Tokyo with Linda ten days earlier. Jane said: "Here I was, an American, with my Swedish friend now living in New Zealand, who I met in Kenya, having lunch at a Vietnamese restaurant at Printemps, a French department store, in Ginza Tokyo – what could be more international than that?" And yes, she said she had a good meal and a good time.

Back at the hotel I updated my diary, which I wanted to have, current every day, I took a bath, also washing a few cloths, and then watched a bit of TV before going to sleep. On the history channel there was a program about the naval battle of the Bismarck during the Second World War. A few days before Bismarck's fate was sealed, Bismarck sank the British battleship 'The Hood' with the loss of 1400 lives after fifteen minutes exchange of fire. Later on 26th May 1941 Bismarck was sunk after a hit by two airborne torpedoes and subsequently 400 direct hits by pursuing British naval ships. Bismarck's sinking cost 2100 lives with 110 saved and imprisoned for the rest of the war in Canada. After the British ships saved a number of Germans they left the rest to their fate, fearing U-boat attacks if they continued their rescue mission. The next program was about how all the Indian chiefs were brought to Washington to sign a major land sale. All chiefs but Sitting Bull signed. Sitting Bull bent down and picked up some dirt and let it drop through his fingers and said that not even this much land would I ever sell to the white man. I thought this History Channel quite interesting.

The next day I woke up at 6.30 AM and picked up the Wall Street Journal outside my 805 hotel room door. Main news for the day was the Oracle $ 5.1 billion hostile bid for People Soft. I also learned that the US unemployment rate had increased to 6.1 % but growth of unemployment had slowed. Another article suggested that poor corporate governance and high executive pay seemed correlated. There was also something about the EU intending to roll back its Euro 112 billion farm subsidies. However we all know that the French will drag their feet as much as they can on any agri reform to avoid political turmoil at home. US Consumer credit grew by $ 10.7 billion in April to $ 1.756 trillion. The Dow crossed the 9,000 line and the latest SARS report said that of about 8,000infected, 780 had died but the spread now seemed to be getting under control.

Just after eight o'clock I was out on Virginia Avenue where I took a right turn and walked towards the city centre and the Mall. One of the first things I saw was a bicycle chained to a pole and everything that could be removed from the bicycle had been removed, stolen – only the body remained. This was a sight almost unthinkable in Japan. The air felt very fresh after some rain overnight and trees and parks were lustrously green. When I got to 23rd Street I turned right as I saw Lincoln Memorial in the distance. I came upon the State Department building from 1960. A plaque said it was the oldest and most senior of all cabinet agencies, instituted in 1789. The department has 250 overseas posts in 180 countries. The head of the department, Colin

Powell is already a national hero who would have a good chance to become president if he chooses to run. As I took some notes outside the building, I thought that someone might think my note taking activity suspicious, and report it to the police. These days the American people is asked to report anything they perceive to be suspicious.

Soon afterwards I got to the Mall and Lincoln Memorial but choose to cross the Arlington Memorial Bridge over the Potomac River to Virginia and Arlington Cemetery. There were plenty of airplanes coming along the river to land at Dulles Airport. Quite a few joggers around this lovely morning of the 9th of June 2003 and the temperature was a comfortable 25 degrees centigrade. At the beginning of the bridge there are two bronze statues and a bit further away another two similar ones. These were all gifted in 1950 from the people of Italy to the people of USA. After crossing the long bridge and seeing some of the many simple white stones on the hill I saw the monument of the Seabees – the US naval construction battalions. They called the memorial 'Can Do'. The further text reads: 'With willing hearts and skilful hands, the difficult we do at once, the impossible takes a little longer. ' 'With compassion for others we build, we fight for peace and freedom.'

I was now approaching Arlington with more than six hundred acres of land and accommodating over 275,000 graves for US servicemen and women and family members. There are still twenty some burials a day on these grounds – not only battle casualties but also long serving and deserving men and women of the armed forces. There are guided tours of the cemetery by bus, but I prefer to rely on my feet and walk to a few key points. As I look into the memorabilia shop I reflect on the need to honour the dead but beware as to not honour war and the destruction, suffering and tragedy that always goes with it. I asked one of the guards how I get to the Kennedy graves and he says: "Just up the hill, you can't miss it" and soon enough I see the sign and find the spot with some of JFK's sayings and the eternal flame. To Americans he says: 'Ask not what America can do for you, but what you can do for America.' To non-Americans he says: 'Ask not what America can do for you but what we together can do for the freedom of man. God's work on earth must truly be our own struggle against the common enemies of man: tyranny, poverty, disease and war itself.'

Besides John Fitzgerald Kennedy 1917 – 63 the grave is also for Jacqueline Kennedy 1929 –74, Patrick 7/8 -63 – 9/8 –63 and a daughter August 23, 1956. The latter two I must admit I never knew of – clearly the lives of the Presidential couple were full of challenges. The grave is on a very beautiful spot with views over the river and the Mall with all the monuments and the Capitol in the distance. Just around the corner from JFK is a lone simple white cross, the grave of Robert Francis Kennedy 1925 – 1968. The inscription next to Bobby's grave reads, "what we need is love, and wisdom and compassion toward one another" and let us "turn the savageness of man and make gentle the life of the world." I reflected that both these leaders had a bit of grandeur sadly missing in the current leadership. After that I went to the memorial amphitheatre and the grave of the Unknown Soldier just behind and saw the change of guards which takes place every half hour.

From there I found my way to the exit and memorial drive to get back to Washington again. As I stepped out of the cemetery grounds I had clocked up 7,700 steps and the time was 10.40 AM. When I had almost crossed Memorial Bridge I stopped at a sign and wrote down 'Welcome to Washington; Anthony A. Williams, Mayor.' I continued towards Lincoln Memorial but before entering I went to the near by coffee shop to have some breakfast. As I walked away with my coffee and muffin two policemen approached me and said someone had reported that I might have been measuring the bridge? I said I was just taking some notes for my diary and that I actually thought that someone might find that suspicious. They politely asked a few more questions and then walked off when convinced I was no more than a harmless tourist. Security is a big issue in the USA post nine-eleven and all the monuments and important buildings in Washington were surrounded by barriers.

When I got to the Lincoln memorial my manpoke showed 10,000 steps and it wasn't even noon yet. Lincoln Memorial was inaugurated 30th May 1922 by president Harding who said: "This memorial is less for Abraham Lincoln than for those of today and for those who follow after." One eighth of the US population were slaves before the civil war and Lincoln felt strongly that the Union could not survive with slavery in some states and not in others. I read Lincoln's Gettysburg address from 1863 inscribed in the wall, and again found it very short and powerful –'government of the people, by the people and for the people.' The Civil War was the bloodiest war America has ever fought with an estimated one million dead men. Looking out over the Mall from the top of the steps of Lincoln Memorial is quite a sight with the large rectangular ponds and the big park with the Washington Memorial and the Capitol behind. The Mall Park is about two miles long and a quarter mile wide and all the museums and monuments are either in the park or alongside it. It really is very inspiring and neatly designed and laid out. Little things I noticed were that virtually all day there is the sound of sirens, mostly from Ambulances, and also the multitude of little squirrels everywhere. Plenty of drinking fountains came in pretty handy in the hot weather. There are also obviously a lot of people around too, but the vast grounds seem to cope well with that.

Leaving Lincoln Memorial I walked over to the left to walk past the Vietnam Memorial. It really touched me when I saw it 13 years ago, perhaps because many of the dead were my age and some from my high school in Michigan were also among the dead. The Vietnam Memorial is beautifully done with just a long black wall with the inscription of the dead soldiers' names. This time I just felt sad that 58,000 Americans (and many more Vietnamese) had to die for what in hindsight looks like a completely futile war and a grave mistake by a succession of US administrations. I continued to walk towards the Washington Memorial with the intention to take the lift up and look at the views of Washington. Once there I learnt that all tickets for the day were sold out and at 8.00 AM the next morning one could buy tickets for the next day. As I wasn't that keen I decided to give it up. I proceeded to one of the Smithsonian museums and saw the nine-eleven exhibition. That was also quite touching with the recording of film and telephone calls and how many very ordinary people were horrifically effected. Many unbelievable and amazing things happened that day and what particularly struck me was how the fourth plane – probably headed for the Capitol – was downed in Pennsylvania through heroic passenger interference.

After half an hour I walked across to Pennsylvania Avenue, took a right and proceeded to the Capitol. I passed the National Archives and the Federal Trade Commission and entered the National Art Gallery and looked at statues. Particularly some by the French sculptor August Rodin (1840-1917) I found beautiful as well as several little dancing nudes by Edgar Degas (1834 – 1917). Because of the overwhelming supply and my limited time (and concentration span) I didn't spend more than half an hour in any museum. When walking near the Capitol and at 16,500 steps I decided to give the Capitol a miss and start my return walk. As I walked there in the lovely afternoon sunshine a tune kept coming back to me all day: 'Varför skola människor strida?' - Why must people fight? In spite of all the wisdom and enlightenment so much of what Washington exhibits conveys assassinations, terrorism, war and violence. Why? When will we ever learn? When will we ever learn?

I also asked myself why everything is so big in America? A medium coffee cup is bigger than anything I've ever seen elsewhere. The same goes for cars, people, health cost, legal bills, egos and ignorance, and perhaps also on the positive side, opportunity and affluence. And when everything is taken into account, it is becoming less and less obvious to non-Americans that America and American life style is something worthy of admiration and aspiration. Is the American star fading? I feel very privileged with my beachhead in Auckland, capital of the South Pacific. I came up to the National Air and Science Museum, but in light of my remembering it from my previous visit and looking at the long security queues I decided to give it a miss. I walked into another little different Smithsonian museum called the S Dillon Ripley Centre and saw an exhibition about health and medicine. Ben Franklin was quoted as saying, "To lengthen thy life – lessen thy meals." And Seneca said that an important part of any recovery is the will to recover.

In the next Museum, The African Museum, a small round one story building above ground, but quite huge under ground, I saw an exhibition 'In the spirit of Martin' inspired by Martin Luther King's many deeds and speeches. This was one of the greatest experiences of the day. Martin Luther King was quoted saying: 'Injustice anywhere is a threat to justice everywhere.' At the age of 35 he received Nobel's peace price – a truly remarkable person, brutally and tragically murdered. The only thing I bought all day was the autobiography of Martin Luther King and I am much looking forward to reading it.

That's it, I thought. At this stage I was monumentally tired and also had a six o'clock pick up at the hotel to get ready for. So I decided to stroll back through the beautiful park, The Mall, to the Watergate Hotel. I crossed 17th Street that cuts right across the Mall and later also Constitutional Avenue to get back to my Virginia Avenue hotel. Upon arrival back at the hotel, my step counter read 24,000, which is about 20 km or 13 miles. Moving around on foot in cities like Washington and New York is the best way as it gives full access to street life, people and moods and atmospheres and also allows you time to think and reflect as you change scenery.

I did some tiding up, ironed three shirts and prepared for dinner as I would be picked up by the Adams family to participate in Jane's birthday dinner. We went to a lovely Virginia restaurant called 2941 overlooking a little lake with lots of birds. The meal was gourmet quality and we had a nice conversation about things past and in future. I related some of my impressions during the day. They were planning to sail on the last QE2 voyage from New York to England in August and then continue to Finland. After dinner they took me back to the Watergate and we said a warm good bye. Knowing they had many friends in New Zealand I said we hoped to see them there soon.

The next day I was up early as usual, made a cup of coffee, checked the news, and got organised for another day. Once out I went to the Watergate supermarket and got some fruits, orange juice and a couple of croissants. Then I headed down towards the Potomac River to go to the Jefferson Memorial. On the river there were a number of speed rowers having their exercise in the beautiful morning. The river looked very brown and quite dirty. This morning all the airplanes were approaching me so the wind must have changed since yesterday. I walked under the Theodore Roosevelt Bridge and then took a short break to have some breakfast. On TV this morning I had seen some discussion as to whether it was possible for a Jew to be both Jew and a complete US Citizen. The conclusion was that it would be a bit difficult because the one might to some extent exclude the other. So I thought: how are Jews different?

I guess one issue is about not recognising Jesus as divine. But then all non-Christians may share that view. I think Jesus was divine. But then I think there is divinity in all life and all human beings. I think that people tend to look for differences rather than similarities. After living in seven countries my perhaps strongest impressions is how similar we all are, with similar aspirations and concerns. Perhaps the misfortune or persecution of the Jews over the years is related to their exclusivity and unwillingness to assimilate outsiders or to be assimilated. Ai to heiwa to kanyo – love, peace and tolerance are foundations of harmony and happiness, and too often these key concepts have been violated or ignored. People should be allowed to be different as long as it doesn't harm anyone else. And although freedom of religion is established in the constitution there has been discrimination on religious grounds in the USA too.

Later at the Jefferson Memorial, completed in 1943 on the 200th university of his birth, I read: "All men shall be free to profess and to maintain their opinion in matters of religion." Other lines of Jefferson's I noted were: "I know but one code of morality for man, whether acting singly or collectively. A free government relies on enlightened citizens. Let all tyranny be replaced by the reason of man" It took me 5,000 steps to get to the Jefferson Memorial located on the most magnificent spot on the Tidal basin with greenery everywhere and in the distance the Washington Memorial and the Capitol in view. I sat down on the steps for a few moments and marvelled at the sights. And inside the memorial, the beauty of the surrounding nature is visible in four directions through the high columns. In the circular memorial Thomas Jefferson's statue is in the middle and some selective wisdom of his is written on the walls. Thomas Jefferson wrote the declaration of independence, which may be one of the finest foundations for government ever written, particularly:

"We hold these truths to be self evident that all men are created equal, that they are endowed by their Creator with certain inalienable rights among these are life, liberty, and the pursuit of happiness." I understand from reading the author Gore Vidal that Jefferson himself had suggested 'created equal and independent' and that he had no reference to the Creator, possibly consistent with the intent to leave religion to the citizenry. Congress however made a few changes to Jefferson's original text. In Vidal's view the changes that Congress made in this respect didn't add any value. Another important feat of Thomas Jefferson's was the Louisiana Purchase from France in 1803, essentially doubling the size of the United States.

After half an hour at Jefferson Memorial I crossed 14th Street Bridge and came upon Raoul Wallenberg Place and then I knew I was on the right way to the Holocaust Museum. Raoul Wallenberg was the famous Swede who worked so hard to save Jews and other refugees and ultimately disappeared in Russia where he probably later died. Outside the Holocaust Museum there was a long queue but I just joined up knowing that nothing would discourage me to see this museum. After half an our including a thorough security check I got through and took the lift to the fourth floor to start the walk through the museum downstairs. Whilst waiting for the lift all visitors were asked to take an identification card, male stories for men and female stories for women. My card read as follows:

Name: Mikulas Diamant; Date of Birth July 10, 1919, Place of birth: Bratislava

Mikulas and his German-speaking Jewish family lived in the town of Hlohovec. His family owned a large farm and his father was a rancher. In 1932, due to declining economic conditions, Mikulas's father began to sell all of his property. Then the family moved to the city of Bratislava where they had many relatives.

1933 –39 My father worked with my uncle in the wholesale paper business. I worked part-time in a workshop as an electrician and I went to high school. In 1938 we began to hear of German atrocities such as the "Night of broken glass." In 1939 the fascists took over Slovakia and I was drafted to the Slovak army. Along with 500 other Jewish inductees, I was sent to a work camp, where we cleared snow off the roads.

1940 – 44: When I returned home three years later, Jews were being transported to Nazi concentration camps. In Bratislava I did my best to remain inconspicuous but ran into an old army friend. Suddenly I was pushed into a Gestapo car. My 'friend' was an informer. The Gestapo took me to their office. They wanted names of other Jews. I saw an open window, and I lept out and fell on my back. Waking in terrible pain, I somehow managed to get to my home. Friends and I planned to escape the Nazis, but one day the SS knocked on my door.

Mikulas survived several concentration camps before being liberated by the Soviets. After the war he emigrated to the United States.

In January 1933 Adolf Hitler was named chancellor and from then on to the German capitulation 8th May 1945 the pogroms continued. The museum had all the horrific photos and stories from the genocide and humiliation of the Jews. It also had many personalised and individual fates recorded. There was a picture of General Dwight Eisenhower at Ohndorf 12th April 1945 where he says that what he saw goes beyond description in bestiality. On the outside of the Holocaust Museum there is a statement from Ronald Regan dated 5th October 1988: " We who did not go their way owe them this: We must make sure their deaths have post humus meaning. We must make sure that from now until the end of days all humankind stares that evil in the face...and only then can we be sure that it will never arise again." Only three million of Europe's pre war nine million Jews survived. Of those who got into concentration camps, the survival rate was less than five percent. The Holocaust Museum is deeply touching and I think it was the most visited of the Washington Museums.

After an hour in the museum I walked back to my hotel and my lunch appointment. My friend Eugene Frese arrived a little late due to heavy traffic between Maryland and Washington. Eugene and I first met at the Harvard Business School in July 1982. We found a bistro on the backside of the Watergate Complex where we had lunch. We hadn't see each other since my 50th birthday five and a half years ago. In the meantime he had suffered a heart attack from the wrong medication resulting in a convalescence of one year. He said he had just finished what he was doing so now he would have more free time. He had just given away $ 10 million of family trust money to some Middle East related charity but he said Uncle Sam didn't want to approve it as a charitable gift. He ordered a Caesar salad with ice tea and I had a salmon salad with water. He gave me a book, which he said, was science fiction and he suggested I give it to my son if I didn't want to read it. I gave him a CD with New Zealand music. Eugene said his family had provided shuldkeiss (business manager) to the leaders of Saxony for many generations before they left as a result of Hugenott persecution. He has two brothers and one sister out in Nebraska where he grew up. One of his brothers is running a large cattle farm, and growing corn as feed. After four years of draught it had been too wet this year and he hadn't been able to plant corn until June.

As we got talking about wine he said his grandmother made 200 gallons of wine a year. This was the maximum annual allowance for one family to make tax free. I mentioned to him a great investment opprtunity into wine in New Zealand but he didn't seem all that interested. I said the challenges we had come up against were frost, birds and discease. To keep the birds out we had nets, noise machines and also someone shooting birds. It had proved very hard to make it work.

He said that in the 1800's in and around their farm in Nebraska, the Platt River had colonies of up to fifteen million cranes that fed there before going to nest in Alaska and Siberia. The river was ideal as it was a mile wide and only a few inches deep. When the railroad came people came up just to shoot cranes from the train or just outside. The same happened to the American Buffalo. The things people do!

He said that for any investment these days he doesn't only count to ten but to a hundred or a thousand before he decides. Most bad investments are from too much haste and not enough afterthought he said. Allowing yourself to slow things down a bit is one of the benefits of getting a little older. We also talked about literature and he said that nowadays it seems students have neither read the old masters nor do they even know titles or author's names. There used to be something called the Harvard five-foot shelf containing about 50 books, which you were supposed to have read before you entered the university. Eugene also said that the recent Iraqi war had not been justified and that he was getting concerned about the turn of events. He had lost three uncles in the war against the Japanese. Three nice young men from Nebraska dying in an unnecessary war. At the end of world war two they tried to agree with Russia to form a world government but Russia was so suspicious so it wasn't possible. But he also recognised Russia's sacrifice and major contribution to changing the fortunes of the third Reich.

I said I had just visited the Holocaust museum in the morning and he responded that when he was there he found it so powerful he had to leave. And still he said he had visited many of the camps in Germany and Poland. I admitted that I too had felt a bit sick at the museum. Eugene was now disinvesting in Europe because his family had no interest. Together with a friend from Harvard University he had bought a castle by the Neckar River and set up Schiller University but now he was getting rid of that too. But he still kept his interests in Turkey and Switzerland. I mentioned I was going to a party in Zurich 9th August and he said we might see each other there, as he needed to attend to some business in Switzerland. His family had owned a great big 70-room mansion in Geneva but they had given it away to the Council of Churches, as they didn't know what to do with it. He also talked about his old friend Vernon Walters who started as a truck driver in the army and ended up a three star general. Vernon Walters had been adviser to many presidents but had thought Jimmy Carter a doofus and didn't want to work for him. Carter was regarded as a disaster as a president but may well be one of the best ex presidents the US has had.

Eugene felt it likely that Greenspan would leave office shortly after George Bush's re-election which no doubt would happen given his strong PR machine. Finally he said he was getting tired of politics and deception and maybe New Zealand might be a good option for relocation. I encouraged him and said we would help in any way we could. He was approaching sixty and said he wanted to get married again if he could find someone nice. We also touched on Sir Edmund Hillary and the 50th anniversary of the first climb of Mt Everest. Eugene said that Edmund Hillary had been working for The National Geographic Society in Washington and Eugene had bought the house he had lived in. I said my son would clime Mt Blanc in July and Eugene said he had climbed Matterhorn. A good guide will drag you through any difficulties he said. Eugene treated me to the meal and as we left the restaurant he advised me to take it easy and not rush into my next job. I thanked him and we both said we hoped we would meet soon again.

Having said good-bye to Eugene, I walked down to the Mall again and sat down on a park bench behind the Vietnam Memorial to make a few notes. After a while I moved to one of the ponds and sat down again, enjoying the beautiful weather. A guy with a fishing rod appeared and started to do some casting. I thought that there would be less than one chance in a million that he would catch anything in the shallow pond with water that didn't look all that clean. Much to my surprise he caught a fish within a few minutes and another four fish in the next little while. I could hardly believe it but it did happen. An hour later

I walked up 17th Street and took a right at the White House just to get a glimpse of it. The road was cordoned off with barriers and there were also plenty of policemen. In comparison to everything else in Washington, the White House looks pretty unassuming as the abode of the most powerful man in the world. I continued up M Street and then went left to find my way to Georgetown for some dinner. After about 15 minutes walk I went into 'Mr Smiths' at 3104 M Street and ordered Cajun stake with shrimps and baked potato. I had a couple of Heineken to go with it and enjoyed the ambiance of the restaurant and felt I had had a pretty full day again. And after dinner I walked in the warm setting sunshine the ten minutes to Watergate Hotel. My Manpoke had recorded 20,000 steps for the day and I was happy.

THE BIG APPLE

June 11th I was up early again picking up the Wall Street Journal at the hotel room door and turned on the TV. Nothing much in the media this morning – markets were flat and more violence in the Middle East. I close my luggage pieces for the fifth time in less than two weeks and go downstairs to settle my account. All going well and I am picked up by the shuttle service at 7.30AM. The driver is from Cameroon and spends most of his time on the cell phone speaking French and driving erratically. I continue to read the paper and an article about a company in Florida firing most of its salesmen just to rehire others at lower salaries. This seems a bit grim and possibly shortsighted to me. What kind of loyalty from staff can such a company expect? On the other hand, if your workforce is overpaid you may need to do something to remain in business. I and the three other passengers arrive safely at the Dulles airport almost two hours before departure. Another shuttle bus passenger and I line up for United Airlines and I say to him: what a driver? And he responds: 'I was quite afraid – it seemed that the driver had been partying all night. ' I asked where he was from and he said Germany and he was on the same flight to New York. Then it was my turn to check in and I was greeted warmly by a very positive lady. She did the check in, tagged my bags, registered my Air New Zeeland frequent flyer number, all very efficiently, joyfully and kindly. I asked her about the airline business and she said it was getting a little bit better. As I walked away I said thank you and that it was a true pleasure to meet such a positive person so early in the day. She also said thank you and we parted ways.

Thomas, my friend from Germany, was already checked in. He waited for me and we went through security together. He said he was from Göttingen University and had attended a three-day conference in Washington DC. I suggested we perhaps share a taxi going from JFK airport to Manhattan, which he thought a good idea. We talked about Germany and he said the biggest problem was the overextended welfare system lessening the desire to work. All recognise the problem, but because of political sensitivities no one is prepared to make the changes necessary. On the Euro he said that Britain would probably never join but he was surprised that Denmark rejected membership. We flew in a very small propeller plane with no stow away room but the flight wasn't full so I could put my things on an empty seat. We got to New York on time and baggage handling was very efficient and we were soon in a taxi asking it to take us to 230 East 51st and Grand Central Station. We got to Grand Central first and I said good-bye to Thomas after exchanging email addresses. Then I got talking to the driver Ayed who said he was from Egypt and on his 4th year in New York. He liked New York a lot. The system was better in America – liberty and the rule of law was wanting in Egypt he said. I said Egypt was the highest item on my list for places to visit and asked him if it was safe. He said it was safer than New York – some people were trying to make out it isn't to harm the tourist industry. He was from Alexandria and I asked him about the historic burning of the famous library and about the underwater cities off Alexandria. He was very knowledgeable and enjoyed the conversation so much that he twice forgot where he was going giving us an extra 15 minutes together. He was very apologetic and I said I didn't mind. 'So you were here for nine- eleven?' 'Yes, I didn't work for eight days' he said and this was because of the very strong anti Arab sentiment after the disaster. Passengers would still occasionally abuse him so he rarely talked to passengers. Ayed felt the nine eleven events were far beyond anything Osama bin Laden were capable of. So who was behind it? He said he had his ideas but didn't want to talk about it. I asked him about the prospects for peace between Palestine and Israel. It would take long and be difficult as nationalism and patriotism were all mixed up with religion, making it quite complex. For the last ten minutes of the drive he had turned off the meter as he had driven too far but we got to the Pickwick Arms Hotel just a little bit later. I shook his hand, said thank you, wished him well and we parted ways.

After checking in and doing some unpacking and freshening up I went for a walk. I went up to 52nd Street to find Bellinis Restaurant where I was meeting my old colleague later that evening for dinner. From there I continued west over Lexington, Park, Madison, Fifth, Avenue of the Americas and 7th to Broadway and took a right to find my old Union book shop on 59th. But much to my surprise it had disappeared so I started to walk south on 8th Avenue instead hoping to find another bookstore. I walked down to 42nd Street and took a left and a left again on 7th to have a look at Times Square. The ticket booth was still there, drawing long queues and selling half price tickets to the same evening's shows. A good system for trying to fill up the theatres. Perhaps the greatest thing with New York is just walking the streets like this looking at people, buildings, shops, traffic etc trying to take in the atmosphere. The buzz and the diversity is unparalleled anywhere – a very special feeling. I was glad to be here again. My last visit was 1999 and before that 1990 and all in all I have perhaps spent three months in this unique city. I asked a Times Square Policeman for directions to a bookstore and he said on the corner 48th/5th and soon enough I found the place. I got a couple of books by Gore Vidal - 'Dreaming War – Blood For Oil' and 'Perpetual War for Perpetual Peace – How We Got To Be So Hated.' These proved to be very interesting. Perhaps the most important thought when disaster strikes is introspection – why is this happening to us – and I also felt all along that the events of nine eleven were just blamed on evil people and that conclusion is not necessarily very constructive. The important question is 'why are these people hating us and can we somehow alleviate their discontent?' Clearly there are many things that can be done and changed but arrogance and ignorance and politics often stand in the way for love, peace and tolerance. It also seems to me that these conflicts are quite 'male' and having more women involved on all levels of society would be good for mankind.

On my way back to the hotel I bought some fruits and drinks. There was now a light rain. Back at the hotel I took a shower and rested a bit before going out for my dinner appointment. As I had twenty minutes to spare I walked 2nd Avenue down to 48th - 2nd Avenue is full of nice looking restaurants - and then took a left towards 1st Avenue. At 1st I saw the UN building just a few blocks away. I thought that it would be nice to do the UN tour, something I had not done before. I continued north on 1st to 52nd Street and then turned left again to get to Bellini's on 3rd. Between 2nd and 3rd I noticed a sign saying ' Don't Honk, $ 350 fine. When I got to the restaurant my friend Jeff White was already there and we sat down to a great Italian dinner. We kept talking so intensely so we hardly found any time for reading the menu. I asked him if he had done the UN tour and he said he hadn't but that he wanted to. I said I intended to do it the next morning. We agreed that the UN must be supported into a greater role in the preservation of peace and harmony between peoples – this is our only hope for a better future for mankind. Jeff said his move back to the USA from Singapore had gone well and they were enjoying it and work was going well.

I ordered a mozzarella with pomodore and then a shrimp risotto and he had prociutto and then some lamb. We shared a bottle of Brunello to top it off and also had a nice Italian dessert. He asked me about my plans and I outlined my thinking. He said he felt the bank never fully realised my uniqueness and talent and he thought I would do better on my own. I thanked him for his kind words and said that my dance with the bank lasted for thirteen quite enjoyable years and that was pretty good anyway. Three hours later we left and said goodbye and vowed to stay in touch and hoping that we would meet soon again. I walked back to my hotel one block away, did some reading and then slept for nine hours.

After a shower and some fruits I was on the New York streets again just after nine o'clock, now heading towards the UN building. On my way there I ran into Raoul Wallenberg Place on 47th Street and along that Street, Katherine Hepburn gardens. Only a few weeks later did I learn that this legend of a movie star died 96 years old. The UN compound goes all the way from 47th to 42nd Street and cover 18 acres. As it is jurisdictionally separate from New York, it has its own stamps, law enforcement and fire department. After some wait for the security check I paid the $ 10 for the guided tour. The tour guide was a lovely looking Chinese girl, Fen, who spoke fluent English. Our group were from Japan, Sweden, Ghana, Texas, California and some other. We learned that originally there were 51 member states, which now had reached 191 with East Timor being the last one to join. The Security Council has 15 members with China, USA, UK, France and Russia – the victorious nations out of the Second World War - as permanent members. Japan and Germany – the number two and three economies in the world are not in this group but this may change in future. One of the signs on the wall said that over 1585 UN peacekeepers had been killed on duty. The dispatch of a peacekeeping force requires consent by the nations involved and approval from the United Nations. The UN has worked hard and successfully to achieve decolonisation. In 1945 seven hundred and fifty million people lived in dependent territories. Now this number is down to two million people in sixteen small colonies such as New Caledonia, American Samoa, etc.

The Economic and Social Council has as a goal to completely eliminate polio by 2005. Another poster showed that the worlds annual spend on arms amounts to $ 800 billion. Thirty per cent of this amount, or $ 240 billion would suffice to eliminate all the worlds' ills in terms of starvation, water shortages, ozone hole etc, etc. So clearly a better order is within reach and doesn't have to be an impossible dream. The financial contribution to the UN is maximum 22 % payable by the USA and 0.001% or 11,000 dollars payable by the thirty poorest nations. I asked if the USA still is in arrears and she said yes – the US Congress only releases money if the UN does this or that and such conditionality is basically contrary to the UN principles. I also asked if the recent events and controversies around the Iraq war had weakened the UN. She said that the system had been severely challenged and its success requires a lot of good will from major countries. The tour lasted for an hour, I thanked Fen for an interesting tour, and then I picked up my backpack, which I had checked with security.

On my way down to my lunch appointment at Union Square Cafe I found another Raoul Wallenberg walk – third time on this trip that I found places named after him. At a newsstand I bought Financial Times and saw that share markets were up about one pct. The share markets had improved ten to twenty pct since March lows. There was also an article about the number of people in the world with one million dollars to invest – the number now reaching 7.3 million or about one tenth of one percent of the world's population. The aggregate wealth of these rich people is $ 7.4 trillion in the USA, $ 8.8 trillion in Europe and $ 5.7 trillion in Asia with the latter growing fastest. There was also more bad news of violence from the Middle East. I met my friend Craig Manning outside the Union Square Cafe on 16th Street and we had another good Italian meal. We talked about life and mutual friends and the future. Craig said his wife was very much anti Bush, which sometimes raised the eyebrows of the Americans. I said my wife very much felt the same way and it may be quite a widespread view that the USA has a seemingly unqualified president, supported in the elections by only one quarter of eligible voters. Questions many ask are: Is this really the best the American electorate can do? And to what extent is the current President just a product of fundraising skills and what attachments and obligations does that imply? Is this consistent with the principles behind democracy? Otherwise they were enjoying the USA and expected to stay another two years. They had been surprised at how cold last winter was and that all needed to buy full winter clothing. There was good skiing in the state of New York, just a few hours away from their residence. Craig also said that as a next career step he wouldn't mind changing tack a bit to do something slightly different.

From 16th Street I walked to Washington Square and towards Church Street and ground zero, i.e. where the World Trade Centre had been standing. When I got there, there was just a large building site and I moved around the fence to find some commemorative signs. I found the spot and there all the names of the nine-eleven dead were listed as the heroes of that day and the event. My friend Eugene in Washington said that the definition of a hero is someone who is dead when I told him that the definition of poetry is that which gets lost in any translation. A big sign on an adjacent building said: THE HUMAN SPIRIT IS NOT MEASURED IN THE SIZE OF THE ACT BUT IN THE SIZE OF THE HEART. Quite a few people had made it to ground zero and were trying to take it all in. A new structure was slowly going up in replacement of what had been. Although it was the biggest insurance claim in history, the subsequent Iraqi war cost even more.

I continued down to Battery Park to have a bit of a look at the sea and the Statue of Liberty. At Battery Park there was a street musician playing jazz trumpet. I asked if he could play 'Just a Closer Walk With Thee' which he did. This reminded me firstly of my fathers funeral where a small band played that and a few other tunes, and also of my visit to New Orleans, the Charles Bridge in Prague and my Jazz friends, 'The New Orleans Naughtiest' in Tokyo where I had heard the tune – my favourite trad jazz piece – before. It is amazing how a little music speaks to the soul and can put you in a good mood. I sat down for while to look at the ferries come and go. These were Circle Line and Staten Island ferries and the water was quite choppy from the many vessels moving around. Then I started the long walk back to 51st Street – I had decided to walk as I think it healthy and also it allows you to see and experience more. I discovered that I could walk roughly one block per minute so the whole walk would be about 75 minutes, as one has to walk about a mile from Battery Park to get to where the streets start to be numbered. I walked to Broadway and stopped in St Pauls Chapel built in 1776, to look at an exhibition of the nine eleven events. The Chapel served as a sanctuary during those confused and desperate days of September 2001. Then I continued my uptown walk and much enjoyed being part of the busy street life spectacle until I reached my 51st Street hotel.

For the evening I had an address of 420 West 42nd Street. This is an area that used to be called Hell's Kitchen and be off limits for decent people. Now it was all changing and the area was recovered to civilization again. I found the new building and we had a drink in their new apartment before we went out to the restaurant just around the corner. Adam and Fiona who I was seeing are New Zealanders who got married two moths ago and Adam worked in my department in Auckland a few years earlier. They had been out of New Zealand for two years and hoped for more time in New York, which they both much enjoyed. After the nine eleven events they had to move from down town because the clean up work ran 24 hrs a day and was so noisy so it was impossible to sleep. It is nice to meet young, positive, optimistic energetic and talented people and we talked and talked until 10.30 PM when it was time to call it a day. At that time it was raining heavily. I helped them back through the rain with my red umbrella and then started my mile long walk from 42nd to 51st Street and from 9th Avenue to 2nd Avenue, i.e. 16 blocks, back in the downpour. Along the streets there were rivers of water and a taxi put a wave of water over my legs. It wasn't too uncomfortable as it wasn't cold and my head was dry. My only concern was the survival of my leather shoes, which were getting soaking, wet. Back at the hotel I saw that my step counter had clocked up 26,000 steps (21 km or 13 miles), which was a new record.

I woke up Friday 13th June, my eldest son's 28th birthday, and saw there was still a light rain. I sent him an email saying I was looking forward to seeing him the next day in Stockholm. This morning I planned to go to the Guggenheim Museum on 87th and Fifth Avenue. I was wearing my light leather loafers from Kuala Lumpur and after a while my right foot was wet as I think my shoe was starting to wear out. At 60th Street just by the cable car to Roosevelt Island I went into a restaurant called the Tramway Diner for a good full breakfast for six dollars. After breakfast I continued my walk uptown and got to the Guggenheim just before ten and had to wait a little as it hadn't opened yet. I paid my $ 10 admission and took the lift to the 6th floor to work myself down. An attendant up there said the museum should be seen from low to high but I decided to stick to my high to low idea. On the top floor was some crazy TV show and four pidgins in a small room full of bird droppings. None of these things did anything for me and most of the museum was like that. One room with the Thaunhauser Collection on the second floor was very nice with artists like Picasso, Cézanne, Gaugain, Degas, Monet and Renoir. I was wondering whether I was perhaps getting conservative not liking much the new exhibition but at least I felt honest about feeling unimpressed. And if others like it that's fine. After half an hour I was through and walked 5th Avenue down to 80th and looked into The Metropolitan Museum. Had the weather been a bit better I would have walked through Central Park celebrating its 150th anniversary this year. Considering the size of the Metropolitan Museum and the limited time left, I only entered the vast Museum Shop, which is quite an experience in its own right. I bought a few nice old replicas and walked back to the hotel for packing, showering and check out.

Five minutes after I had done all that my airport transfer arrived to take me to Newark Airport. There were three other passengers, French-speaking Africans, and as I was the last pick up we headed straight for the New Jersey Airport. The check in queue took half an hour and I was informed that the flight was full and on time. The scale showed 27 kgs for my two check ins, and in addition I had my three carry ons but that posed no problem. I had a hamburger and a beer and I bought a bottle of Whiskey and sat down to wait for the flight to Stockholm. After two weeks of travelling out of Tokyo through the USA from west to east I felt I had experienced all I had hoped to.

FLYING TO SWEDEN

On the flight I sat next to Addy, 21, from Connecticut, on her way to St Petersburg. She was boarding a bit late and I helped her stow her bag and clothes away in the overhead locker. (Not all clothes – just her jacket.) Addy was attending university in Ohio and wanted to be a writer, perhaps particularly of cook books. She was well informed and also critical of the current US administration in Washington DC. "Don't think that all Americans support Bush and the things he does," she said. We talked about Hillary Clinton and her new book and she said she would trade Hillary for George anytime. We talked about literature and we both had enjoyed Hotel New Hampshire, The Fountainhead and Dostoevski. Her ancestry was half Swedish and half English and she asked many questions about the Nordic countries and Russia. I showed her the book I bought the day before 'This is New York' by E B White and she said she had loved other books he had written including Charlotte's Web. I told her that I read E B White on the recommendation of Gaucho Marx who, according to my reading of Marx books, held White to be his favourite author. Again I felt lucky to have good company and that it is something spring like and lovely with young, sensible, optimistic people who are ready to just step out and make a mark on life. Addy had signed up for one semester of Italian studies in Firenze and I said I couldn't think of a nicer thing to do.

Arriving in Stockholm early Saturday morning after seven and a half hours flight I said good bye to Addy and wished her a good holiday. I got into the new terminal at Arlanda and had to walk about a mile to get to the baggage claim. Kristina, my son's girlfriend, met me. Kristina is on the finishing touches of a doctorate in microbiology, expecting to be ready by December this year. She is a role model for good health and a nice, friendly, lovely, intelligent person so I think Max has been lucky to find her. She was picking me up in a new smart SAAB car so I travelled in style. We arrived at my mother's house just after nine o'clock and she came out to greet us. I had seen her only two months ago when she visited Tokyo and we went down to New Zealand for a week together. That was quite a trip for her at 83 years of age. As always when coming to Sweden it struck me how green and fresh everything looks and how clear the air is.

At noon we had lunch in Stockholm with Max and Kristina and my sister Agneta at Mosebacke with great views over the City. We had salmon, new potatoes and white wine with that. Max and Kristina were elegantly dressed as they intended to proceed to a wedding after lunch. As Kristina doesn't drink any alcohol she is usually the designated driver. Mother and sister and I went for mile long walk through the Old Town of Stockholm to the Hey Market where we parted and we took the subway to our suburb. In the evening I watched a bit of Stockholm Marathon, which started at two o'clock and had a maximum allowed time of six hours. As I had a dinner invite for seven o'clock I saw some of the late runners moving slowly towards the goal. I got to my friends – Claas and Else-Marie's – place, which I thought lovely, and had a vodka lime followed by trout, salad, new potatoes, white wine, and straw berries with ice cream and white chocolate sauce and coffee with a little glass of Japanese whiskey. After the dinner we took a walk in their neighbourhood in the bright summer night seeing several wild rabbits in the middle of the city. The next day I went out to my younger sister's Ylva's (and her family's) place on one of Stockholm's many islands and we had lunch with her family in their garden overlooking the lake. At that time my sister like myself was self unemployed after just having left Deloitte's but within a few weeks she had signed up with a new employer as CFO. I also visited the grave of Georg Olsson, 1920 – 1999, my late father buried in a beautiful piece of nature by a little lake, about a mile from his home. My mother's garden had grown a bit wild since my last visit and I cut trees and bushes and the lawn and tidied up as I had been doing once a year before.

In the week following I met with a few ex colleagues over lunches and dinners and prepared for our mid summer celebrations out on our island two hundred kms south of Stockholm. We got out on the island on Wednesday night and on Friday about forty people gathered outside to prepare the flower pole and to dance and sing with all generations for half an hour and then have coffee on the lawn. This all worked out well and for the candle light dinner at our house we were fifteen people having roast, new potatoes, bread, plenty of red wine and many other things. Again there was plenty of singing at the dinner and afterwards people were talking and some were playing games. As this is the shortest night of the year it is light until 11.30 PM and then gets light again at 1.30 AM. It is quite a unique experience. People are very happy to have put the long and dark winter behind them and trying to have as good a time as possible. We played some volleyball, went swimming, boating, fishing, hiking and canoeing and all tried to make the most of it. I stayed on the island for two weeks before returning to Stockholm.

Sweden is a good country to live in with many positives. People are well educated, the society is quite egalitarian and women have perhaps more prominence than in many other countries. On the negative side are the climate with a long and dark winter and taxes, which are the highest in the world. High taxes can easily become an infringement on liberty and independence of the people as the bureaucracy that high taxes inevitably creates wants to regulate in detail how people live their lives and who is eligible for the vast sums of government support and hand outs. Less for you to decide on – more for the government to decide on. I hope the European co-operation and influence will encourage Sweden to be a little bit more middle of the road. I sensed that many people felt me and my family lucky to be living in a civilised country without the two drawbacks mentioned. But to be fair, any country including New Zealand has its issues and needs to improve and change to meet popular demands. I believe that the Nordic countries and Australia / New Zealand are amongst the best societies in the world with the down under countries coming out a little bit ahead. One of the benefits with a beachhead in both is the opportunity to enjoy two summers every year. Another benefit is that the whole world is between Sweden and New Zealand so travelling from one to the other, it is possible to include any world destination at little or no extra cost. I ask myself what I have done to deserve all this? Perhaps I am just very lucky.

During my six weeks in Sweden I went back to the island for two weeks enjoying a heat wave with excellent weather. Every day we – I and my friends, usually six to ten people in one two or three high speed day cruisers - would bring food or coffee and go to the outer islands to view the waves rolling in and to sit on the polished cliffs and swim in the Baltic Sea, which at this stage was quite warm at perhaps 22 degrees. I also had a chance to go with my son Max to Dalarna to see my house there and to do some painting and maintenance work together with him. We worked all day, went for swims in the lake mid day, and took a sauna and made good dinners together. We achieved a lot and had a good time. I made a point of saying hello to all the neighbours who I hadn't seen for four years. It is a really nice place, fully renovated and with beautiful fireplaces in every room. Max enjoys going there with his friends so I have decided to keep it although I can't draw on it much. In Stockholm I had a few more lunches and also went down to the local lake for a swim a few times, and tried to tidy up my mothers garden. There were a few trees that were invading her space and I cut them down improving outlook and light intake. Six weeks felt a bit long but in hindsight it was all very good and valuable. With good access to Internet I could entertain my network all along and also type my notes whenever I felt like it.

The last day of July was the day of my departure and Max picked me up to take me to the airport. My mother was up early to cook me some breakfast. I would have to believe she is one of the most 'Genki' (alert and energetic) 84 year olds I have ever come across (and of curse a wonderful mother). We had probably spent more time together this summer than anytime since my school days, which is good given my 17 years of living overseas. Max arrived in gym gear as he intended to do a workout before going to his office. We talked a bit about his future and his upcoming MBA studies. With full time work and half time study he will be busy although he is also very keen to retain some time for himself and his many hobbies. He is very independent, very fit and very reliable and is lucky to have a lovely girlfriend, beautiful, pleasant and talented. As we approached the airport the signs direct us to a parking area but as it is only a quick stop and exit he ignores the signs and drives me to the door. A taxi driver advices to be quick or we will get fined. I tell the helpful taxi driver that this is the only airport in the world where you can't leave a passenger at the terminal entrance. Perhaps this is part of an anti car pro public transport campaign. It reminds me of my sense that a shadow of intolerance, bureaucracy and self righteousness is cast over Sweden. Anyway we unload and say good-bye in less than a minute and Max is on his way to the gym and I on my way to Scotland.

SCOTLAND NEXT

In the airport I head for SAS check in queue and there a lady asks to see my ticket and she says this ticket can be processed by the self check in machine. But I have two check-in luggage pieces? 'Doesn't matter: those can just be left at the luggage counter.' So I move over to the machine and feed my ticket in and it says 'can't read your ticket!' Then I go back to the queue and the lady suggests I haven't done it right so she advices me to go and ask the assistant to help. I find the assistant and she feeds my ticket in and the machine says 'can't read your ticket.' The assistant tells me that the machine can't read my ticket. I thank her for her help and go back to the first lady and say that her colleague told me the machine can't read my ticket!! To say that I was annoyed would be overstating it but there is nothing much charming in the experience either. After all this she asks me to check in at the business class counter, which I do. I know the airline industry is in trouble and perhaps this is the background to many frustrated staff and passengers. I picked up a complimentary Financial Times as I stepped onto the plane.

The flight was 90 percent full but as luck would have it there was room to stow away my hand luggage and the seat next to mine was empty. The SAS in flight staff looked like they were all about to retire. Arriving in Copenhagen one hour before my British Midland flight from gate C 28 was due to depart to Edinburgh I thought there was plenty of time but proceeded to my gate anyway as I had little interest in shopping. This proved to be a good decision as pier C unexpectedly had a passport check with a very long queue leading up to it. Many people were nervous about missing their flights but I was in good shape. Being at my gate twenty minutes before departure and with no people there I concluded that the flight must be rather empty. An unenthusiastic SAS staff told me I could only bring one piece of hand luggage and that my tennis rackets had to be checked. I asked if the flight was full and she said 'almost' which went against my own reading. She gave me a tag for the rackets and told me to leave it before entering the plane. The plane was less than half full and I hung on to my rackets and stowed them overhead easily together with my bag. The on board staff were a couple of Scottish girls providing a nice change to the dispirited people I had encountered earlier.

Bertrand Russell's line 'Excess virtue is a vice' kept coming back to me on a daily basis in Sweden. There are so many politicians with a greater tax take than anywhere else in the world and wanting to do so much good to the people. The result is a sense of paralysis and lack of independence and freedom for a large group of people. Jean-Jacque Rosseau says in his 'The Social Contract: 'Liberty consists less in doing one's own will than in not being subject to that of another; it consists further in not subjecting the will of others to our own.'

You may think Sweden a good country for losers, but not even the losers are happy as they often feel trapped and caught in a system totally lacking in incentives to improve their situation. My judgement here may be a bit harsh but visiting my former home country only for a brief time each year I can see how government is creeping into the minutest details of people's lives and this has little attraction to me.

Flying into Edinburgh I notice the two impressive bridges over the river Forth just before landing twenty minutes ahead of schedule. Baggage delivery is swift and I get to the meeting area before the plane's official arrival time. After a little wait allowing me to finish the chapter in my book of love stories, I see Haruko and sneak up on her and give her a hug. She points to where John is and I give him a hug too – long time no see and such a good friend and soul mate. Soon we are in their dark green Jaguar heading north over the bridge to get to Cullen. John runs thru the program for my nine days with the time divided between Cullen, The West Coast islands and then Edinburgh for the arts festival. Sounds perfect to me. The landscape is green, rural and open with very few trees, reminding me of New Zealand. It is easy to see how the many Scotsmen came to feel at home in New Zealand. My friendship with John goes back almost 25 years and Haruko came on the scene just a few years later.

As we drive north John and I dive into deep philosophical conversations picking up from our many email exchanges and the last time we met in Prague two years earlier. As we are both amateur philosophers and perhaps more enthusiastic than professional our discussion goes all over the place and making Haruko in the back seat opt for a nap. What is normally a three hours drive turns out to be a six hours drive after a few stops and scenic detours. John points out to me the distinct line as we leave the low country for the Highlands. The Highlands was quite lawless as late as to the middle of the 18th century, and highlanders ransacked and burned low land villages, in much the same way as the Vikings in the past. A key factor in civilising the north was the building of many fine bridges to make the land more accessible. We stop at Stonehaven to visit the Dunnottar Castle from the 12th century. A bit cold it was, but a beautiful location on a cliff by the sea and full of history. We get to Cullen 6.30 PM and drive up to the huge mansion The Cullen House, previously inhabited by the Earl of Seafield.

My hosts' place is two stories of about 150 sq meters each and with huge windows and wonderful views over a green wall of nature and a little creek called The Punchbowl. Very tranquil and very beautiful. The building has eight share-holders with roughly the same size 'apartments.' It dates back about eight hundred years and looks like out of a fairytale. The upkeep of something like that was probably eating into the previous owner's, The Earl of Seafield's, finances to the extent that he preferred to sell it and live in the nearby dower house, that also quite magnificent. The ground floor with bedrooms and bathrooms are all in white stone almost like a wine cellar. And the first floor is essentially one big room with beautiful ornaments in the ceiling and some very large windows and wooden shutters – all really tastefully done. That main room reminds of Versailles or the Prince's gallery in the City Hall of Stockholm. On the building outside their apartment there is an old text in stone reading: 'Hope ye Anchor of Faith'. John says he thinks it would be the perfect motto for me as he says I epitomize the rationality of optimism.

We have a dinner appointment with some Swiss people also living in the building at the local town restaurant called 'Seafield's Arms Hotel and Restaurant'. We are eight people altogether and we begin with drinks, beers, whisky and wines. We order from a big menu and I have crab cakes and lamb. A good meal, a warm evening and some old and some new friends. It feels exciting and fantastic to just drop down in anew environment so different and yet I feel so much at home with these generous and friendly people. Nothing feels exotic to me anymore and I don't mean that in a negative sense but in a positive. No matter how different landscapes and buildings may look, the ultimate beauty is in good people and good people make me feel happy, contented and at home. The next day we take a long walk through Cullen along the coastline. We cross over a fantastic stone bridge – Scotland seems full of them – and a pretty little golf course is situated along the beach. We are out for about two hours, talking, looking, and each enjoying the conversation.

On August first, the Swiss National Day, the Swiss people, Peter and Eliane Schleiffer, arranged a party for all in the building, about twenty or so people. As it was a fine night, tables were laid out in the garden. The host was serving Racklettes, i.e. the Swiss cheese and potato dish, and a special machine had been brought up from Switzerland for the purpose. This cooking was quite labour intense and the host was tied up with this task for at least an hour. There were other delicacies too and plenty of good wine, some of it from the host's vineyard. The diversified group of guests were quite formal at first but as the evening wore on happiness, song and laughter spread around the table. I contributed a few songs and jokes too, always enjoying a new audience. The next day we drove around to Elgin to do some shopping and we also looked at the icehouse on the premises. The icehouse is a round cellar like building where ice was kept for year around use in smaller iceboxes. There were plans to convert it to a wine cellar for the inhabitants of the mansion. All these houses and bridges, dams and roads must have required enormous labour input to be constructed but I guess labour was the one thing that was abundant and cheap in olden days.

John cooked a beautiful Soufflé' on broccoli, cheese and of course the usual flower, eggs, butter and milk. As we were having some Sicilian chardonnay 'Planeta' whilst cooking I tried to write down what he did as he progressed but it all got a bit complicated and in the end I couldn't make much sense of my own notes. I shall have to follow the cookbook when I try it myself. Key is to not open the oven for the 40 minute cooking period. I also noted that there is a lot of labour involved and that there must be easier ways to feed yourself. Although I must admit that the end product was very delicious and I admire John for his tenacity and sincere interest in food and wine. After the South African white we had a superb Shiraz from Australia, my favourite wine. For desert we enjoyed lots of homemade ice cream with fresh rasberries. Living like a king among genuine good friends! Life couldn't get much better. We finished off the evening with a sauna and a beer. Haruko skipped the sauna.

Next day we drove away towards west Scotland for our visit to Mull. The road through Inverness and along the many lakes and canals is very scenic. We arrived in Oban at 1.30 PM after driving through some rain and went straight to the ferry which we had booked for six o'clock. We tried to get on the two o'clock one and just missed getting on, but were in a good position to get onto the four o'clock one. This turned out to be perfect as it gave us two hours to look around and get some lunch. Oban is another Scottish stone fishing village, very quaint and pretty and possibly a bit slow off-season. We had lunch at nice hotel restaurant overlooking the bay and managed to get a little bit of a feel for the place. On the top of the hill is a building called the tower, round with many arches making it looking a bit like Coliseum? The founder had it built to alleviate unemployment among masoners and put a statue of each of his relatives in each arch. Nice idea if you have the money.

After just under an hour on the ferry we arrived at Mull and started to drive towards our hotels. When we tried to book the night before it was quite full so we ended up booking one room in two nearby hotels. It is good we got the early ferry because it took us an our and a half to drive the one lane roads to the hotel sites. We just had time to check in and have a quick shower before assembling for dinner. The three-course dinner cost thirty pounds excluding wine. We were served cured herring as a pre starter, then a chicken mousse and for mains halibut and sea bass and with that we had a good Chardonnay. For dessert we had coco cake. Another real treat and after dinner John drove me back to my hotel and Haruko joined as well – to ensure John didn't fall asleep, she said. Two years prior John had been on a motorbike in Greece and fallen asleep and had a very close brush with death. He hit some rocks on the side of the road and his first memory after the accident is bleeding profusely and hearing a roadside doctor say 'There is nothing I can do for this man' making him think he had only minutes to live. After some convalescence he came out his old self except for a small becoming scar on his forehead. Psalms 90:12 refers: 'Teach us to ponder how few our days are that we may live each one wisely'.

My hotel, Calgary Hotel, was very quaint and one of the girls working there was a Kiwi from Christchurch so I talked a little with her before going to bed. The next morning I went for a long walk before the 8.30 breakfast looking at the beautiful bay with a white sand beach and hundreds of sheep climbing the hillsides. Very tranquil and picturesque and not too dissimilar from New Zealand. After breakfast I was picked up by my friends and we drove towards the island of Ulva – same name as my sister's meaning wolf and her husband's name is Ulf which also means wolf so you don't want to mess around with them - to catch a boat out to Staffa Island. The weather looked a bit iffy at first but improved as the day progressed. We found the ferry and had half an hour's wait there, which was very nice and relaxing. Some guy was fishing lobster or crab just outside and we see how he emptied his overnight cages. Very calm, very idyllic. There was a little ferry across the water to Ulva for four pounds and return free. I thought it a bit expensive and John suggested it might be better to have the first leg free and then charge ten pounds to take people back.

Our motor yatch picked us up for the four hour trip to Staffa island and we were a group of maybe fifteen people. The weather was now lovely with about 25 degrees and no wind. The captain drove up to some small islets full of seals who didn't seem much disturbed by our presence. About an hours trip out in the sea we came to Staffa Island. The formations of pillar looking staffs, all being pentagonal, is just out of this world fantastic. We were told there is a similar island on the Ulster side of the sea. We landed on the island and got to go ashore to view Fingal's cove and also to climb up to the high plateau of the island. Mendelssohn was here to view the island and composed "Fingal's cave" part of "The Scotch Symphony" to try to capture the wonder of it all.

The three of us walked around the island covered in grass and bird droppings and with the most stunning views over the open sea in one direction and the Scottish coast in the other. The weather was now brilliant and quite a few people from various vessels were coming onto the island. But all were behaving very well and it didn't seem to impose at all on mother nature and the bird life.

After the Staffa visit the boat rounded the island of Ulva and we saw Puffin birds and many Porpoise, which is of the dolphin family. After the boat trip we drove to Tobermory, which in the evening sun presented a very lovely face. We walked around and looked at the shops and all the happy people and sat down at a pub for a few beers and chips. We also booked for dinner at what looked to be the best restaurant in town. A bit later we had a good meal there consisting of soup and trout and a good Wolf Blass Chardonnay to go with it. We stayed the night in Tobermory, intending to take the second ferry the next day at nine thirty am. I suggested we park our car in the ferry queue before we have breakfast just to ensure we would get a place. When John and I drove down in the morning our car was first but when we got there after breakfast it was very busy. After about an hours drive, we tried to get on a ferry to Isle of Skye but it was just too full and we decided to drive back to Cullen instead.

We got there just in time to pick up the prime fillet that John had ordered the week before. His Swiss friend had given him cooking instructions for doing delicious meet. One starts with the best well hung piece of meat one can find, then fry it in a very hot pan to seal it and put it in the oven at seventy degrees for three hours. John fried the meat and put it in the oven and then Haruko looked after it whilst we went for a ten km walk through the woods up to a mountain top to command a great view over the nearby land and sea scapes. During this 13,000 steps walk we saw heaps of chanterells but John didn't want to pick them without a knife to cut them rather than pull them up, in order to not jeopardize their return next year. I said I never heard anything like that but we left them anyway. They do cost a fortune in the delicatessen shops and they go very well with good meat. It was a very good walk and we came back Haruko said the meat was done so could we please get ready for dinner. Again we had a bottle of white for appetiser and then some red wine. The meat was really fantastic and we ate the lot together with some fried potatoes and plenty of salad with tasty garlic dressing.

John had also served Scotch every night and had me taste different brands and kinds. I learned the difference between Highland and Island whisky the former a little bit darker and the latter having a little bit of a smell of the sea. John felt it was worth paying a little extra for good whisky as the improvement in quality often outweighed the difference in price. The following day we drove to Dufftown Golf course and John and I played a round of eighteen holes. The location is very pretty and the course holds the highest located T-off in Britain. This day was over 30 degrees centigrade and there was a lot of climbing uphill on the course so quite a taxing affair. We both enjoyed the golf though and afterwards proceeded to see some whisky distillers. On our tour at Glennfiddich, I learned that whisky is the same as beer except that the former is distilled and I also had many other useful things pointed out to me. The whisky tours are free and come with some tasting of samples at the end. Most distillers seem to have a shop and also a small restaurant on the premises. For dinner that night we had Cullen Skink, a local soup containing potatoes, smoked Haddock, onion, pepper and salt. Quite good taste. We also had the rest of the meat and some good wine to go with it.

The next day we were to drive the four hours from Cullen to Edinburgh. But before we started our journey, John took me to the local Castle ruins on the sea and we got there in the morning fog. On the field leading down to the castle there was a structure about 15 meters around and perhaps six meters high, which John asked if I could guess what it was. I tried lighthouse, or grain storage, or a place where a fire could be lit to warn inland people of approaching invaders from the sea. He gave me good marks for my guesses but said it was a Doocote or Dovecot. The intent was that pidgeons (old Scots word 'doos') would come through the open top and nest there and when full of doves a lid would close and the Pigin pie was only a matter of a little effort and time. John also told me that when some friends of theirs visited this Castle ruin their dog jumped after a bird and fell a great distance down on the rocks. They left the dog for dead but when checking the next day the dog, much to their relief and amazement, was running up and down the beach.

When we were on our way south the fog had lifted and the weather was fine and quite hot. I dosed off in the next to driver seat only to wake up by a swift acceleration as we were overtaking a big truck in a curve. I thought it lethal, but subsequently realised that John before the curve had seen that all was clear. Anyway, that woke me up to be more sociable. We stopped again in Stonehaven to have some homemade ice cream. In Edinburgh we went to John's favourite shop, a delicatessen called 'Valvona and Crolla' on Elm Row. It had a great supply of the most magnificent hams, salamis, cheeses, breads, olives, artichokes, biscuits, wines and everything you might want for a delicate ready-made meal or dessert. The flavour of the shop is Sicilian and I was reminded I have never been to Sicily and I must soon! John and Haruko bought a little of almost everything and I got a six-pack of Sicilian wines to go with it. The afternoon sun spread light and warmth over the city and the festival arrangers must be overjoyed with the weather.

We got to the apartment located in on Eyre Crescent in the New Town area, quite centrally really and next to the Botanic Gardens. The apartment was in the process of combining two smaller apartments into one larger and although much had been completed, like kitchen and bathrooms, a lot still remained to be done. The hall to which one stepped in from the front door had no less than ten doors which all had been beautifully prepared for painting. John was essentially doing it up himself. Their main abode is on Hampstead Heath in London but they are spending more and more time in Scotland. After showers and checking emails we had a bottle of White and some of the fine delicatessen just bought. Good bread, hams, salamis, olives and cheeses and some wine to go with it shared among good friends – what could be nicer? 'Companion' and 'company' comes from Latin – 'cum pane' with bread! Makes sense.

Just after seven we walked out into the balmy August evening and took a taxi to Pleasance Courtyard to pick up some tickets for tomorrow and see what tickets we could get for the current evening. We got tickets to an 8.15 PM show – a standup comedian Jo Caulfield of whom the program said 'back at her delightful bitchy best'. It was entertaining but a bit raw. Jo asked a handful of people in the audience what's your name? Where do you come from? And What do you do? And from there on she just improvised. She picked on me and tried to be intimidating but couldn't quite figure me out I think so I got away lightly compared to some others. She managed to keep the audience laughing for an hour and most people seemed to enjoy themselves in spite of shocking use of language and insinuations. After the show we had some beers in a very busy bar. We decided to walk back thru the pretty streets of Edinburgh and finally stopped at 'Cumberland Arms' for a night cap beer. I felt the city reminded me a bit of Prague in that there are so many beautiful historic buildings and I felt very pleased to be there in good company. Doing something for the first time again!

In the morning we went for a walk through the nearby Botanical Garden. Quite a large area providing a nice lung for the city, which isn't that large anyway at around 300,000 inhabitants. We ran into a school class studying plants with their teacher. There were many old ladies and also some young ones walking their little children and others all enjoying the meticulously kept gardens. From one point there is a great view over the city, which is quite hilly, and its skyline of churches and towers and the castle in the distance. Our one hour walk registered 5,000 marks on the step counter. We had a good breakfast with eggs, bread, croissants, salami and tea and talked and read the newspaper. Big bombs had gone off outside the Jordanian embassy in Bagdad and also at the Mariott Hotel in Jakarta, both killing about fifteen people and wounding scores of others. The paper also showed a picture of Amrozi bin Nurhasyim, 41 years of age, and all smiles although just sentenced to death for his role in the Bali bombings a year earlier. August 7th was the five-year anniversary of the Nairobi bombing killing 220 and destroying the American Embassy there. So much violence where there should be love, peace and tolerance. We must try to understand the reason behind all this rather than just fire away at the symptoms.

A special supplement to 'The Scotsman' containing all the festival events of the day showed no less than 130 events before 1.00 PM that day. In total there are more than 1500 events at the fringe part of the festival on a subsidy of just 64,000 pounds. The main festival is subsidised with two million pounds and the whole spectacle is expected to generate 136 million pounds to the local economy. The exact financial return may be difficult to calculate but it sure feels good to be there and will no doubt be a booster for Edinburgh and its people. As we had a lunch invitation with Roger Gifford out of town that day we got underway just before noon and drove north over the bridge to junction number nine and then to Glennfarg and Aberangie. Roger's place sits just at the foot of a big hill and it is visible from the motorway, perhaps three miles in the distance. A small road led up to the mansion of some thirty rooms, again looking like out of a fairy tale. No one I ever knew in Sweden or New Zealand would have a house like that but in the UK and the USA I have sometimes visited these fantastic places and often found that the people inhabiting them are just as normal as you and I. Beautiful living and beautiful setting, but also no doubt a lot of upkeep and maintainance. 'We are owned by what we own!' (Nietzsche)

We were greeted with pink champagne, white wine and red wine. Roger showed a little bit of the house, which was full of antique furniture and paintings looking like they came out of a museum. There were another couple there too, Jim and Masako and their two children George and Ken, all from Tokyo. They said they had picked these names for the very Japanese looking boys because they were easy to write in Japanese. The food was ready – a beautiful meat pie – and then all sorts of accessories like many vegetables and salad and bread. We sat at a grand table in the kitchen, which had a magnificent AGA stove. These are lovely and will keep a whole house warm in the winter. After a great lunch with good wines and cheeses we moved out in the well-kept garden for coffees and desserts. The weather was perfect and I thought life was pretty good to me. Roger and I worked together in London in the late 80's and then he worked in Tokyo so we met both in New Zealand and Tokyo and had kept in touch during the years. We share a passion for singing, he probably being a notch more of a singer than I. This makes me recall what my singing teacher in Auckland told me:

'I am not so sure about your singing, but I have never seen such self confidence before!'

Roger was hoping to rent his place to hunting parties. He said these were organised for parties of about 10 hunters and for 5,000 pounds there would be 200 birds allowing each shooter 20 birds each. This is quite big business and part of corporate entertainment. Anyway, we thoroughly enjoyed the afternoon and all had a good time. Haruko appreciated the chance to speak some Japanese again and also played very nicely with the two small boys. Jim, the boys' father originates in Illinois and works for Caterpillar in Japan.

When back from this lovely excursion we all had a snooze and I prepared some tea before we were to see more of the festival. John checked his tickets and realised they were for a one o'clock performance which we obviously had misses. But we would no doubt find something else. Haruko felt a bit tired and opted to stay home for the evening as John and I took a taxi back into festival territory. We got tickets to 'Instruments of mass destruction' by Rainer Hersch. He had a great one hour show, perhaps more positive and less cynical than the one the night before. The Iraqi war he felt was just an endeavour by the Americans to teach us all some Geography. Who in the world would know what Basra was before this war? He used many musical instruments in his show and played the piano quite well himself. In the end he said that the festival was a non-profit organisation – wasn't meant to be but that is the way it turned out. And any surplus from his show would go to needy children. His children. One of them needed a new car. He also said that between 40 and 60 percent of all cast die in the famous Operas with Verdi topping the list and that on a per hour basis more people die in Opera than anywhere else. He was a great performer and at the end of the show he received a standing ovation.

On our way back we stopped at the Bailey pub for one lager and one Guinness, served by a lovely Australian girl. I didn't pick she was Australian but John heard it immediately. When we arrived back at the flat just before ten o'clock Haruko had prepared a lovely supper with wine, bread, pate, Parma ham, and tomatoes and we had a last good supper together. After the meal John suggested we have a last glass of whisky together before a short night as I had to be at the airport by 5.30AM. I set the alarm for 5.00 but true to my nature I woke up fifteen minutes earlier and turned it off. I said good-bye to my great hosts and wished them welcome to New Zealand. On the flight to Frankfurt I sat next to Aureli from Lousanne, returning home after six weeks of language school in Edinburgh. She had just finished her law studies and was taking a break before starting to work. After four days at home she would travel India for another six weeks. Good choice I said and we shared some impressions of India, perhaps the ultimate tourist country.

ZURICH AND THE LOVE PARADE

I arrived in Zurich on schedule and after some confusion as to what conveyor belt my flight was on I found my bags. I went to the railway office and asked for a second class ticket to Zurich and Kilsberg. I was told that was 8.50 francs so I asked how much is a first class ticket and was told 11.50 so I changed my mind to travel in style. The train arrived promptly and I got my four pieces of luggage on to the train, which seemed to be in a hurry to move on. This is Switzerland where everything is on time. As instructed, I left the train at Zurich Hauptbahnhof to find platform 14 and the train to Kilsberg. It was very hot and I had to wear my red jacket and Borsalino hat as I had no where else to put them. I did get quite sweaty and later learned that the temperature had reached 36 degrees that day. I had to wait half an hour for the second train and I saw lots of people dressed for participation in the love parade. These were mostly young people with almost nothing on providing a bit of distraction and making the wait seem shorter. I also heard music from many different sources in the distance. But it all seemed pretty innocuous and nice. I read in next day's paper that the parade attracted 900,000 participants and there were only eight arrests and 118 taken into hospital. The train to Kilsberg took only fifteen minutes and when there I looked for a taxi. As I couldn't see any, I asked the bus driver just outside and he inquired as to where I wanted to go. I said 'Schwandenstrasse,' which he identified on his map and said he would get me very close. Perfect – and the bus trip was included in the train ticket.

The bus driver told me when to get off and I soon found my bearings and the 36 street number I was looking for. This was the abode of Ruth Seger and her friend Raine who we had never met. We would be attending the same party in the evening and when my friend Carita Riesen told her friend Ruth that some people would be coming all the way from New Zealand the latter immediately offered to take us in for the night. When I pushed the door bell there was no-one at home. My wife, Linda, should supposedly have arrived from New Zealand via Singapore early in the morning that same day, so I thought they might be out shopping or perhaps trying to meet me at the airport. I just took out my book and sat down to read until someone showed up.

Half an hour later Ruth came and we greeted each other. When I asked 'Where is Linda?' she said Linda had missed her plane in Auckland. This I thought strange. Instead of flying west to Singapore she had flown east through Los Angeles and London to try to get to the party on time and she was due any moment but Ruth hadn't been able to see her at the airport. Ruth had a wonderful apartment overlooking Lake Zurich. She suggested I have a shower which I thought a great idea and then we sat down on her balcony with a cold drink and had a great chat about who we were and what interests we had and how the world works.

Ruth is a lovely easy to get to know person. An hour later a taxi arrives and I hurry out to help with the luggage. Linda has now been travelling for 35 hours and is a bit exhausted and also mentally worn after a lot of difficulties finding replacement flights for the ones she missed. I did feel sorry for her to have had such a challenging route to get to here, but all is well that ends well. After a shower and a cup of coffee she was ready to go to the party. Ruth went to Zurich to pick up Raine who had been watching the love parade and when he arrived we all moved along to the fifty year's party of Carita.

Carita and I worked together at PKBanken in Stockholm for two years in the early eighties and we probably hadn't met since, so almost twenty years. However we had stayed in touch and we did enjoy each other's company so this reunion was very nice. Carita lives a bit further out from Zurich in Waedenswil. When we arrived the Champagne was already flowing and people were mingling and having finger food. Carita looked pretty much the way I remembered her, blond, stylish and perhaps a bit enigmatic. A big twenty-year's absence hug was exchanged and we were all into the party as if it was next door. A couple of other old colleagues/ friends were also there but most of the twenty five or so people were new faces, some from Finland, some from Sweden, and perhaps most from Switzerland. Many as it turned out were unemployed affected by the economic downturn and the rationalisation that had swept through banking. Carita married late, had one daughter, Roxanne, then divorced, and remarried a much younger man from Palestine.... He was responsible for the food of the evening, which was of Middle East/ Lebanese type and very delicious. Roxanne, a very cute little twelve-year-old, played a few tunes on the

Saxophone before dinner. As we sat down Carita gave a speech wishing all welcome and also introducing each and every person in the room, which was a good idea, given that many hadn't met before. Seating arrangements were by languages, and our table was Swedish/ English. I had the pleasure to sit next to the hostess. There was also plenty of good red wine and people relaxed and got happier and happier as the wine flowed and the evening progressed.

Carita's sister Ilse from Helsinki gave a very personal and sensitive speech about their closeness and friendship and Sara, Ilse's daughter translated the speech to German. This was the only formal speech of the evening. I also said a few words of appreciation and friendship and sang 'The Best of Times is now' emphasizing the passage: 'hold this moment fast, and live and love as hard as you know how, and make this moment last, because the best of times is now.' Then there was plenty of joyous singing by different groups. After dinner a belly dancer appeared looking very Middle East but Carita assured me she was a local school teacher. Some school teacher!! After this professional performance guests also started to dance. Ilse asked me if I were able to dance Finish Tango and I said that would like to learn so we tried it out. And I found it most enjoyable and not too different from the basic steps I always apply. Linda got into a deep conversation with one or two people and I tried to move around a bit to get to know those at other tables as well. Everybody seemed to have a good time and when I, a bit after midnight, surprised that Linda had lasted that long after her extended travel, suggested that we take a taxi home, Raine said he would drive the car home. At about one o'clock, well wined and dined and danced, we arrived back to Ruth's place. It struck me that I hadn't talked that much to Carita but at least we had spent time and had fun together and hopefully we can have a follow up later in Europe or New Zealand.

After a hot night, temperatures were around 30 degrees all night, we woke up at around nine and Raine cooked a fabulous breakfast which we had together on their balcony with the nicest of views over the rural landscape and the church bells sounding regularly. Breakfast consisted of eggs, fruit salad, toast, orange juice, special coffees, jams, cheeses and anything else we might want. No efforts spared. We had a lovely hour on the balcony under the marquise talking and eating and enjoying the new company and friendships. Both Ruth and Raine were in the IT business, she in the software side and he in security side. Ruth was also fluent in Spanish and had written a paper on Don Quijote. I said I read it last year and was totally fascinated by it and would send her a few of my notes and reflections. Linda gave them a couple of bottles of fine wines from New Zealand and some other little things.

It was now getting on a bit and we had a 12.07 train to catch to Frauenfeldt so they kindly drove us to Zurich Hauptbahnhof. On our way there we saw the many parade participants waking up in their tents. It must have been awfully hot in a tent when the sun rose and temperatures went above 30 degrees again. We felt very lucky and privileged to have been invited to such a nice party and also to have been looked after so well by our new acquaintances, Ruth and Raine. In thanking them we also naturally invited them to come and stay with us in Auckland. We have extended such an invite to many, but because of the distance there is but a small trickle of visitors who find their way to our Pacific Island. In the meantime we shall remain cyber friends.

Just before one o'clock we arrived in Frauenfeldt to see Guiseppe and Doris, who so kindly eight years prior had looked after Felix when he spent a year in Switzerland to learn German. Guiseppe met us at the station and took us, and our light luggage, to their new home ten minutes away. A great top floor apartment with balconies on both sides, one for morning sun and one for evening sun. Doris had prepared a huge salad for lunch and we enjoyed the meal together. Guiseppe, now retired, came from Sicily forty years ago and Doris was still active as a language teacher. He is an agile nice looking man in his early sixties and she is a warm and lovely person, a few years younger. Between them they speak Italian but Doris also speaks German, French, English and Spanish. For me this was another first as I had never met them, but Linda had seen them both in Switzerland and in Sweden. As I had built a picture of them based on descriptions, I felt I recognised them too. After finishing the meal Doris said it is just too hot to go out so she suggested we rest a bit and then make an excursion a little later. Kampeki desu!! i.e. perfect. A little snooze in the afternoon is one of the nicest things that can be bestowed upon you.

Linda brought them a couple of books and I gave them one of my last copies of Carpe Diem, the book I put out for my fiftieth birthday.

After the rest we went to a beautiful Kartaus (Chartreuse) Kloster nearby. The cloister is five hundred years old and now fully restored to original condition. The restoration must have cost a fortune. It is beautifully located on a hill side with spectacular views over the rolling landscape. We spent an hour there, looking at all the different rooms, the church, and some art exhibition. Around the grounds were hops and vines for the making of beer and wine. We sat down in the garden café' and enjoyed their own cloister made beer. A cool beer on a very hot summer's day is one of life's delights.

They then drove us a short distance to Stein am Rein, a little picturesque town where time seemed to have stood still for three hundred years. In the approach to the town there is a nice bridge over the river and from the sides of the bridge children were jumping into the river in the warm afternoon sun. It looked so idyllic. We parked the car and walked into the fairy tale looking square with buildings all adorned by art and paintings. Buildings had wooden inlays and were three or four stories. As we approached the main square the music from harmonicas met us and the whole place seemed to sway and dance with the music. We were offered to sit down and have Piccata Milanesa with risotto, which we agreed was a good idea and we had some wine and beer and water to go with it. Having a good meal outdoors in this wonderful environment with happy music filling the air cause me to state: Ich bin glucklich! – I feel happy. We enjoyed the food and the atmosphere for about an hour and then went for a little walk along the Reihn. The weather couldn't have been nicer as it had now cooled down to 28 degrees. The heat spell meant low water levels in the river and also caused problems for the farmers. People were sitting at outdoor cafes and restaurants along the river and it all seemed quite like paradise – wundershon, wonderful, subarashi, underbart. It was all like the Promised Land in the Bible.

We were back at the apartment at around nine o'clock and sat in the dark on the balcony for another hour seeing the sky going from purple to almost black and in the distance the lights from the air planes leaving Zurich airport. As a night-cap we finished off two large bottles of water which seemed the thing to do after such a hot day. After a long chat we all retired to bed. I realised the hosts had given up their bedroom and slept in their respective 'offices.' In these times of Internet communication it seems people like a little office space of their own. We also learnt more things about Sicily. It produces more wine than Australia, it has five million inhabitants and it is two thirds the size of Switzerland (which is about half the size of Scotland) and it is on roughly the same parallel as Tokyo and Auckland, the latter of course being southern hemisphere rather than northern. Switzerland now has about seven million people with very low population growth but strong pressure from immigrants. We discussed immigration and agreed it needs to be structured and orderly to minimize abuse of systems and resentment among locals. The direct democracy in Switzerland with the many referenda may seem ideal but has its problems too. Quite often it is hard to explain the issues fully and there is a lot of questionable ways of winning voter support.

At breakfast we talked about Doris' pilgrimage from Switzerland to Santiago in Spain which distance she had walked by foot over several years and holidays. She now wanted to start some new walking project. This year they had just walked 'Piemonte' in North Western Italy and found it beautiful and quite unaffected by tourism. They were keen to also visit New Zealand, which we tried to encourage. She told us that the friend she had done her long walks with had both her sons in hospital after a serious fall mountaineering, which killed the third member of their group. I was thinking of our son Max and his interest in climbing, and was hoping he would go into some less risky sport. Linda however was confident that he is a very careful and responsible person. After breakfast we were taken to the Frauenfeldt Bahnhof to catch the train to Zurich Flughaven. There Linda checked in with Swiss Airlines, which I understand is nearly broke for the second time, and I checked in at Singapore Airlines before we had some drinks together. We said good-bye for another five to six weeks and I asked her to look after herself and not miss the flight back and of course also to have fun. My flight was half empty so I had three seats to add some comfort to my travel. I slept a few hours after lunch but wasn't really too tired so I just rested rather than slept. As the plane was all dark to help people sleep I didn't want to put my reading lamp on.

As I sat there in the dark I reflected as to what the highlights of my trip had been. <u>For the USA</u> my sailing excursion in Honolulu gave me a real sense of happiness. Seeing old and new friends in four cities was very good as were my walks in Washington and New York City. The trumpeter in Battery Park who played 'Just a closer walk with thee' on my request will remain in my memory. As for Sweden, seeing my mother and son and the light life with old friends on the island in the Baltic stand out as very pleasurable. Going by boat to the outer islets in the Baltic for swimming and a picnic is a very unique experience too. In Scotland the sense of feeling so at ease and at home in a totally new environment was great and a tribute to my hosts John and Haruko. Home is where your friends are. Great times, nice dinners, new restaurants. Boarding Staffa Islands on one of the nicest days of the year was also a heavenly experience. In Zurich I was reminded of how idyllic Switzerland is. Nature is ever present and you don't have to take many steps to see a mountain, a lake and some cows. All seems so clear and high quality. Switzerland offers a very good life style to most of its people. Add to that the good party and our meeting with long standing friends in Frauenfeldt.

Next is Singapore and the return to New Zealand.

SINGAPORE OR TEMASEK

Arrived on schedule and as usual in Singapore I was in my hotel room within one hour from touchdown. The hotel, The Pan Pacific, gave me early check in and late check out at no extra cost. Singapore must be the easiest place in the world to fly in and out of. At the airport, Changi, they have also wisely provided some extra comfort for passengers like free local phone calls, free City tour for transit passengers, and comfortable space and chairs so passengers can have a rest. I think this makes a lot of sense and if I have a choice I would always prefer stop-over in Singapore and that would be my recommendation to other travellers as well. Upon arrival at eight o'clock in the morning I didn't feel like sleeping so I went for a swim in the pool. I have come to really like my swims. I am not a proficient swimmer but the carelessness and weightlessness experienced when swimming lifts my spirits and my soul.

I slid into some slacks and a light shirt and set off to my moneychanger at Tower Five of the Suntec City. I gave him a stack of Hong Kong Dollars, Pounds, Swiss Francs and Yen and in less than a minute he handed me the equivalent in Singapore dollars. I had done my head count before so I knew he was in the right ballpark, in fact it was a bit more than I had calculated. In Japan this exchange would have taken no less than fifteen minutes as in the service industry in Japan, time is of no essence. I shot up to my old office on the fifteenth floor and gave all the girls in the reception a hug. I really loved my time there two years earlier and believe I had a unique relationship to staff. In the bank I saw my relationship managers to regularise my file. Subsequent to 'nine eleven' the 'know-your-customer' requirements have increased in order to prevent money laundering and terrorist money transfers. If files are not in good order the bank faces fines and challenges to its license.

I had lunch with a friend at a Clark Quay restaurant overlooking Singapore River and we compared notes as to recent personal experiences. Walking back from the lunch I bought a few books as well as some ties and a pair of Hush Puppies shoes to replace the ones I had worn out. Then I went for a snooze at the hotel. I slept like a log for two hours but then felt fine again. My dinner appointment was at Singapore Cricket Club, also with a friend from previous visits. The Cricket club is in an old colonial building and very well located at the Padang right in the centre of Singapore. The Padang is a large grass area surrounded by trees and some fine buildings on one side and the river and the sea on the other side – a great location. As we sat down on the veranda, some girls were playing netball right next to us and a bit further off there was a doubles tennis game going. And as the sun is setting, the lights on the many high rises come on and make quite a pretty scene. The general Manager for the Cricket Club is an old friend of mine and he came up and wished me welcome back. Also some of the staff recognised me after four years absence and said they were happy to see me. I am so pleased I kept my membership as I think it is the nicest club I have ever belonged to. Passing through the bar on our way out there was live music from a band of three so we stopped for a beer night cap before saying good bye and taking taxis to our respective abodes.

As I woke up rather late I went directly to the hotel breakfast room to have one of these fantastic oriental breakfasts offering anything anyone could possibly want. I had an omelette made to order, guava juice and fruits and also some pastry with my coffee. Perhaps I over ate a little but overeating in the morning is not so bad. Everything was good except the coffee, which tasted like mud. After breakfast I went for a meeting with the bank's auditor who I happened to run into when visiting the branch. Over a cup of coffee I gave him my account for the state of affairs in Tokyo and Asia. I also said that I think auditing needs to consider a refocus. The single biggest value in a successful company is the intangible good will value. The building and preservation or loss of this value is usually not audited at all for lack of scientific method. However as things like team spirit and customer satisfaction are key to value creation and success, these things should also be addressed by auditors. We had a good meeting and he thanked me for good co-operation for a few years and wished me all the best. I also handed in my old pair of Hush Puppies shoes to the Tower Five shoe-repair shop to have them resoled by the next day.

I needed to hurry back to the Hotel as my friend, Yong Wah, was going to pick me up soon for an afternoon of golf followed by a dinner. He was on the dot in a nice Lexus jeep and we had a warm greeting after about one year's absence. We were going to play golf with his wife Dorcas and his good friend Ken Thai, ex MD of Price Waterhouse, Singapore and now a professional director. First we went to Yong Wah's house as he wanted to show me his drift wood sculptures. His hobby is to collect driftwood and then bring out the art in it by carving.

He showed me some fantastic pieces, really first class art work, one which I thought was a lying Hippo and one that looked like an eel. They were perfectly polished and rounded and when he showed me his work in progress I found this equally impressive.

He said that he had recently been asked to give a presentation at a conference in Brunei and said he would if he could talk about driftwood. The arrangers asked for a summary of the speech but he said he didn't have any and they would have to trust him to make it interesting. So he talked about how you find these weather-beaten crooked pieces along the shoreline. And a bit like people, you have to watch them and think a bit before you know what is really in them. And then you start to mould the piece in a way you think is suitable but more often than not you find as you go that something else comes out. Each piece is different. Yong Wah made it a point to not declare what he had made but left it to the imagination of the spectator. Quite fascinating really and I am sure his presentation would have been worthwhile. Yong Wah is a very agile man in his early sixties and very curious, knowledgeable, understated and kind hearted – a real credit to the human race. His main occupation nowadays is as company director. Each year he spends a few months in Methven, just south of Christchurch, New Zealand, where he has a farm.

Before we went to the golf course he also showed me his garden with many cacti and a Kepel tree which, if you eat its fruit, makes you smell like violet. One sultan down in Indonesia had prohibited his people from eating the fruit, as he wanted to preserve the pleasant violet scent for himself. There was also a drum stick tree and he said the Indians called it 'Muringa' and used it for medicinal purposes, i.e. to reduce high blood pressure. When at the golf course, The Singapore Island Country Club, we were waiting for his wife and daughter to arrive, he talked about reflective listening. He said the Chinese character for listening (old character, and he drew it for me on a piece of paper) has six components: ear – king – ten - eyes – one and heart. In listening the ear must be at the centre, and the one you listen to is the King of that moment, no matter who it is, and you must be as attentive to everything the speaker does as if you had ten eyes and you must listen as if you and the speaker had one and the same heart, i.e. empathetically. This makes a lot of sense and Yong Wah was kind enough to send me the 'listening' character over email later.

The two ladies arrived and we had some lunch and a little later Ken Thai arrived too. The skies looked a bit dark but then Singapore is often like that and it has the highest incidence of lightening of any place on earth. We got into our buggies and drove from hole to hole. Ken had a good day and Yong Wah who has the lowest handicap didn't have such a good day, Dorcas played well and I was a little bit behind, true to my higher handicap. There were lots of monkeys on the course which might be annoying to the locals but which I think quite charming. And we enjoyed ten holes in good weather but then the rain and the siren put an end to the game. It didn't really bother me as I had already had some good fun. I was taken back to my Hotel with instructions to meet a few hours later at The Parnakan Restaurant of the Negara Hotel. I stayed at the Negara Hotel at my first visit to Singapore in 1970 so I knew well where it was, just behind Orchard Tower, off Orchard Road. With two hours to go before dinner I went for another swim. Then I walked over to the City Hall MRT station and took the subway, in order to not find myself stuck in the Hotel's taxi queue when everyone else is looking for a taxi. My own view is that taxi in Singapore is too cheap which results in demand exceeding supply and during peak hours or rain it is very difficult to find one. The MRT which is new, and meticulously clean and efficient, took me to Orchard Road and I walked a bit to get to Orchard Tower. These were the very yards I would normally walk the dog when living in Singapore so a bit of nostalgia crept over me. Going through Orchard Tower to the back I walked passed some tailors and inevitably the tailors hone you in when they see you. They say things like 'where are you from?' or 'Please take my business card' just to make you stop and converse with them. And once you do that they are very good at making you buy something from them. I have learnt by experience not to pay any attention and just walk by.

Parnakan food is Chinese-Malay food, i.e. Chinese cooking with the added spices of Malaysia. It is very good and tasty. We were eight around the table and I had Christina on one side and Yong Wah on the other. Christina was wearing a lovely red silk blouse and I said to her: 'My favourite colour is red'! ' I know', she said, and smiled. Christina is chief financial officer of Keppel Investments where my good friend Chin Hua is CEO and he and his wife Trina were also attending the dinner. Chin Hua and Trina were educated in Auckland so have half their hearts in New Zealand, a bit like my family. Christina brought me two presents, a fine little wine carafe and a CD with no less than six bible versions on it and Chin Hua also brought me a CD with Jazz music. Again I thought myself very lucky to be a guest of some of the loveliest people of Singapore, they all, of course, of Chinese extraction and I being a Swede from New Zealand. We are having this deep wonderful friendship going since a few years back where none of us would leave any stone unturned when it comes to assisting, helping or welcoming the other.

We ate many of the Parnakan dishes and the owner was singing and playing the piano supported by a guitarrist. Yong Wah and I walked up to the musicians to sing a couple of songs – Tennessee Waltz and Boroung Ka Ka Tua. We sang enthusiastically together and none of the other guests left the restaurant so I guess we didn't do too badly. After the dinner Chin Hua's chauffeur took me back to the hotel and I thought back about another great day in Singapore. Next to Sweden and New Zealand I feel more attached to Singapore than any other country. But I also know that I can live and love it anywhere as long as I strike up some good friendships with the people. That is, I believe the cornerstone of the good life. Back at the hotel I read a few pages of Confessions before turning the lights off.

The day of my departure I started out in the pool. My friend picked me up at the hotel and took me to Raffle's Hotel to have breakfast in the Tiffany's Room. My successor in Singapore was leaving his position and felt that his exit hadn't been handled well. I listened to all his comments and advised that at the end of the day the best is to let by-gones be by-gones and in spite of imperfections in management and procedures just try to stay positive and move on in life. The key reason for his frustration is no doubt the bank's reluctance to do any Asian business and that can kill the enthusiasm of anybody. That is the material issue that any future employer can understand and accept. When it comes to issues like poor handling, lack of integrity and honesty of corporate officers, that will always be a more subjective area which is best forgotten an not referred to. The world is full of imperfect people and we mustn't let that bring us down. Anyway, we had a good breakfast and it is good to talk through issues of grief with a good friend and colleague.

Later in the morning I had a coffee with the HR manager of my previous bank and we talked about this and that including mutual acquaintances, many of whom now had left the bank. She asked me if I had any advice on how she could learn more about conflict resolution and motivation. I said there are no easy quick answers but recommended reading, learning and listening to broaden the mind and give more experience and confidence to deal with people and new situations. I also recommended her that when faced with a 'people conflict situation' to ask what the fair and best solution is and then try find the rules to support it rather than just looking for the rules and then apply them. One must try to be more than just an upholder of rules and policy – one needs to show personal judgement and empathy as well. Over time one can see some patterns in most human behaviour and that can be picked up by experience. She is very professional and a good friend and I hope and think she will do well in the bank. I picked up my repaired shoes and returned for my lunch appointment at the hotel.

For lunch I saw another good old friend who took me to the Japanese restaurant of the hotel I was staying in. I had a sashimi meal, which was nice light food compared to the many substantial meals I had been eating. He is an Indian Singaporean and he said his business had been going very well and also that India was doing well. I said to him that I am fascinated by India and how warm and kind people are there. Indians seem so deeply spiritual that I have come to think that all religion originated in India. The one thing I struggle with in India is the class system and the fact that there is such a thing as the untouchables. He said that this structure was relatively new and that is now being phased out. That system is just powerful people formalising their superiority and that has happened in most societies. On another subject he said he felt New Zealand was an attractive option for retirement but that was probably five to ten years away for him. He was on his way to a second holiday in Japan, which he and his family had loved at their first visit. He is a wonderful guy and a good friend who I expect to see in New Zealand from time to time.

We said good bye and I went for a walk before returning to my room to put all my things together. I had time for another swim and thereafter read a little and took a taxi to the airport.

Very efficient check in, perhaps partly due to the flight being only half full. Again I got three seats next to each other so could spread out a little. The flight was uneventful and due to a strong tail wind we landed one hour before schedule.

BACK IN NEW ZEALAND

After landing I bought my three litres of tax-free liquor that NZ allows you to take in. I picked up my bags and was then approached by a customs officer, who asked to see my passport. He asked me where I came from, why I had visited so many countries on this trip and he asked to see my ticket. After about five minutes I had satisfied all his questions and could move on. Perhaps it was my red jacket and straw hat that attracted his attention. He was polite and kind and I didn't mind. Felix came to pick me up and we drove into town. Felix seemed happy. There was a bit of overcast about twelve degrees, which was almost 20 degrees less than I had lived with the last month. But that was ok – New Zealand is coming out of winter whereas Europe is heading into fall. At the house I greeted the dog and the cat and later in the day Andre' when he arrived back from school. I went out on the veranda and saw the palm trees and the ocean in the distance. The garden looked nice with olive and lemon trees, a fig tree and many herbs and flowers. The new PC in my little office was working well and I could check my emails. The house is full of good books and music. I went to bed to catch a few hours of sleep thinking that it is nice to be home again. I felt very happy to think I had such a lovely house and family and so many friends on this Pacific Island that I have chosen to call home. This was the end of my trip around the world. I had walked well over 10,000 steps a day during my extended holiday. Now I would continue to enjoy The Second Lease of life to include much tennis and outdoors, entertaining friendships here and abroad, good wine and food, music and community activity, reading and writing, supporting the children and planning future travels. Life could be worse.

25th August 2003

A taste of paradise

Longitude 85 degrees west! Latitude 45.5 degrees north! There it is in the middle of nowhere. Petoskey, Michigan! 99.9 per cent of the world population never heard of it! All my passion for better life balance suddenly seems totally irrelevant. Here people don't need to dream of Utopia. This is Utopia!

I am sitting at a picnic table by the waterfront looking at all the boats and yachts moored there. It is Saturday morning of July 16, 2005. There is a slight haze but otherwise clear and the wonderful sunny weather seems to continue for ever. It is already 75 degrees at the start of what looks to be another very warm summer's day.

But for the soothing rush of the rapids of the Bear River as it runs into Little Traverse Bay of Lake Michigan there is not a sound this tranquil morning. Every half hour a bell announces the passage of time which otherwise seems to stand still. Although the highway – the US 31 – runs between the boat harbour and the City, any sound of traffic is absorbed by a thick belt of lustrous trees.

Suddenly two people are gliding by in a parachute drawn by a motorboat, which I can see in the distance but cannot hear. Perhaps it is the distance and the slight easterly wind that takes the sound out. Or is it just that Paradise is liberated from obnoxious noise?

On my left side is the 400 ft brake water constructed many years ago by military engineers. It provides a great walk out to the now derelict light house. At the end of the break water by the light house there is a metal ladder allowing access from the water. This was probably put there for emergency purposes a long time ago but now it makes the pier a very popular spot for enthusiasts swimming and diving. At this early our there is no one on this pier.

I decide to go out there and change my shorts for togs to enjoy a morning swim in the clear, lukewarm water. A few minutes later I dive into the lake. Weightless in the water surrounded by beautiful views! I experience a feeling of intense harmony and happiness. Swimming very slowly I can hardly believe the tranquillity of this place. Fate brought me here forty years ago and I am still intrigued over the reason for such good fortune.

As I look up towards the City it looks all green and the only building towering over the green is the spire of St Francis' Catholic Church. The rest of the town is nicely bedded down in the greenery. I cannot but reflect that surely this is the way God meant for man to live in harmony with each other and with nature.

Today the annual Arts in the Park event takes place with over one hundred exhibitors of arts and crafts, putting out their work for inspection and sale. After another swim I will walk up and check it out to enjoy the people, the colours and the buzz of the event. Perhaps I will run into someone I know.

From the Visitor's center brochure I have learnt that the population of Petoskey is around 7,000, which trebles summertime. Visitors are now coming throughout the year as all seasons are nice up here with skiing in the winter and spectacular colours in the autumn and many fine flowers in spring. But the basic population is big enough that there is a genuine feeling of permanence rather than one of just a limited season resort. Life here is real and not superficial.

As the city is located on a slight slope, the "ocean" is visible at the end of all streets that run from east to west. It is not really an ocean but the size of Lake Michigan gives an impression of an infinite body of water. And it is pleasing to the eye and soul to walk down a street with brown brick buildings and plenty of green trees on either side of the street with the vast blue lake at the bottom of the street. Every clear weather evening the blue lake turns golden by the setting sun. Most of the town as it stands today was built in the late 1800´s.

For me this picturesque city has a third dimension as well. The reason for my presence today is the 40th reunion of my high school class, the class of 65. Although I have led a rich and varied life with many high lights, my teen age year here has etched itself beautifully into my memory.

As I am about to do my second swim, two blond and nicely tanned young girls appear in their bikinis. One is Michelle 17 and the other is Lander 11. The six years' age difference between them is not obvious. I ask where they are from and they say Lansing. They giggle and laugh and jump in and out of the water whilst I complete my second swim. I tell them I am writing a few notes about Petoskey and the beautiful morning and that they fit right into the idyll.

The morning haze is lifting. It is getting warmer. Sitting here by the sea with a good book and a note pad and the ability to dive into the water from time to time is rather ideal on a day like this. But as I am a bit of restless soul I will soon move onto the Pennsylvania Park and the arts fair. In so doing I leave the car by the waterfront where there is ample free parking.

Downtown Petoskey is accessible through a tunnel under the highway. On my way to the tunnel I pass the old Grand Rapids Railway terminal building, now restored to former glory and housing the local history museum. The railroad which survived for nearly one hundred years stopped running in the 1960's. There was also steam boat service from Chicago in the early 1900's.

I remember my time in Petoskey forty years ago as quite idyllic and charming, full of learning experiences and excitement. Being an amateur philosopher, I have thought that in order to be able to give love one needs to have received it. Similarly, in order to work for a better world it helps having experienced it personally. I believe Petoskey gave me that insight into what the good life and the great society might look like.

Passing through the tunnel under the highway leads me to Petoskey Street with old brick buildings and many nice shops. I turn left on East Mitchell Street to get to the Art in the Park location. Cars move slowly, always giving preference to pedestrians crossing the road. People of all ages dressed well and colourfully are congregating towards the park. In the park I find particularly the silver smiths interesting, as anything I might buy needs to be small.

Walking around I run into Pattie from my high school class and I think I recognise one more lady but as I am a bit uncertain I refrain from approaching her. Later that day I see her again at our reunion party and tell her I saw her in the park.

What a perfectly lovely morning! What a great experience! I am glad I made the effort of my twenty five hours trip to get here from New Zealand. Slowly I walk back through the tunnel to the marina and my rental car.

Petoskey has elevated my life to a new level. Thank you, Petoskey! May you continue to inspire people the way you have influenced and inspired me!

July 2005

The Wells Tavern

It doesn't get much nicer than this. I and my friend John Watson from Scotland are having a beer at the Wells tavern in the crossing of Christchurch Hill and Well Walk in the heart of Hampstead. This is post a show we have just seen in the little local New End Theatre. It is about 10.30 PM and we each have our pint and some chips in a bowl. Yesterday we ordered half pints and a succession of them so today we went straight for the real stuff. We found a table outdoors and in a summer's night it is particularly pleasant to be outside.

It is very quiet and still. Surrounding the pub there is a park across and many trees. And of course stylish brick buildings from several centuries ago all tastefully designed and maintained to the highest standard. Real estate in this sought after area is now so valuable so no owner can afford not to look after their property well. The roads are narrow and it all feels a bit like a live museum. Nowhere else in the world have I experienced anything quite like it.

There are four or six little tables outdoors and two or three people are sitting at each one conversing. It is all done with low and subdued voices as to avoid disturbing the peaceful evening. John and I are discussing this and that, I can't really remember what. It doesn't matter. We much enjoy each other's company and we haven't seen each other for two years. I tell John that if this place and moment doesn't represent paradise, I don't know what would.

I recall the book 'The Stone Boy' telling the story of some brothers who bought a small farm where rumour had it that a treasure was hidden somewhere. When the brothers had been looking and digging everywhere for forty years without finding anything it dawned on them that it was the farm itself that was the treasure. Sitting here in Hampstead talking to John, I feel that life doesn't get much better.

When listening to a presentation in Tokyo three years prior the speaker quoted Goethe saying: "The best thing in this world is gold. Better still is the sun. But best of all is good human conversation." That is what we are experiencing.

We have corresponded about designing a new religion. Many have tried before us. What drives us is to try to perhaps extract that which is beautiful and uplifting from several religions. That which can unite all, and which in the name of harmony and tolerance doesn't put one model in contrast to another. I think we agree that love is the essence of life but often the magnificence of love gets lost or confused and diffused by overzealous interpreters of religion.

We know we only have three days together so we won't solve the issues here and now but we vow to get together again and progress our thinking. This lack of tangible results of our discussion doesn't matter. The key is that we have met up again and that we are enjoying a precious hour in each other's company with a glass of beer in a beautiful setting.

21st July 2005

Las Vegas....

Finally got there after four successive delays in Auckland and a very tight transfer in L.A. Queuing up for immigration I met a girl from Sydney just ahead of me. She was going to take a bus to San Diego to spend three months there and later to move to London with her boyfriend. She was a little bit large but her olive skin and warm countenance made her quite attractive all the same. It was nice to have someone to talk with for the 45 minutes wait in the meandering queue. As she knows I have a connecting flight she offers me to pass her in the queue. I said thank you but also that I wouldn't dream of passing her. 'I think I'll make it and if I don't there is always another flight.' As we were waiting, they announced on the loudspeaker system that the luggage from our flight would be taken off the conveyor belt to make room for the next flight. Another risk in terms of not finding the luggage!

When it was her turn for immigration I said good bye to her and soon was called to my own counter and got through after being fingerprinted and photographed. I went straight to the off loaded luggage but in spite of checking twice I couldn't find mine. Given that it was only 45 min to my Las Vegas departure, time was precious. I went to the Air NZ desk and said my luggage isn't there. The attendant asked what it looked like and accompanied me to check and after not finding it among the unloaded luggage said 'is that it' and pointed to an item still on the carousel. There it was. Lucky day! I grabbed the case and hurried towards US Air and my next flight.

US Air was at another terminal so I had to go outside and moved with great speed to the next terminal now being down to 30 min from departure. As I walked into the US Air terminal I found myself in the arrivals hall. There were two more levels in the building. I went to the lift and got in with the choice of 'ticket level' or 'departure level'. I choose departure level but once there quickly realized that I couldn't get rid of my suitcase there so changed again to the ticket level. Now there was only 25 min to departure. I gave my suitcase to security and they said please wait until cleared. A few minutes later it was cleared and I was given a boarding pass. 20 minutes to go. Now back to the departure level and looking at two security check queues – one long and meandering and one short with an x-ray looking machine to step through. I asked the staff why this queue was shorter and was told that many people are afraid of the machine and prefer to go through the manual check. So given my time pressure I choose the short line. I took off my shoes and took out my computer from the back pack and emptied my pockets and lined up for the x-ray machine. I passed through without problems but now down to ten minutes to departure time.

I hurried to the gate and got there realizing I had five minutes to spare. I reflected that most people would not have made that connection. I also thought that flying even long legs is easy and the challenge with travel nowadays is delays and connections and changes of terminals and security delays. Every stop adds a lot of risk for stress and things going wrong. I don't mind for myself – having a strong heart and low blood pressure - but I understand that less agile or experienced travellers will find it challenging and cumbersome.

I arrived in Las Vegas after the 45 min flight. The flight was more than full and US Air offered any passenger willing to travel three hours later a round trip ticket to anywhere inside the continental USA in exchange for voluntarily giving up their seats. Upon arrival at the Las Vegas airport I got my transfer to my Alexis Park Hotel. The transfer was very quick as the airport is situated almost in the centre of town. The hotel looked nice and I showered, unpacked, changed clothes and walked 10 minutes to the Strip. The Strip is the ca four miles long Las Vegas Boulevard with all the fancy hotels and casinos. It is totally unique to Las Vegas and it is a bit crazy and tacky but also fun and fascinating. Coming up East Harmon Street by the Harley Davidson Café I made a left turn and walked south to take in all the impressions of the dazzling lights, hotels, shops and many pedestrians.

At this stage around 7 pm the sun was setting. I ran into a half price ticket booth and after asking for options decided on the Crazy Horse Show at the MGM hotel and casino complex with show start at 8 PM. This was a few blocks further away but I got there in time for me to have a pre show beer at the casino bar. Even at the bar stools there are gaming opportunities for patrons by electronic boards for each patron.

The show consisted of 10 – 15 beautiful girls elegantly but lightly dressed performing various sensual dancing numbers. This was mixed with film pictures from the original Crazy Horse shows in Paris celebrating the beauty of female form. The audience was mostly couples sitting around small tables with a drink. I thought it was very tastefully and well done and on balance a good value cabaret experience. I walked out feeling I had been well entertained and happy to be on this trip and holiday visiting a place I have heard much about but never visited.

At this stage I had been up for perhaps 24 hours so I just had a quick bite at the Scottish restaurant and took a taxi back to my hotel. The hotel had advised to not walk at night but take a taxi for security reasons. Subsequent evenings I walked back anyway, deciding that at the early hours that I would normally return the crooks and hoodlums weren't operative yet. I think it is after midnight and especially in the small hours of the morning and particularly if drunk that the risk starts to increase. Since I rarely last to after 11 PM and don't drink much and always am very cautious I normally feel rather safe. Back at the hotel I fell into bed and slept like a log for ten hours.

The next morning I woke up just before ten and I can't remember when I last slept that long. I showered and made a cup of coffee after figuring out how the coffee maker worked. I put on a pair of shorts and my red polo shirt and wore my black hush puppies without socks. I noticed what a nice pool the hotel had and regretted not taking any swimming gear. At the front desk I asked for directions to the nearest shopping centre and was told it was about two miles away along Flamingo Avenue. 'The main shop there is a Target. What's your transport?' 'I am walking. Half an hour's walk is just an invigorating way to start the day.' Very few people walk to get anywhere in the land of the automobile. He said it could get a bit hot to which I responded that I grew up in a cold country and enjoy the heat.

I walked with my shoulder bag under the clear blue sky with virtually no other pedestrians and only light traffic. I was warm but not hot and felt terrific. In less than half an hour I was there and found the Target. Not many people shopping on a Tuesday morning in a suburban Las Vegas shopping centre. I found the blue jeans shelves and realized I would have to try a few to gauge my size. I looked around and could see neither people nor changing rooms, so I just dropped my shorts on the floor and tried a pair of 32/32's. 32 waist was just a little tight so I looked for the next up and at first I saw only 34's but two more full inches would be too much. I seemed to remember that they stepped up two inches at a time but then I saw a pair of 33/32 and they fit perfectly. I put the Wrangler Jeans at incredible $ 17.95 in my shopping basket and put my shorts back on. My continued shopping included some large T-shirts and a pair of soft gym shorts that I figured also could serve as swimming trunks in the afternoon. After putting three or four other little things in my basket I went to the check out and was amazed at the $ 46 total for all the chosen merchandize.

I asked if there was any book shop nearby and was given directions to a Barnes and Nobel book shop five minutes away. I found the book shop and asked the knowledgeable shop assistant for a few books I had read about in The New York Book Review the week prior. Unfortunately they didn't have any of the three books I asked for. They were probably too hot off the press. But when I asked for the book my wife wrote 'Astrid and Veronika' she said she had five copies.

The book which was written in New Zealand two years earlier was working itself around the world in an amazing way. The first estimate was that, being a first novel, it would sell 1,500 copies in New Zealand and that would be it. Now it had sold 60,000 copies in Sweden and 10,000 in New Zealand and 90,000 copies in the USA. It will also be published in Holland, UK, Germany and Italy this year and I have been negotiating with Japan. I bought 20 % of the stock (one of the books) as I felt it so fantastic that even a place like Las Vegas would carry a book written as a university paper by my wife in New Zealand. It would be a nice gift to Linda's mother in Sweden.

Leaving the book shop I spotted a sign saying 'Great Salads' and as it was now noon I thought that would be a nice place to take my lunch. The $8 salad buffet including ham and pasta, soup and ice cream was great and tremendous value. The girl who brought the drinks looked nice and friendly but when she turned I noticed she had a bottom 2-3 times normal and I couldn't but help reflect that it is strange how sometimes extra weight concentrates in only one spot. After looking after me well and asking me several times if I was happy I thought I would leave her with a good tip to recognize her commendable conduct and effort.

This restaurant experience brought back a memory from attending Harvard Business School for a summer finance course some years ago. One of my co-attendants when I asked him what business he was in said: 'We are in bathroom china and one of the few companies that like to hit new bottoms every month.' Another one of my co-students was treasurer of Northwest Industries. Understanding that 'Northwest' was a conglomerate I asked him what their main product was. He responded 'male underwear.' Thinking this was a little unimpressive for a large corporate I asked him what the future might hold for the company. His response was: 'Longer term we hope to get into female underwear!'

Just outside the restaurant there was an Italian cloths shop and I went in to look at a new jacket. I was the only customer in the shop and the keeper called out to me from the back of the shop – 'What do you want?' 'I'd like to buy a jacket.' 'Is it for you?' 'Yes!' – then to my astonishment he said: 'I can sell you nothing – you are too little.' 'Not even a tie?' 'No, not even a tie!' This was not only a sign of giant America but the shop was in fact a tall boy's shop. I was surprised and perhaps a little amused thinking that not only a tie could he sell me. When later in my hotel room I noticed that the 'large' size I had picked for T-shirts was too large for me although in New Zealand 'large' would fit me like a glove. But in America I am obviously merely 'Medium.' Nothing wrong with being 'Medium' per se! On TV later I heard that 6.2 million Americans are now morbidly obese up from 4 million five years ago. The definition here is being more than 100 lbs overweight.

I left the shop and started the walk back to my hotel. Having bought a few postcards I looked for stamps in a shop and was again reminded that the US is unique in charging a premium for stamps. The 75 cents stamps I needed could be obtained for one dollar each. But then all countries have their peculiarities. In Stockholm 'public' toilets can only be accessed by paying 75 cents equivalent. New Zealand has neither of these anomalies. Close to my hotel I walked past a bus stop with two girls waiting for the bus. They asked where I was from and said they were visiting from California. 'Did I need company?' I said thank you, but no thank you, and continued to my nearby hotel. I reflected that Nevada and Las Vegas is just across the border from the Greater Los Angeles area and Reno in from San Francisco and gambling and stage shows are not the only forms of entertainment on offer for visitors. Garments were on sale everywhere with the text: Las Vegas – Sin City.

Back at the hotel I put on the gym shorts I just bought and went to the hotel pool. The large pool had about 25 reclining deck chairs but only one other couple there. I rested a bit in the therapeutic sunshine, read a little in my book, 'The Audacity of Hope' by Barack Obama, and went for a swim in the cool but clean and refreshing water. I managed to squeeze a brief nap in after my pool visit before the evening program.

For the evening I had booked tickets for the show 'Mystere' by Cirque Du Soleil at Treasure Island. I got mid-priced tickets @ $82 including tax and having seen this circus company twice before in Singapore and Auckland my hopes and expectations were high. Treasure Island is one of the great hotels cum casino and theatre complexes on the northern part of the Strip. On my way there I walked past Venice with canals and gondolas and also Paris with a half size Eiffel Tower, all in glittering lights. At the Treasure Island I had a pre show dinner at the Vietnamese restaurant.

Entering the Theatre people were already laughing entertained by a 'jester' walking around doing different pranks to and with the audience. Cirque Soleil is a total experience devoid of any low points and the very opposite to boredom. The show started with people coming down from the ceiling and a small orchestra playing and a couple of professional singers to provide back drop for all the performances. These are either 'jester-like' or displaying the utmost of breath taking acrobatic skills. Regularly people from the audience are drawn into the shows as well. Before arriving in Las Vegas it had been recommended to me by friends who had been there recently and I did find the show a true highlight. Recommended viewing!

After the show I walked the Strip southward and stopped at a few casinos for a couple of beers and to try my luck at the slot machines. My bets were quite limited as I am well familiar with the fact that on balance the house wins and the odds are stacked against the players. Perhaps a bit like religion you really need to believe in it for it to work for you. It is a little strange, materialistic and perhaps tacky to have acres upon acres of gambling rooms with tens of thousands of one armed bandits. But for a one time visit there is a degree of amazement as well. Although each time I sat down I was winning at some stage I always continued until my initial limited bet was lost, which perhaps is the experience of most players. I learned from a tour guide that Las Vegas should really be called Lost Wages. Chances of winning big are miniscule and chances of losing your bets are major.

At 6.30 AM the next morning I was dressed and waited outside the hotel for my prearranged pick up for the Grand Canyon Tour. Always being on time is just part of my upbringing and nature. No pick up at 6.40AM. Knowing there was a flight to catch @ 7.40AM I got a bit restless @ 6.50AM and asked the bell captain to please call the operator – Pappillon Tours.

He got the message that for some reason there would be no pick up and could I take a taxi to Boulder City airport. The bell captain found a taxi and told the aged driver to please drive to Boulder City airport. The driver said that is a long way, I don't know the way, and who is going to pay for it? After a few phone calls he read out to me the road description and was convinced the Tour operator would pay the fare. He started the long drive and I noticed he drove just a little faster than the speed limit.

He told me he was from Persia and had lived in USA for 32 years. He married a Turkish lady and they moved to their new country. He still had quite an accent and spoke a little un-distinctively as a sign of old age. He told me he was 75 years old and that he had a son who is a doctor. The reason why it took a while to get the instructions for directions he said is that 50 % of the people out here can't tell the difference between north and south. Another 50 % of people wake up every morning after a night of substance abuse, drugs or alcohol.

This makes the taxi business a little more challenging. I am not sure if he meant that 100% of the people are 'nutty' or if the two halves of population he mentioned were fully or partly overlapping. Together we navigated the way to Boulder Airport and got there 7.35 AM with a small margin before departure. I thanked the driver and wished him well and saw that he got paid. I also told the lady behind the counter that it was disappointing that the pick-up didn't work and that no-one called me to say they wouldn't be coming. If it wasn't due to my own initiative I would have missed the Grand Canyon Tour which was the purpose of my long trip. Without apologizing she said she understood I was disappointed.

Five minutes later we were airborne for Arizona and Grand Canyon. It was a small 16-seater plane with big windows for maximum visibility. We flew over the Hoover Dam and were told that Boulder City grew out of the barracks for the workers building the dam. Boulder City is the only city in Nevada where gambling is prohibited. And they claimed that the Hoover Dam was the biggest construction job in human history. I wasn't sure I believed that, thinking The Great Wall of China must be bigger. We were told that the concrete was poured 24 hrs a day for two years to complete the dam. That is enough to build a two lane highway across the entire USA.

The purpose of the dam was to regulate the water flows down stream and to generate hydroelectric power. It was built during the depression 1930-1931 and was finished two years ahead of schedule at a total cost of $49 million. Today that is no more than the annual compensation of successful Wall Street bankers but in those days of deflation and depression a dollar was a lot of money. We continued to fly over what looked like desert. Suddenly the landscape changed as we got to these huge rocks and valleys with the Colorado River at the bottom.

We landed in Tusayan (Indian for 'little or no water') in Arizona on a high plateau of 7,000 ft. That is higher than the highest point of Sweden and thus it was much cooler than in Boulder or Las Vegas. I thought it might be cold so I wore a t-shirt under my shirt and also brought a light jacket. I should have brought some socks also because my bare feet in my shoes got a bit cold. We were met in Tusayan by a jolly driver who said he felt his job was a laugh and the day he didn't feel that he would resign. He would take us to two vantage points in

Grand Canyon National Park. We passed two types of trees growing in the park – Ponderosa Pine and Utah Juniper. He said there were plenty of animals and he asked us to look out particularly for Elk, Coyote, Mountain Lion and some smaller animals. We did see a roving Coyote on the road looking like a somewhat downsized German Shepherd.

After 30 minutes drive we got to one of the look outs with stunning views over the mighty Grand Canyon. We were standing 1,500 meters above the river and there were rocks and buttes as far as the eye can see. I brought my little digital camera but the depth and grandiosity of it all would not be possible to capture on camera. From information signs I learned that the Colorado River is 1450 miles long. It has an average with and depth of 300ft and 40 ft respectively with 160 rapids, some with 10 ft big waves. Nowadays 5,000 people a year make the trip of the full river in what looks like safe rafts but it would still be very dramatic and challenging and wet! The trip from source to the Pacific Ocean takes ten days. As demand for this trip exceeds allowed throughput one needs to apply early. Next to the river there was a green belt but otherwise very dry and barren.

After half an hour's stop, the driver took us to a second vantage point to take in the amazing view again. Trying to take it all in I suddenly saw a parallel to religion or more precisely the bible to what unfolded in front of me. You can either focus on the beautiful mountaintops or the life giving river 1,500 meters below. Or on the sharp steep sides in between! When I read the Bible a few years ago I captured everything beautiful, everything elevated, all the mountaintops. It would have been equally easy to look only at the sharp and arid declines that suggest that nothing can grow here, neither man, nor plant or animal. Breathtaking experiences require contrasts. If it was all high plateau or deep river flat, the beauty would be absent. But because of the parts that are not pretty but very dramatic, the beautiful parts stand out and the total impression is amazingly spectacular. Much of what the Bible says is atrocious and despicable, but perhaps the darker chapters help show the inspiring parts even more clearly. My preference is to see the beauty and perhaps try to appreciate the opposites as necessary to help us see and focus on that which is divine and beautiful.

Later when in Sweden I similarly reflected on the uninspiring, dull wet and cold weather and how it is very unappealing, but the effect of the first warm summer days on plant and people is unique and impossible to achieve in a place which is pleasant and lovely all the time. And even the welfare society which tries to take away all risks and lows also deprive many of the chance of experiencing achievement and satisfaction of a job well done.

The Grand Canyon was the goal for this stopover in USA and I did feel that these views and the sense of eternity looking out over this spectacular landscape had a profound effect on me, well worth the effort of getting here off the beaten track. A few years earlier I saw an advertisement by 'Emirate Airlines' with the question: 'When was the last time you did something for the first time?' It reminded me of the need to do something new regularly in order not to stagnate and be overwhelmed by routine. Later on this trip I planned to go to Nashville based on the same thinking. My son Max went there and said it was terrific. Later in the year I plan to visit Ho Chi Minh City to learn more about life in Vietnam. And of course Linda, my wife, is experiencing the trip of her life, travelling through USA to promote and talk about her first novel which has now sold in excess of 150,000 copies. I am so pleased her artistic talent, which was always there, has manifested itself in this spectacular way.

Standing at the edge of Grand Canyon I could see horse tracks as people could rent mules to get down to the bottom of the great rift and back, without exhausting themselves. These were one or two day tours. There are also opportunities for shorter raft trips on the river and to go by helicopter up and down the gorges. After a couple of hours of absorbing the magnificence of Grand Canyon we had lunch and watched the Grand Canyon movie on a huge screen with dramatic pictures from helicopters and rafts.

Among my fellow tour participants I befriended a lady from London and a couple from Frankfurt. There were quite a few Germans in our group and also English, Australian and some Spanish speaking. In Las Vegas Spanish is frequently heard in the streets and restaurants. They all seemed very nice and friendly.

In the afternoon we flew back over Grand Canyon and did it all backwards and landed safely in quite strong winds at Boulder airport. The driver of the van that took us back was a worried soul and he kept complaining about how difficult it was for him to figure out in which order to best deliver us back to our hotels. He also worried that traffic would cause great delays. Like most worries in this world, these were unfounded. The traffic was no problem and half of us alighted in the centre of the strip anyway to make his task a lot easier. I said good bye to my friends and went to the half price ticket booth and got a ticket for an eight o'clock show at The Stratosphere.

After an hour's nap at my hotel I took a taxi to The Stratosphere, located at the northern most end of the Strip. I heard the taxi driver had an accent so I asked him where he was from and he said Hungary. I asked him if Hungary was better off now post communism and Russia. He said lots of problems remain. Everything is about money and many are unhappy. Most state assets have been sold out. I suggested that at least people could travel freely now. He said that before they weren't allowed but now they couldn't afford it. And Russia's influence even before 1989 was pretty limited anyway. He felt that the divide was increasing with big business on the one side and the hard working lowly paid people on the other. He felt that was the case in America as well. I said a lot of Hungarians came to Sweden in 1956 which he knew and he said he had tried Sweden for himself but found the weather and cost level equally depressing. I suggested that that was a good reason for me to live in New Zealand. Thirteen dollars later we arrived at the Stratosphere, I paid him $ 15 and said good bye and wished him good luck.

I took a pre show dinner at The Stratosphere. The show was 'American Superstars' with impersonators of Elvis, Britany Speers, Michael Jackson and two others. It was all very well done and I thought the 'others' best because I weren't familiar with the originals and it thus gave me a new experience. Overall quite lively and well put together performance. As this was my last night in Las Vegas I decided to walk the three miles along the glittering Strip back to my hotel. I stopped for a beer and a little gambling but was back in bed before midnight with a wake-up call for 7.30 AM for my flight to LA.

The flight from Las Vegas was an hour late but that still left me with a 2.5 hrs in LA for transfer. The Lufthansa flight was also an hour late so there was no problem. Passengers were offered 600 Euro and free hotel if they volunteered to take the next day's flight. Obviously the flight was over booked. I couldn't see if there were any takers.

On my way over the Atlantic I saw the film Rocky Balboa about the retired boxer making a come-back. From that film I picked up these lines which stuck with me:

"Let me tell you something you already know. The world ain't all sunshine and rainbows. It is a very mean and nasty place and it will beat you to your knees and keep you there permanently if you let it. You, me, or nobody is gonna hit as hard as life. But it ain't how hard you hit; it's about how hard you can get hit, and keep moving forward. How much you can take, and keep moving forward. That's how winning is done. Now, if you know what you're worth, then go out and get what you're worth. But you gotta be willing to take the hit, and not pointing fingers saying you ain't where you want to be because of him, or her, or anybody. Cowards do that and that ain't you. You're better than that!"

I thought my three days in Las Vegas had been a fun diversion. Now I was looking forward to seeing friends and family in Sweden before my next new experience in Nashville and meeting up with Linda in Washington and New York. Two days after New York I would attend a concert by Auckland Chamber Orchestra, of which I am the chairman, and life would be back to normal. I am lucky to enjoy a pretty nice and appealing normal life.

13th April 2007

Nashville...

Memphis you can skip but Nashville is special. That's what Max, my son in Sweden, told me a year ago. I arrived Saturday 28th April 2007 after a detour from New York. The airport was clean and without the exhausting business and overload of many major airports. Got my bag, found a taxi and 20 min later I checked into the Broadway Holliday Inn. I was told it was a busy week end as on Saturday the annual Nashville Marathon would take place with twenty or so bands along the route. All smooth and efficient so far! The flight was four hours late out of New York but having a good book to read I didn't allow that mishap to influence my good humor. Anger dwells only in the bosom of fools. After a shower and a change of clothes I was out in the lovely spring afternoon before three o'clock as I had also gained one hour by the time difference.

Clean wide streets and a clear blue sky and half a mile's walk to the part of Broadway where it all happens. Even at this hour in the early afternoon there was live music in every bar and restaurant and lots of people in and around the venues. It looked and felt like one big party with orderly and well behaved people.

I stepped into the 'Legends Corner' and the famous 'Tootsies' and the music was full on. I didn't feel like starting drinking so early so I walked out and watched the street life and enjoyed the balmy sun. Just as I wondered where I could buy myself a cowboy hat I stumbled upon a 'hats, boots and leather' shop. I wanted a nice rather quiet hat, realizing that too fancy a hat would look out of place anywhere but here. I found one that fit me, my taste and my budget and walked out of the shop with a smile almost as big as the hat, ready to try one of the bars. After a beer and listening to three or four songs I strolled around a bit more, browsing some of the shops.

For the evening I had bought tickets to the 'Grand Ole Opry' in Opryland twenty minutes drive away. I walked back to the hotel to get ready for the evening and show. After checking emails and a bit of a wash I took a cab to Opry Land. It proved to be a huge complex with a 4200 room hotel, shopping malls and the 4,500-seat Opry Theatre. At the entrance of the theatre there was a good sounding quartet playing country music.

The show was divided into five half hour slots with a new band for every slot. People screamed and whistled at some of the artists that came in suggesting to me that the person was well known and perhaps a star. But to me they were all new and unknown. I have to admit that the musicians were very accomplished, displaying lots of skills and enthusiasm. Several popular performers looked really old, like 75+ years. One of the nice things about this place is that slim or fat, young or old, smart or shaggy no-one seems to notice or care. The key is to have fun and be happy, using catchy music as a catalyst. After a long day and having moved through a lot of time zones coming across from Europe I felt a little tired and I left fifteen minutes before the end when the several thousand audience would be out there looking for a taxi. I found the taxi I needed to take me back downtown to have my dinner.

At this stage, Broadway and the side streets were teeming with people and some of the restaurants had thirty minutes wait to be seated. After a while I found a nice looking little place on 3rd Ave South. I ordered a Miller Lite beer on tap and a fillet mignon and enjoyed the entertainment. This time there were two young people – a guy playing the guitar and a girl singing – both performing to the highest standards. I got my beer and steak sitting on a high chair in my new Cowboy hat. I felt good about life and my lot. The staff looked after me so well – I was asked at least five times if I was happy and had my glass replaced as soon as it was empty. I left about an hour later and walked the streets for a while, inhaling the unique atmosphere before returning to the hotel. It had been a long day and I was ready to fold.

The next day, Sunday, I was out on the streets at 8 AM after my ordinary morning routine including a good breakfast. The sun was rising and it was obviously going to be another gorgeous day. At this hour not much was open and streets were deserted but for a few homeless people asking by passers for spare change.

I stopped by the Second Ave Ticket Booth finding it closed as I expected and decided to go back a little later. I continued to the riverfront park which looked really well kept and pretty in the early morning sun. After a while I found a spot and sat down to just bask in the glory of the morning, looking at the Cumberland River and finishing my book. Four impressive bridges were visible from where I sat as well as the new football stadium across the river. As I looked up from my book at one stage a huge barge passed on the river. The morning was very quiet and tranquil with few sounds to be heard.

After about an hour by the river I walked north and had a look at Fort Nashborough. The signs there reminded me that it was just over 200 years ago this was frontier country with frequent battles and other hardships. It also struck me how rich and fertile the land looked and how the Indian tragedy in giving it up corresponded to the fortune and good luck of those who came instead. I turned left and once again headed towards the ticket booth. The 10 AM trolley tour around town was full but there was a 10.30 opportunity to join a lunch cruise on The General Jackson wheel steam ship on the Cumberland River. The Cumberland starts in the Appalachian Mountains and runs to the Ohio River which in turn flows to the great Mississippi. I decided to join the cruise as I couldn't really roam the streets all day long. The pickup coach went to three or four hotels before arriving at the ship a little before noon.

The bus driver was about 65 years old and a local farming son. He talked about the hardship of small farming and how his father was a share cropper until the son was 16 when there was enough money to buy a farm. I asked him about farm prices and he said it starts at about one million dollars and yields are low and don't allow for much debt. The driver told us that Nashville is the capital of Tennessee since 1843 and has about 600,000 inhabitants. Including the surrounding counties the population reaches about 1.5 million. The bigger city, Memphis is about 215 miles or three hours drive away. During the civil war Tennessee was the last to leave the union and the first to rejoin. Business in the area is pretty good, the biggest sectors being healthcare, banking and finance, government, tourism and music with healthcare employing about 100,000 people. Tourism and music employ 20,000 and 14,000 respectively. The tourism numbers struck me as a little low but sometimes it is difficult to fully calculate all the effects and implications of a business sector like tourism. He also said that many foreign firms had chosen to place their American head quarters in the area. We drove by the head offices of Nissan and Bridgestone, both own by the Japanese. No less than 15 Nashville companies have annual turnover in excess of $ 1.5 billion. Average annual family income in Nashville is $ 80,000 nearly twice that of surrounding counties. The driver said he doubted that number as most new jobs seemed to be rock bottom McDonalds and Wall mart jobs.

As the day before was the annual Nashville Marathon run several people on the bus and subsequently on the riverboat had come for that event. I suggested to a few exhausted and sore runners that if you want to go 25 miles it is smarter to use a bicycle as running that far regularly will wear your joints down. Many of course had made their participation a fundraising event which provided a better motive to go through all the agony. Although the area looked pretty flat one senior runner said that wasn't the case at all but it felt more like San Francisco.

Upon entering the ship we had to join a big line and as we progressed in it the reason for the delay was that every individual or couple were photographed steering the mighty General Jackson. A bit tacky perhaps but contrary to my custom I actually went along with it, splashed out, and bought the framed picture for $ 20.

True to my nature I struck up conversations with people in the line and later on the boat. When asked if I was there on holiday or business I explained about my wife's book tour around the US and how I had come to support her in Washington and New York also finding time for my own detours to Grand Canyon and Nashville. As I said her book was selling like hot cake around the world, inevitably people asked about the book causing me to write the name of the book and the author on the back of my business card. I must have been through that process at least 15 times on my trip and if each of those buys a book and convinces ten people to the same and then they convince ten and then ten again – another 20,000 books would be added to the current sales of 170,000. 'Penguin America' had said 'Astrid and Veronica' is a word of mouth book and I was certainly trying to put my mouth behind it.

On board the ship I got a cold Budweiser from the front deck bar and sat down on an empty chair at a table with a couple from Wisconsin and we got to know each other quite well during the 20 minutes that preceded the lunch call. We discovered that we both had had lunch at Al Johnson's Swedish restaurant in the Door County in northern Wisconsin. It was a glorious spring day and the big white steamer moved soundlessly down the Cumberland River which banks were lustrously green and again I was reminded that God's Promised Land surely couldn't look any nicer than this. Paradise is here and now, it can't get much better. After a little while of absorbing all these idyllic impressions we were instructed to go down into the main dining hall for lunch and the big show. I estimated the number of people there to 400, quite a big room and group. As it was well organized it all flowed pretty effortlessly. I asked a lady if she was in the queue. She said yes and asked where I was from as no one around here uses the word queue. I said New Zealand and she said she was from southern California outside Los Angeles. My wife's aunt lives in that area too, in Hemet, California. 'You're kidding?' She couldn't believe it as that was exactly where she lived. Small world! So that was all quite exciting and I ended up giving her too my card with the name of Linda's book on the back.

The food looked good and I brought it to my table # 2 just next to the stage. The other people at the table were the ones from my pick up coach. There were two or three pretty girls there but I ended up sitting next to their mothers or grand-mothers. This didn't worry me and I established that one was from Orlando and one from Detroit so I talked about Florida and the elections and storms with the one and about my year in Michigan with the other. And I also mentioned joining my wife's book tour after Nashville. I asked the lady from Orlando and her daughter if they weren't having desserts. They said no – to many calories. After inspecting the dessert table I decided to take their cue and refrain from the indulgence myself and got myself another beer instead. Returning to the table I said to the ladies – thank you for helping me avoid a meaningless dessert with brown cake, brown sugary sauce and whipped cream. Who needs it anyway?

The Tim Watson show started at 1.15 PM and was well delivered by another group of accomplished musicians. Tim himself played the violin but said he never learned to read scores of music. He played the violin behind his back and under one leg. At one stage he invited a lady from the audience to play with him and she held the bow and he played loud and energetically by moving the violin over the bow. Amazing skill level! His jokes were a bit drawn out and some I had heard before but he himself as well as the audience seemed to appreciate them. He was also praising the veterans, the president and God and although I considered that slightly out of place, I realized it may have audience appeal in this 'red neck' country. As all looked pretty happy I wasn't going to lose my good mood. The issues are complex and the front line soldiers in Iraq (or earlier in Vietnam) didn't create the conflict. I only hope that more Americans understand that for every American casualty there are ten Iraqi, and more often than not, innocent women and children. I hope for more love and less hate and fear. One quote from Harry S Truman comes to mind: 'The only thing you can be sure to prevent by war is peace.'

After the show I returned to upper deck and just enjoyed the beautiful day and the calm river with a few leisure boats passing us. The ship docked and we all got back to our coaches. The driver said he would take us anywhere we wanted to be dropped off. A sign above the driver said: 'Gratuities are not against company policy!' The driver also told us a joke: This woman in Canada drove to the liquor store to buy her husband a quart of Whisky and on her way back she picked up an Indian lady hitch hiker. After a while the passenger asked what the driver had in the bag between her legs. She responded 'A quart of whisky for my husband.' And the Indian lady nodded and said 'that seems like a good trade to me.'

Before they left the bus, the beautiful daughter of the old lady from Orlando leaned over to me and asked about my wife's book and if there is a web site. I wrote the name of the web site on the card and gave her. She looked at the front of the card and as she didn't have her glasses she asked: what do you do? So I said I have a few directorships.

I read and play tennis, drink wine and travel. She laughed and said: 'that's the kind of job I have been looking for.' When the two of them left the bus the driver thanked me over the speaker system for making her laugh. Up to that moment she had looked totally stern and totally disinterested in human contact.

The driver asked me for my hotel but I said I was happy to get off anywhere downtown as we're all living in the city. We were let off on Broadway close where we had boarded the bus. As the fine weather continued I decided to take a walk on the Shelby Pedestrian Bridge across the river to get a good view of downtown from the crest of the bridge and from the other side. I sat down on the grassy slope down to the river bank for about an hour, tending to some notes and enjoying the glorious day. The sun reflected in the river and it all looked like a big streak of gold. I walked back heading for Tootsies thinking that on a Sunday afternoon there should be ample room for me to enjoy the music and atmosphere at the icon establishment. All around Tootsies there are similar places like 'Legends Corner,' ' Second Fiddle', 'Blue Grass Inn', and 'Honky Tonk Heaven'.

At five o'clock pm this Sunday in late April the music at Tootsies was flowing. I found a small table with a high stool, ordered a beer, and took in the music and character of the place. On the right next to the entrance door, three musicians were playing some great music. The venue is about 5 yds times 15 yds with a long bar along the left side. Two beautiful young petite blonds were running the bar generating lots of revenue and tips I'm sure. A bottle of beer is $ 3.25 and you are offered one dollar back and the balance goes into the tip jar. The ceiling is all black with three equally black fans for cooling the air. There are also four large speakers in the ceiling to make sure that the sound is spread evenly throughout. People are sitting on the bar stools or just standing around with their drink. Further in there are some shelves with purple T-shirts, caps and the like for sale to the patrons needing some evidence that have been there. Next to the T-shirts there are three vintage motor cycle helmets. Everybody looks really happy with their drink and chatting – some dancing - and listening to the performance.

Now a young girl is joining the band. One of the Patrons tells me she is 'Krystal Marie' which I have no reason to doubt. Her voice is outstanding and with her three songs she spellbinds the excited audience. Then she takes the tip bucket and walks around to get it filled up and all seem to contribute some funds. I tell her she is a great singer and she smiles and the world smiles. The musicians are three guys all looking and dressed quite differently cherishing as it seems freedom and diversity. Some red neon lights and a Miller Lite neon sign bring a low light to the room. Everyone of notoriety has been here and the right wall is covered with old photos of when so and so visited Tootsies. Perhaps 40 people in the room quite comfortably whereas the night before there was quite a line of people waiting to get in. A new player around 65years of age steps up on the stage and says: 'I will show you how good these guys are by playing a tune they never heard before.' And with a bit of a trembling start all the players are into it after a little while and even do their solo parts to this new tune totally in harmony with each other. Another surprise is that smoking is allowed - one of the last bastions. Of course I don't smoke but I am not too bothered if others do.

After half an hour the band takes a break and I move on to 'Legends Corner.' Here is a formidable guitarist 'Chris Casello' a base and a drummer, all very professional. The guitarist says between tunes that there ought to be a $ 5 cover charge to support the musicians but there is none and patrons are encouraged to consider this when asked for a contribution. After fifteen minutes this band too takes a break and I walk out after putting my fiver in the bucket. I walk back to my hotel which I left eleven hours earlier. I check my email and squeeze in an hour's nap before going out to look for a place to eat dinner. I check a few places but some are too bar-like and some too restaurant-like and I prefer something in between so find myself returning to the same place as the evening before. In a bar only, the food may not be great, and in a formal restaurant, you'd rather eat in the company of one or more friends.

The staff recognize me and attend to me right away – a T-bone steak and a glass of Pinot Noir. The wine is delivered right away with a glass of water. Over the bar counter there is a silent TV showing a game of total boxing, i.e. also kicking and hitting each other lying down. Quite atrocious really but I have a hard time taking my eyes off the debacle. The steak arrives and I order a Budweiser to go with it and find myself enjoying another great meal. The waiter tells me that tonight is Karaoke night but after a few songs by a good female singer it's time to leave. The night is balmy and calm except for the music seeping through the bar doors and open windows. Two days into it I reflect that it has been a worthwhile and fun experience and I return to the hotel, ready to fly to Washington DC the next day. An old friend at the World Bank has invited me to stay with them for a couple of nights. I am very much looking forward to seeing him again and to discuss some world issues. And it will be exciting to meet up with Linda to hear firsthand about her 'road show' across the nation.

7th May 2007

Post Scriptum.

I spent one day walking around the Mall in Washington DC. Crossing Arlington Memorial Bridge I walked up to the Lincoln Memorial and again read the inscriptions on the wall. The Gettysburg address I am well familiar with but the other inscription from Abraham Lincoln's second inaugural speech I hadn't read in detail. These words stuck with me as suitable guidance for mankind: 'with malice toward none, with charity for all.' I also looked at the Korean Memorial as well as the Monument of the Second World War. The first was striking whereas the second was mostly grand and impersonal. It is a fine balance I think between remembering heroic sacrifice and glorifying war. Sometimes it seems that all we are proud of is wartime exploits. Most people engaged in war are losers. War is always a sad tragedy for those who have to engage in it. People gave their lives for peace and not for more war.

After being taken out to dinner by the Adams, my host family, the night before, I had lunch with Jim Adams again and also my other long time World Bank friend, Tom Tsui. For dinner I went out on the metro Red Line to Shady Grove where my old class mate Linda picked me up and showed me around their farm a little further out. It was nice to talk to her forty-two years after we graduated from High School.

And then I met up with Linda, my wife, and joined her whirlwind book tour in Washington DC and New York with dinners, receptions and signings. Her recent book career is almost beyond comprehension in terms of her great and spectacular success. I am very impressed with her achievement and sincerely happy for her.

Saigon...

Stepping out of Hotel Rex in central Saigon at noon wondering a little bit where to head. Equipped with the hotel map my intent is to stroll for a few hours just taking in atmosphere and street life. But less than twenty steps away from the hotel entrance a man approaches me and says he will show me Saigon on his motorbike. 'Drive slow and careful' he says. I hesitate a little, as it deviates from my plan but then think it perhaps a good idea and I can always cover the immediate vicinity later. Wearing shorts and a my red short-sleeve Hawaiian shirt, black hush-puppy loafers, a beige Singa Beer cap from Thailand and a shoulder bag, I swing up behind this guy and we are away. I have also asked about the cost and the numbers he mention takes it to one dollar to go from A to B or ten to fifteen dollars for all day. So cost is not an issue. No-one is wearing helmets here but that doesn't really worry me as the traffic moves rather slowly and wearing a proper helmet in this heat would make life very uncomfortable.

Saigon is full of light motorbikes, at least thirty of those for every car. Perhaps that is one way of easing congestion as if it was all cars, traffic would come to a permanent halt. Most bikes have two people on them, girls and boys and young and old. I am a little surprised how untidy it is. Not that litter is an issue but more the lack of proper sidewalks and the sense that infrastructure is pretty basic. But around the city centre things are in much better shape. I have had the impression that Vietnam would be ahead of some of its neighbours but perhaps the chequered history, with the many wars, has delayed progress. I expect that Hanoi probably is a bit tidier and I also have formed the opinion that Vietnam will be a rich country some day, starting from behind perhaps, but with a sense of purpose, and a strong desire for growth and development. I am sure it will come up to first world standards in half a century or less.

My driver asks where I want to go and I say just around the city centre. He drives slowly and carefully as promised. Particularly in intersections it is quite chaotic but somehow the traffic flows and I have no concerns for safety. We go to the Binh Tay market Pagoda and he lets me off to have a look around at the old Chinese Pagoda there. It is full of incense and I motion to take my shoes off but the guard shakes his head and says no need. It is quite pretty and mystical as these things are but I don't need to spend a lot of time here as I have seen many temples before. I do buy a packet of incense for winter evenings and mornings in Auckland. There is some kind of spectacular deity at the far end centre of the building.

I reflect that no-one can really believe that this symbol creature can do anything much for humanity, so perhaps the meaning of religion lies more in its promotion of peace of mind and perhaps respect for those preceding us and all the miracles around us and a hope that our good deeds and prayers will affect the randomness of life in our favour. The power of positive acting and thinking! Perhaps most people are middle of road as far as religion is concerned and in that middle most religions have a great deal in common. Love, care, respect for the elders, treating your neighbour well and being kind, generous, forgiving and compassionate. This is part of the golden rule which by its proven win-win philosophy holds out the best hope for improving the global common weal, making universal good sense.

Across the road from the Pagoda is a food market which I look into. The bags of strongly coloured lentils and spices look mystical and attractive and whatever I point to is one dollar a kilo. I buy one bag of red peppercorns and one bag of lentils of together perhaps half a kilo for very little money thinking it will make good ingredients in a soup a rainy day in Sweden. And there are sure to be one or two of those during the month I am about to spend there. In New Zealand of course all import of food stuffs is strictly prohibited so I wouldn't think of bringing it in there. Now the rain is pouring down and the driver says it doesn't matter as he has a rain coat. Luckily I have one too but I suggest I go and have lunch somewhere until the rain stops. I am not keen on driving in the rain but that is what we end up doing. A short trip to the restaurant he recommends turns out to be half an hour to a small place at the other end of town. At this stage I am quite wet but it isn't cold so it doesn't matter a great deal. And it feels a bit like an adventure to challenge nature in one of these large growing third world cities of great renown for all the drama it had to endure in the 1900's.

The restaurant looks pretty average but there are nice young ladies serving and I order a plate of pork with vegetables and noodles and a jug of beer. When I ask for the name of my driver he gives me his card, which says Pham Van Minh, driver tour. I pour some beer for him. The waitress puts a major block of ice in his mug whereas I refrain from ice. My father taught me many years ago that when in marginal countries you don't drink tap water and you avoid ice. He would also include salad and many other things as taboo but I have long since moved on from that advice. Nowadays I never take any inoculations but thirty years ago I would have had two or three before any trip to 'the third world.' I think risks have reduced and also I am particular to try to pick decent restaurants which look clean and tidy.

After the jug of beer is gone he orders another one but I am thinking that the driver shouldn't have too much. He is reasonably modest in his consumption and I am unconcerned. He tells me he was born 1957 and has a bullet wound in his hip. That he says is why he is limping. I ask him if it was a Viet Cong bullet or an American one and he says VC. He doesn't seem to have any bitterness about it. I guess they are all glad it is history and not much use dwelling over past miseries. He tells me he has three children the oldest a daughter at 19. She is working but the other children are at school.

I ask him if the city is called Saigon or Ho Chi Minh City and he say either one is fine. I think I hear him say it's not worth arguing over it – people can say whatever they want. There are so many silly things that lead to confrontation and hatred in this world so let us all try to be above that and cherish what is good and important. He didn't say that but that is what I would like to understand from his comment. It is about 2.30 PM and he says he has already had some lunch so I end up eating the lion share of the food. And drinking most of the beer but leaving a little both food and drink for the house pig, assuming there is one. I wonder if there are many tourists in town and he says, no, this is low season. People like to come here when it is winter in the other countries, to escape cold and dark. But this time of the year there are fewer visitors. I tell him I am ready to go back to the hotel for a nap as I started the day in the small hours of the morning in Bangkok. He says the War museum is really close and I should see that first.

After five minutes on the moped we are at the War Museum which has a small entry fee which I pay and get a little brochure. Outside the museum there are some American military hardware like two airplanes, a tank and some big artillery pieces. Inside the museum there are lots and lots of photographs from the war. At least half of the visitors seem to be foreigners. The pictures are horrific. And it hits you like a fist punch what an immense tragedy the whole thing was. We all know there were 58,000 American dead and perhaps half a million wounded but those numbers would have to be multiplied by 10 – 20 to get to the number of dead and wounded Vietnamese. More bombs dropped by the Americans in Vietnam than all bombs dropped during the whole of WWII. And 70 million tons of chemicals released to the detriment of people and vegetation. What a colossal tragedy with no obvious benefits whatever. How can these things happen? A combination of excess power and serious want of wisdom and care! And now the Iraqi war seems to be a repeat of it all. When will they ever learn?

A couple of lines come to mind from the book I just completed reading – The Anatomy of Melancholy by Robert Burton, written 1621: *bellaque matribus detestata* – wars of mothers loathed - *quod stulte suscriptur, impie geritur, misere finitur* – begun in folly, continued in crime and ended in misery. This last line seems equally applicable to many if not most wars, including recent ones in Vietnam and Iraq. Perhaps if we have more mothers or at least females in executive positions in government, things would look up? Our traditional way of making politics is not a great success story.

After twenty minutes of contemplating the horrors of war I am on the bike again en route to the hotel. We stop again at the Notre Dame Church built in the late 1800's. Quite a beautiful, big and impressive church reminding of the French period of influence! I walk through the church but don't really find reason to stop for anything in particular. I tell the driver I can walk back from here, thank him and give him 200,000 Dong. He says he is looking forward to showing me more things tomorrow. Outside to the left of the church is another impressive building which proves to be post and telecom building. On my way over there I am attacked by a young lady wanting to sell me some postcards and books. I say no but end up with ten postcards and a little book by Graham Green – The Quiet American. Starting my walk back, a big dark cloud comes up and suddenly my driver pops up again and says 'maybe rain – I will take you to the hotel.' And a few minutes later I am there, thanking him again.

I check my emails of which I have received sixty in two days, eighty five percent being junk. At home I have a program that quickly deals to the junk but here I have to delete them manually which, although irritating, is not too arduous. A bit like credit cards, internet and email now reaches out to absolutely everywhere around the world it seems. Not only available everywhere, but also instant and precise. Truly a revolution in communication! It is now five o'clock and I decide to have a pre dinner nap. I wake up by someone knocking on the door. It is the night maid wishing to open the bed and put some chocolates on the pillow. The knock wakes me suddenly and I wonder why someone is waking me up at seven when I haven't asked for any wake-up call. That is when I realize it is seven at night rather than seven in the morning. I gratefully receive the chocolates and have a shower before going for a walk.

As I am not really hungry I walk the streets for a while looking at the buzz. Two ladies on a scooter drive up to me and ask if I need a massage. I decline their kind offer and continue along a rather dark avenue with the odd vendor selling tourist garments, cigarettes and sunglasses. As luck would have it I stumble on a busy night market and find a few things which I can't abstain from buying. One is a short sleeve cotton shirt with a quilt like pattern and Vietnamese buttons and collar. It looks great but I do know from experience that what looks great in India, Japan or Vietnam may look contrived, loud and out of place in your own country. But I am so happy so I buy it anyway. And later I see a similar garment for ladies – this one a sleeve less vest. I consider buying it for Linda, my wife, having found what I think is the right size. But after some hesitation I decide against it thinking that there is only a 50 % chance that it is the right size and a 30 % chance that she will like it. This puts the success chance at 15 % and my basic training in arithmetic suggests the odds are stacked against a buying decision. It is difficult to buy things for someone with a very clear and decided taste. The downside of an exquisite taste is that most things look trite and ordinary. I don't suffer from that problem being partly colour blind. The next day I found a coral bracelet which looked really nice and the only question mark was that it was embarrassingly cheap, but she wouldn't have to know that of course. When we recently visited New York together she fell by misjudging some stairs and her favourite coral bracelet broke. I bought the bracelet thinking that the meaning of a present is more as a token of appreciation than a matter of value or utility. It is the thought that counts.

After a little more than an hour of walking around I returned to the four-star Rex Hotel and went to their roof top bar for a beer and a sandwich. There were not many people there but a Philippino band of four played and sang popular songs whilst I had my late evening snack. Before calling it a day, I read a little in my book about an American in Kyoto. It is well written and brings back fond memories of my own two years in Japan.

The next day I woke up at six and started to write a travel note. I didn't feel too much happened the first day but if one scrutinizes the mind, it works constantly and continuously during our waking hours, so if I only can identify and decipher the muddled thoughts they are all there, some making more sense than others. A full breakfast was included in the room rate and I enjoyed the fruits and the cooked breakfast with a made to order omelette. After breakfast I was ready for my second day of Saigon. As I wanted to go for a walk on my own this morning, I considered going out the back door to avoid my acquaintance from yesterday. But I decided it was more ethical to talk to him and explain my intentions so as to not prevent him from pursuing other business opportunities. I did that and also said that the day following I would be ready for a tour again.

In going out on your own you stumble on things in a way you don't if you are with a guide. You may lose out in some ways but you also gain the pleasure of being in charge and making your own choices. As this idea crossed my mind I thought that perhaps my wife's often being contrary is for the same reason. As long as you are guided and cared for you don't develop your own path finding skills and you are not learning by making your own mistakes. So if for no other reason than to exert your own independence and make your own decisions you may end up being contrary. But how about making 50 % of decisions each? I think it is a bit like dancing the foxtrot or tango – it only works by natural leading and following, taking and giving. If you have to analyse it and agree to percentages the desired sublime quality of a relationship is unattainable.

My five hours walk in mixed sunshine and heavy rains ended up quite liberating and satisfying. When the rain started I put on my rain jacket and when it stopped five minutes later I took it off. Strangely I found myself wetter when wearing the rain jacket than when not. At about 30 degrees an extra water proof layer locks in the body heat and perspiration sets in. But it wasn't really uncomfortable. And besides, I like some challenges, given that my normal life is so pleasurable and free from obstacles and tribulations. For good health, a bit of adversity needs to be sought out and enjoyed. And I did enjoy a vague feeling of overheating and exhaustion.

I intentionally walked to a part of town where there were many restaurants just to check it out for the evening. However, before noon it all was pretty quiet and locked up. I had a good map so I knew where I was at all times and also how to walk back. There were plenty of motorcyclists and rickshaws that wanted to look after me and who could have taken me back but I was committed to walking.

Some street vendors, often children or girls approached me with their wares but I said no thank you to all. The day before I noticed that the locals did not say no to unwanted selling approaches, they just ignored it. If you say no you have already entered into a dialogue and discussion and the following question may be why? And then you are hooked for a prolonged discussion and dialogue where you may end up the looser. I did give some money to a mother with an infant but with some other beggars I just looked the other way.

Just when I decided to turn and start back I came across a shop that looked like a pharmacy. Realizing that the one thing I forgot to bring was sun screen lotion I wanted to buy some. The pharmacist didn't have a clue what I was on about but luckily another customer helped me and I got my sunscreen. The other customer asked if there was anything else and I said I would like to buy tooth paste as well. This was not included in the pharmacy product range so I had to settle for the sun screen at 42,000 dong which sounds like a lot but is actually less than three dollars. I thanked them and continued my walk.

Taking a right turn I ran into the helpful interpreter again and she asked if I found any tooth paste. I said I hadn't. Follow me and I will show you where to buy some. And very near there was a little shop selling toothpaste. I bought the smallest tube available at a very modest cost. I asked the kind lady who helped me how it was that she spoke English so well. She said she was an English teacher. She said she lived just nearby and would I like to come home with her. I said that is very kind of you and that it would be nice. Twenty yards further away we stepped into a little room off the alley with a few people around a table. I was introduced to her mother, brother and sister in law. The brother lived in Calgary, Canada. They all seemed very friendly and thinking it natural that my friend brought a stranger to her living room. The brother got up and said he was busy and the mother asked if I wanted a drink and went out and bought me an ice-coffee. And I had a chat to the quite petite English teacher for perhaps half an hour.

Her name was Thanh Tran Thi and she was born 1953, but looked younger. I had already in the street asked her about Thich Nhat Hanh but probably because of my poor pronunciation it took a little while for her to catch up with who I meant. Of course she knew him. He was living in the USA and was not so much read in Vietnam for political reasons. He is a Buddhist monk and writes beautifully.

Thanh Tran said she wanted to travel to Canada to see her brother and sister in law but her visa had been refused twice at interviews with Canadian authorities. The first time they said her bank account was too small to allow her a tourist visa and the second time when she applied for student visa to study English she was rejected because her English was found to be too good. I said I thought that was terrible whereas all countries engage in some similar activities. She had just been approved for a US Visa so now she intended to visit USA instead. She asked me what the US was like. I said it is a wonderful country to visit because people are very open and friendly and generally the weather is good and people are happy and optimistic. Perhaps the main draw backs are incompetent politicians in Washington, particularly the current administration, and a scary level of religious fundamentalism by many Christians. We both agreed that religion should be between the believer and God and that it is more a matter of conduct, i.e. love, than form and dogma. She was a Buddhist and I declared I have a lot of sympathy for Buddhism, not being religious myself.

I asked her how she was free in the middle of the day when she was a teacher. She said she had some classes in the morning and some again in the afternoon. Knowing that character is as important as skills, how did she teach children with that in mind? She said there are ways to ensure that the values are held high by the way you approach your teaching. Most schools now are co-ed whereas before the war single sex schools were very common. We agreed that mixed schools have the advantage to better prepare students for the realities of life. I said that when I have recruited people I have always looked for character as much as skills and most people would be better off, if they had to make a choice, with slightly less skills and more character but most schools and employers didn't really seem to comprehend this.

I said I had visited the War Museum and thought the war particularly tragic, cruel and unnecessary. She shrugged her shoulders and said that is how humans behave and she didn't seem to want to dwell more on the subject.

I said I remember one Thich Nhat Hanh story called the Stone Boy where two brothers had bought a farm because they heard there was a treasure there somewhere. They dug and dug for forty years when exhausted, they suddenly realized that it was the farm that was the treasure. We agreed that paradise is now and the key is to open your eyes and appreciate it. She gave me a few pc printouts on Buddhism which I read in the evening. After exchanging email addresses I said I had to move along in order to not overstay my welcome. This was a wonderful encounter with a person who seemed to be as fine a person as I have ever met. And with today's impressive communications technique she is a potential friend for life – amigos para siempre.

Coming out of her room there was a fine rain so I put my rain jacket on but the rain soon stopped so I could remove it. I walked past a wet and flat 100 Dong bill on the ground and made the calculation that since 100,000 equals 7 dollars, 100 Dong equals 0.7 cents. I left it on the ground for someone in better need.

Half way back to the Ben Thanh Market which I intended to visit, the skies really opened and I had to seek shelter as did many cyclists. I found a little shop that kept me entertained during the rain shower and I bought a few nice little wood framed mirrors and some well made beauty boxes that would make good little presents. This is also where I bought the coral bracelet mentioned above from three young graces who all engaged in tailor making the bracelet to my liking. They said they were all single and could I please bring some boys for them to marry. When I mentioned I had three sons they all shone up. I bought one rough coral bracelet and one with round polished pieces, the former being much cheaper that the latter but I sensed my wife would prefer the rough more natural looking one.

I moved on the Ban Thanh Market and found it very busy and active. As I stepped in I was courted by five different sales people wanting to sell me shirts and shorts and whatever I might need. One alert and keen girl went through so much trouble to sell me a pair of shorts but I seemed to be just in between sizes and nothing fit so to her disappointment I moved on and found another shop which provided a better fit. Nowadays I am keen to try garments on as things come in such different shapes even if the waist measure is correct. In this kind of market there are no changing rooms, but the lack of such never worried me. It takes a couple of seconds to change trousers and even without trousers you are no more undressed than on a bathing beach. Post market I found a little restaurant and had a good Vietnamese meal with a couple of local beers. After all that it was time to return to the hotel and have a rest.

And in the evening I asked the hotel for advice on restaurants and they recommended a nice Vietnamese one only five minutes' walk away. This was in an area I hadn't yet discovered and there were plenty of restaurants and bars and quite an evening buzz. After dinner I walked around a bit but felt quite tired so made it an early evening.

For the next day I had decided to take the hydrofoil out to Vung Tau which is an hour's ride on the Mekong. I had misread the timetable and missed the boat so would have to dream up something else. It was now Thursday and the weather looked great after earlier rains. As I stepped out of the hotel I was 'assaulted' by another moped driver who asked what I wanted to do. I said I didn't know but that I would like to see the Mekong Delta and perhaps go by boat on the river. He said he knew just the place and would take me there. I asked him how much it would cost and he said thirty dollars and I looked surprised given that I had paid 15 dollars for the previous day. He said this is far out of town. And I said; if it is that far, I am not sure I want to go there by moped. So he quickly corrected that it isn't that far and we agreed on 25 dollars.

But it was pretty far – 70 km one way which took an hour and a half. He stopped just outside Saigon and said he was picking up some helmets as you are not allowed on the motorway without helmets. I forgot to put on my sunglasses and dust and specks hit my eyes during the entire trip. Not very comfortable but it all went ok and we didn't have any rain! We got to the town of My Tho and the office of the river tour operator. There was a young lady there who said this would be a private tour for me only at the cost of sixty dollars. The tour would take me to two islands and include several snack meals and music and rowing a small canal.

I thought that all sounded ok and she and I walked to the landing and the boat with the driver set out on the mighty river. I learned that the Mekong starts in China, runs through Laos and Cambodja, and has a total length of 4,000 km and 250 km in Vietnam only. Impressive statistics! It obviously is the key provider of irrigation to a huge agricultural basin feeding perhaps fifty million people. The girl told me her name was Nguyen Thi Thuy Trang and that she was 35 years. She looked younger and wore an elegant yellow shirt and smart slacks. When she guessed my age she was 14 years short of the actual saying 'You look much younger and stronger than that!' which put me in a good mood. The river was quite busy with three car ferries going back and forth to the Unicorn Island and many smaller vessels as well. The weather was still good, nice and warm and some light clouds.

The Unicorn Island, our first stop, is a very lustrously green, tranquil and beautiful island. Our first destination was a fruit restaurant where we were given a big tray of mixed fruits to eat. There were small bananas, papaya, pineapple and two other nice tasting fruits, the names of which escaped me. As we enjoyed the fruits a small band played on local instruments and sang local songs. All very nice and tranquil and the island looked like a real oasis with little sign of the last several hundred years of development. Our conversation was a little bit difficult at times due to pronunciation difficulties but most of the information got through anyway. Then we moved to a canal in the middle of the island where a number of small row boats were lined up to take visitors through most of the island back to the big river. Thi Thuy Trang and I got into a boat and one paddler in front and one at the back propelled us swiftly and quietly through the jungle to the open river. We would have met twenty other rowboats in the narrow canal on their way back to the mid island landing to pick up new passengers.

On the way over to the next island, the Coconut Island, I was offered a coconut drink and at the island there was a coco nut candy making 'factory.' Most of the work was manual and there were five ladies in the production chain. It all looked pretty basic but tidy and nice and the candy was delicious. I bought a pack for almost no money at all of these nicely hand packed goodies. We also stopped at a honey making place and had some nice honey tea with snacks including ginger chips made in a way I haven't seen before. I got a pack of those as well although I had decided to stop buying things in order to be able to fit it all into my luggage.

My charming guide and hostess said that's it – unless you wish to have lunch next door and I said it would seem a good idea and please join me for lunch. We took the boat a little further and came to a jungle restaurant. There were a number of coconut tree roofs covering separate tables and we got our own little 'hut.' Thi Thuy Trang recommended Elephant Ear fish so we ordered one of those and also some rice and vegetables and meat and some drinks to go with it. She drank water and I asked for a local beer. The fish arrived beautifully cooked and in a stand where it was kept on even keel. The waitress made us a number of rolls with rice paper (edible) filled with fish and vegetables, a bit the way Peking Duck is served. It was all very delicious.

Behind Tri Thuy Trang was a big water buffalo lying on the ground clipping his eras a little every now and then. She told me she had never been to Hanoi or to any foreign country. Her husband is a chauffeur and in small country town like this pay levels are very moderate.

She lived with her husband's family which was the norm whereas her brother lived with her parents. She said she was very happy because she got to meet so many nice people through her job as a guide. She didn't have any children and thought me lucky to have three boys. We got water melon for dessert and ate that and continued to chat a little. I asked for the bill which came to $ 8.50 for the two of us which I rounded up to ten dollars. We returned to the boat and found the river quite choppy as there was a strong wind with some dark clouds coming up in the distance. I said I hope I don't have to ride the moped through rain all the way back to Saigon. She asked me why I came on a moped rather than in a car to which I am not sure I had a good answer. But I did say I found it more exciting. The boat driver negotiated the waves quite cleverly going across the river with side wind and then against the wind at the other side exactly the way I would have done it myself, all to keep us from getting too wet.

I gave her 100,000 tip which she seemed quite happy with and said it had been a good fun time. Just as we stepped into the tourist office the skies opened and a tropical rain came pouring down. Luckily it finished after fifteen minutes and then we got lucky and had no more rain on the ride back, which felt shorter than going out. This time I wore sunglasses to help protect my eyes from dust and particles. I believe the speed limit for mopeds was 60 kph and he added about 10 kph to that where conditioned allowed. It still took one and a half hours to travel the seventy kilometres. What I forgot was to put sunscreen on my arms and knees which were exposed to the sun for the entire trip and therefore got quite burned. Back in Saigon the driver asked if I would like an hour's massage at a nearby place. After sitting on the bike for three hours and feeling a little stiff I thought that a brilliant idea and got a good rubbing up by a very professional masseuse.

For the evening I felt like a light meal having eaten a bit too much lately and all wisdom suggests your good health benefits from eating less, particularly in the evening. I went back to the district where I ate the day before between the streets of Dong Khoi and Ba Trung just next to the open area of Nguyen Hue. This seems to be where people gather in the evenings. There were lots of Japanese restaurants but I didn't really feel like eating Japanese this evening. I saw a place which looked quite nice and asked if they served soups and found that they had ten choices of soups. I settled for one with Chinese spinach and shrimps and ordered a beer to go with that. It was just what I wanted, light and tasty. I much enjoyed the soup and paid the bill for 93,000 after rounding up.

I was feeling quite exhausted after my long moped trips and my eyes were tired. But as this was my last evening I decided to go for a walk and look at the night life and have one or two beers before doing some packing and retiring for the evening. Quite a lot of people moving about this Thursday night and some foot ball game was on, featured on large screens in many of the bars. As I walk around a corner the same young lady I saw the first evening on a Vespa drove up to me and asked if I was looking for company. I said I was only looking to have a beer somewhere. She said that if I joined her on the bike she would show me twenty girls in fifteen minutes and I was sure to like one of them. When I wasn't interested and walked away she drove off in eager pursuit of other opportunities. After a couple of beers in a noisy street corner bar I went back and filled my roller suitcase with my old and newly acquired things making it bulge a little. However, as it is quite modest in size and weighed only 14kgs leaving New Zealand I knew I was quite comfortably inside my weight limit.

The next morning I finished my packing and had breakfast giving up my favourite tailor made omelette for vegetables and fruits. When I checked out I noticed that the names of the very tidy young ladies that served me were My and Dung. It is strange how some words or names common in one culture can become almost impossible in another. I had told my driver to meet me at 8.30 in the morning to take me to the hydrofoil boats to Vung Tau. After checking my luggage with the concierge only bringing what I needed for the day's excursion, I stepped out of the hotel at 8.30 am and the driver was there. I had read up on Vung Tau on the net and learned that it is a large island outside the mouth of the Mekong and the beach resort of Saigon. So I had my swimming togs, my book, sunscreen, raincoat, mini camera, sunglasses and some plastic bags to put my shoes in and any wet gear after swimming. I didn't really know if there would be swimming opportunities but thought it good to be prepared.

The hydrofoil went down river past many ships and docks at great speed and because of wet windows it wasn't possible to see all that much. All seats were assigned and we were given water and a napkin and later sea sick bags. I don't think anyone got sea sick but the last bit was pretty rough. Besides the wind, the weather was perfect. I was thinking that although quite random, my program had been perfectly adjusted to the weather. Murphy's law suggests that anything that can go wrong will, but I think it's corollary is equally valid, that things turn out well if we don't worry too much about them. The ticket price was 120,000 Dong each way and I booked to return at 2 pm. Upon arriving at the island, the hydrofoil parked next to five other similar boats so we all had to step through those to get ashore. I thought that being in a wheel chair here would pose quite a challenge. Arriving at the landing, there was a little bus waiting and I asked where it went. The hostess asked where I was going and I said I didn't know. She suggested I'd be better off in the bus than out in the sweltering sun so I went in hoping to get to a nice beach with holiday restaurants.

I didn't realize how large the island of Vung Tau was but after fifteen minutes I jumped off at a spot where I could see the sea nearby. Walking towards the sea a moped caught up with me and the driver, who wore a helmet, said here is no good, I will drive you to the proper beach. I hesitated a little but thought it made sense to rely on someone with local knowledge so I jumped up behind him and rode the extra five km needed to get to where the action was. Since I arrived in Saigon I got the impression that people were generally honest and theft and fraud rare. I felt safe which is always nice. We got to a beautiful bathing beach and the driver taking me there agreed to pick me up again at 1.15 pm for the return trip with the hydrofoil. I asked if there were any changing rooms and was pointed in the right direction but was stopped as I first needed to buy a ticket for 2,000. I got the ticket and went in and changed putting my dress shoes in a plastic bag and the rest of my clothes in my shoulder bag.

I rented a deck chair and a table for my things for 30,000 and went for a swim. Big waves and nice water temperature and the water seemed reasonable clean. Plenty of people on the beach and many in the water! They seemed to eye me as a strange yeti from the north but always with a smile and I didn't meet one unfriendly person during the entire visit to Saigon. When swimming I kept an eye on my things but they seemed safe there on my rented mini table under the parasol. When I got back to my chair I was offered a beer which I accepted, thinking, why not – I am on holiday after all! Life could be worse I thought, as I sat there feeling like a price, viewing the blue ocean with a tiger beer in hand! After a bit of reading and a second swim I was ready to move on. I bought another shower ticket and asked if they rented towels. No, but I could buy one just across the aisle. I picked a little pink one and paid a dollar for it. The shower was a pipe without mouthpiece and no hot water but it all worked out nicely and very comfortably. I managed to dress without soiling my cloths in spite of the floor being all wet. My socks and dress shoes I put on outside where I could sit down and after wiping my feet with the pink towel.

Just above the changing rooms there was a grand restaurant with stunning sea views. When I arrived it was all empty so I got top service. I ordered a sea food platter and a beer and the young waitress was keen to have a conversation of sorts. She said she had 'only two years of English at school so not so well speaking.' We went through the 'how old are you' routine and I learned she was twenty-one and my own age I already knew. Another nice, keen, friendly individual! Just after 1 PM my driver arrived a little early to take me to the hydrofoil. He said it was just nearby which sounded strange to me but he said afternoon sailings were different from morning arrivals. He knew what he was talking about. He took me to a fine villa which I could inspect for 15 minutes before going to the landing nearby. I paid him 50,000 and he seemed very happy with that.

It was now quite windy and the trip across the open sea was choppy. I sat next to a French guy who had lived in South America for many years loving it. We talked about tourism, South America and many other things. I asked him about the new French president but my new friend didn't like him as he was too George Bush like. I read another chapter in my book and fell asleep for half an hour. The trip took half an hour longer than expected, probably because of the strong wind. At the arrival point my driver waited for me and we were off. I asked to be taken to the Ho Chi Minh City museum which I had seen was nearby. He took me there and I spend 20 minutes getting an impression of the museum. In essence it depicted the evolution of Saigon as a city from early times. I bought a nice little compass at the museum shop. I have come to much appreciate museum shops as they often have some interesting old replicas. And although I must admit a weakness for shopping, 90 % of what I buy I buy to give away. Going back to the hotel he said he could take me to the airport on his moped but I said no – too much luggage.

I picked up my luggage at the hotel and changed cloths in the hotel rest rooms and typed away on my pc for an hour before it was time to leave for the airport. At 5.30 pm I took my baggage to the Hotel front and both my previous drivers were there to guide me from the door to the taxi. Nice of them to come and say good bye and another reason may have been to receive final gratuity. I gave both of them a gratuity. The traffic was intense particularly the innumerable people on their mopeds. Sitting in the car admiring the intense buzz on the streets and contemplating my four days in Vietnam I thought the trip a lot of fun and very worthwhile but doubted I would ever come back. Saigon! Gone with a sigh!

13th July 2007

Yangon

'You process passengers twice as fast as your colleagues,' I told the check in lady at Stockholm Arlanda airport. I gave her my tickets and said I was going to Yangon. She said I would have to collect my luggage at Bangkok to take it through customs. I protested that I wanted it checked to my destination and she said all Thai destination needs to go through customs at Bangkok. 'But this is Yangon, Myanmar?' and she realized her mistake and said she could do it. She also gave me the two boarding passes required. The check in took twenty minutes leaving me a little over two hours before departure, most of which I spent trying to use up my ninety minutes minimum internet ticket. After double security checks, each necessitating unpacking my lap top, the flight was on time and all went smooth.

I had an aisle seat and next to me were two Thai ladies who said they came from Skelleftea. They were going home to Hua Hin after their annual three months stay with their boyfriends in northern Sweden. I said I visited Hua Hin a year ago and really enjoyed it. One of them, Suwenee, spoke reasonable Swedish and the other, Srisawoord, spoke English so we managed to communicate rather well. We didn't venture into any deeper discourse but I am sure we all gradually felt like friends. Srisawoord asked me if we could swap seats so she could have easier access to lavatories, and I saw no reason why not. Two bad movies, 'Spiderman and Fun in Acapulco' made me stick to my book and also sleep a few hours. After a ten hours flight and a swift transfer in Bangkok I arrived in Yangon about nine o'clock Sunday morning.

Arriving in Yangon was easy. I had the required visa and my luggage arrived in good order. I exchanged US $ 100 at the official airport money changer and got 45,000 Kyats, only to learn as I stepped into the taxi that the inofficial rate was 120,000 Kyats for US$ 100. The government operated on the lower rate and the market paid more than twice the official rate. I just reflected that this is not the first time I have this kind of experience in a new country and the only thing to do is to not bother but to see it as a learning expense. Money changing and inflated taxi prices are the most obvious ways to fleece new comers. I asked the driver where I could change another $100 at the better rate. He said he had 120, 000 and sent a big bundle across to the back seat. I took out $ 100 and gave him. After a while he asked if I had finished counting the money and I said I didn't think it necessary, that I trusted him. I saw the bundle was twice the size of the previous bundle I had received.

The taxi driver was the son of an Indian Ghurka soldier from the war and he was informative and helpful. From the business card he passed on to me I saw his name was Nanu. He took me to the beautiful Kandawgyi Palace Hotel where I was greeted with a drink and many nice ladies looking after me. Like my previous visit to Vietnam, I gathered that this was off season, allowing extra time and service to each visitor. We had landed through heavy clouds and it was still drizzling. I was given a beautiful top floor room with a view over the magnificent Kandawgyi Lake in the middle of Yangon. It was now about five o'clock in the morning in Sweden and although I felt quite tired, I decided that a few hours exploring would be wiser than going to bed right away.

Luckily my shorts has many pockets enabling me to accommodate the 160 one thousand Kyat bills that I had acquired as well as my wallet and other little things. I could see the mighty 'Shwe Dagon Pagoda' from the hotel and I decided that would be a suitable target for my first walk. Although it looked enormous from up high or from the street where its main entrance was, from the ground it was invisible due to the many tall palm trees. After fifteen minutes walk in the what I thought was the right general direction I stumbled upon the temple and realized there were about one hundred marble steps to negotiate before arriving to the main Pagoda area. Many little boys must have thought I looked different or funny as they tried to chat with me and also get some money and in some cases sell little things. The whole Pagoda area was bare foot territory so the boys tried to sell me a plastic bag as a shoe container. All along the many stairs there were shops selling temple memorabilia like Buddha statues and such things.

When I reached the main level I was told it cost five dollars to proceed. I realized that this was only applicable to foreigners but also thought that was all right. Just as I paid my due, a young man stepped forth and said he was the resident guide. Instinctively I thought I don't need a guide, but thinking about it again I considered it would be worth it. Without some expert comment even beautiful temples and churches are difficult to fully appreciate. The guide told me he was born 1978 and his name was Nandar. He wasn't married. He had spent six months in Korea working very hard in a factory in order to generate some capital. His English was a little weak, but his knowledge about Buddha and what we saw compensated for his lack in language skills.

The temple or pagoda was built in the 11-hundreds and it contains no less than 26,000 Buddha images. He explained that the Myanmar people traditionally were not very religious but they had come to be devout Buddhists. He also explained that Buddha is not seen as a divine creator but rather as a teacher on life issues – how to be good and live well. The Myanmar religion doesn't contain much superstition, but is more about seeking to live life in the best way possible. Meditation is a key component of that realization and he said he himself meditated half an hour a day in quietude followed by fifteen minutes of recanting texts that provided good guidance for desirable conduct. It all seemed to make a lot of sense to me. Unfortunately I found myself saying 'I see' and 'is that so' to many things I couldn't hear or understand.

Nandar did carry a small parasol which I initially thought was ridiculous, but after a while in the tropical heat on the white marble floor with the mammoth cupola in gold, which reflected all the sun rays, and due to my deficit of sleep, I almost felt faint and came around to thinking that the parasol was probably a good idea. I did capture that the top of the pagoda at 326 feet has 3,154 gold bells and 79,569 diamonds and other precious stones, the biggest diamond weighing 76 carats. The essence of Buddha's teaching is 'loving kindness' (compare Paul's letter to the Corinthians 1:13) and I tend to agree that if people get that right, most other things in life will fall in place. I have thought that if Jesus would have come across someone like Buddha he would have said or thought – I can do no more for this man – he is already a reflection of things divine.

Nandar also said that the temple contained the world's largest bell - which he showed me – weighing 24 tons. When the English tried to 'steal it' the bridge they took it over collapsed and it was recovered and put back where it was meant to be. A truly huge bell with an amazing sound to it! Although I felt a little faint at several times I much enjoyed the tour of the Pagoda where people were meditating all over the place. They were not praying but rather meditating, trying to focus the mind on things important, like reverence for parents and the concern for loved ones, and setting the mindset on good will towards all.

After an hour of that I was all templed out and felt I needed a light meal and a nap to build on the three or so hours I had slept the night before. I found a rickety taxi which took me back and at pool side by the beautiful lake I had a club sandwich and a local Myanmar beer. After that I pulled the shades and slept deeply for two hours waking up quite groggy. But a shower and a glass of water set me right such that I could pursue another expedition.

This time I walked towards the downtown area. It was very hot and a little longer than I anticipated but after twenty minutes I passed the main railway station and found myself in the core of the city – which now counts five million inhabitants. In what looked like a sewer or dirty river, a young naked boy was washing or bathing. I also reflected that the state of repair of pavements was pretty similar to Laos or Africa – charming in some ways but not very impressive. Several little boys and some others asked me for money and I gave some away. Two very young children greeted me with 'Hello monkey,' making me smile. There were chicken and stray dogs on the uneven pavements.

Downtown was rather busy, but as it was Sunday it probably was less busy that normal. Some market activity was still on but mostly contained food stuffs and some other cheap goods – a lot less colourful and interesting than the markets I have come to know in Thailand. I thought a little of Havana as I walked the alleys because the old housed looked a bit derelict and quite charming but run down – as I imagine that Cuba would look too. Suddenly I ran into a small barbershop so

I went in and asked if they could tidy my hair up. They said yes and in five or ten minutes my excess hair was all gone through the hands of a pretty and competent Burmese hairdresser. When I asked what it cost she said 500 Kyats, which is less than fifty cents and I thought of the offer I had seen two days earlier at Drottninggatan in Stockholm for a special price haircut at US $ 35. This was seventy times less! I did give her a 100 % tip and felt quite happy that I was tidy again at such a reasonable cost.

I had a divine pre dinner massage and then some BBQ pork with vegetables at a nearby restaurant – all worthwhile and very pleasant. When I got back to the hotel by ten pm I decided to try out the night club which was all about Karaoke. Because of the off season time of the year I found myself alone with ten local girls and we sang the typical Karoke songs for about an hour – Diana, There's a House in New Orleans, Dancing Queen, Yesterday, Tennessee Waltz etc and I found it quite enjoyable. And I am sure the cost was no more than one tenth of what it would have been in Tokyo. By 11 PM I was ready to fold up to gather strength and energy for tomorrow's adventures.

After the traditional great Asian breakfast I called Nanu, my driver from the day before and suggested he take me to the Yilepaya temple at eleven am that morning. That was the temple he had mentioned, which is situated in the middle of the big river. He confirmed he would pick me up at eleven and I went for a walk around the lake just outside the hotel. I soon realized that the lake was in an enclosed park area so I had to pay one thousand Kyats entrance (again, special higher rate for foreigners) which I was happy to do and started my long walk on the board walk which almost entirely surrounds the lake. Forty-five minutes later I realized I wouldn't be back by eleven if I were to encircle the whole lake, so I decided to go back the same way I came. Very pretty walk and park and the obvious target for young lovers who adorned all the benches by lake side! It got quite hot and for a little while it rained too so upon my return to the hotel I was quite wet. I rested for a little while and changed shirts and was picked up by my designated driver as agreed.

He told me that the pagoda we were going to was about one hour outside Yangon which proved to be spot on. The average speed we travelled with was about 40 kph due to the poor state of the roads with frequent serious pot holes. One reason for calling Nanu rather than taking the first available taxi was that his Indian/ Nepalese background gave him a good command of English. And if you are to spend at least two hours with someone in a car and learn about a new place, it is helpful if you speak the same language. Soon after we left Yangon it started to rain lightly. The road was like one long stretch of patchwork and we moved slowly to avoid the many pot holes. Along the road were groves, fields and dwellings which reminded me of my time in Africa or driving in rural Malaysia. I asked him about his family and he said he had two daughters 24 and 22 years old, and one son aged 11. Big gap I said and he said with Buddha's help he finally got a son. The eldest married daughter was a dentist and the next one had a law degree and was now adding IT skills. I suggested they were very well educated which he agreed but then it isn't very easy to get a job. His wife ran a little business selling gem stones at the market. During school holidays they taught their children Nepalese so as to preserve their command of their mother language.

He explained the people of Myanmar were free to travel to foreign countries but the earnings levels and the limited convertibility of the currency made it hard to contemplate foreign travel. He said he had never been to any foreign country but would like to visit Nepal and India and perhaps Thailand. Several times he had to stop and pay small amounts of toll for using the road. After half an hour we crossed a very long bridge over the Bogo River to Suriem. The bridge was about ten years old and constructed by Chinese engineers like many other Burmese bridges. And this one, unlike most others, also had rail tracks on it. He commented that during British rule they were run by foreigners but at least the British added a lot of infrastructure and organization. During the four years of Japanese rule in the early 1940's there were no rule of law at all and the Japanese just did what they wanted.

When I touched on the political situation he and my guide yesterday said it was not suitable with a military government but against a well oiled and armed organization it isn't all that easy to argue for a change. He said that Aung San Suu Kee was still in house arrest and was liked by most people but no change could be anticipated in the near future. When in Auckland, I had learned at an Asia seminar that the major neighbors of Myanmar, China and India, are more interested in stable relations with Myanmar than who governs it, so a little like the situation between the US and Saudi, stability and the continued access to raw material is more important than alignment with stated ideals.

The driver also told me that Yangon has about five million people whereas all of Myanmar has fifty-five million. The second city is Mandalay in the middle of the country, seventy km to the North. He described Mandalay as quite an industrial town, much smaller than Yangon and with lower buildings since it historically has burnt about three times. Its traffic is dominated by bicycles and motorcycles whereas in Yangon the car dominates. I asked if there were river trips from Mandalay to Yangon but he said the boat which takes about five hours goes from Mandalay to Bagan which is about one fifth of the way between the major cities.

I said that in Southern Burma there looks to be a wealth of islands in the Andaman Sea and wondered if they were attractive. He said he once went down there with a Swiss friend but the area is run by the military so not very accessible for visitors. He went through another road toll and the attendant didn't have the change to return so just waved him past. As we were rolling into Kyauktan, the town with the river temple, it started to rain more intensely. We got out of the car and I was attacked by young girls who wanted to sell me things. One tried to sell me small bags with what looked like popcorn but I said no. She was very pretty so I took a portrait photo of her instead and offered her 200 for the modelling. She refused to accept the money unless I took some of her popcorn which I then did. Nanu told me that the island palace is surrounded by big fish and the 'popcorn' was for feeding the fish. In fact all the things they were selling were designed for visits to the palace.

I paid 4000 Kyats for the transfer from land to the island which allowed us to travel in a covered boat. This proved useful as the rain was getting heavier by the minute. We had to leave our shoes in the boat as all temples are accessed bare foot only. At the Palace I had to pay a small entrance fee again and received a fancy ticket stating the full name of the temple as 'Kyaik Hmaw Wun Ye Lai Pagoda.' I looked around at all the little rooms and meditation spots hurrying when in the open to avoid getting soaked by the intense monsoon rain. I also thought it was nice to go bare foot on wet marble in the tropics. It is funny how something small like that can make you feel happy. I found a place to off load my fish food and the big fish were jumping to get their share of it.

After about twenty minutes of looking at the different rooms I felt it enough and that we should challenge the deluge and try to get back ashore. This time the boat was full of passengers, trying to avoid the rain and we were shipped safely to the main landing. Nanu told me to wait under the cover while he fetched the car. He asked me if I wanted to look at the local market and I said if it is under cover I might take a quick look. I spent ten minutes there and as it was mainly a food market I didn't think I would buy anything but ended up buying some sandal wood incense.

Nanu asked if I wanted to have lunch and I said I could if there were any decent restaurant. He said there wasn't so we went back to Yangon, getting there about three and a half hours after departing. When he asked me if he were to take me back to the hotel I suggested he drive me to the main post office so I could obtain some stamps for a few postcards. The post office is on the fashionable Strand together with the British and Australian Embassies and the famous Strand Hotel. Stamps for an overseas post card were 30 Kyats, equal to one fiftieth of what it would cost in Sweden. So little by little I was clawing back the loss I experienced from my initial dealing with the Myanmar government at the airport. I paid Nanu the thirty dollars or 36,000 Kyats we had agreed, which was probably a bit rich, but I thought if he spends that amount of time driving me around, thirty dollars is quite fair and didn't want to bargain.

I sought out an internet cafe to check emails and looked for a place to have a late lunch. There were plenty of eateries but most looked a bit basic. I found a place with a proper menu that looked clean enough and thereafter had some chicken and cashew nuts with a local beer before taking a taxi to my hotel for an afternoon nap. In the evening I followed the same pattern as the previous night with a massage, dinner and some karaoke. I think I experienced 'the law of diminishing utility' in terms of massage and karaoke. The tough massage that felt so good the night before felt more like torture the second night and I also got my fill on karaoke. I noticed that the song 'Carol' (Oh Carol, You are but a fool) was accompanied by film pictures of two young Asian girls dancing through the streets of Stockholm's old town, reminding me of the beauty of my birth town.

When I opened my curtains the next morning there was a little squirrel running on the wood level outside. And beyond through the palm trees, the lake with the amazing wide boardwalk built in the lake and stretching for miles, making it all like a picture out of a fairytale. After breakfast I decided to walk to the Bogyoke market about a mile and a half away. A bit long to walk in the tropical heat but I welcomed the exercise and the chance to take in the environment enroute. I noticed that several people were carrying parasols as protection from the sun. It struck me that almost no tourist were to be seen. Probably not too many here and those who are wouldn't walk the streets. When I passed the railway station and turned right on Bogyoke road I was approached by an Indian looking man asking me if I wanted to change money. Although this particular man wasn't very confidence inspiring I did change fifty dollars and got a good rate.

When I got to a Hindu temple I realized I was on Anawrahta Rd rather than Bogyoke Rd so I took a right and right again to get to the market. I started on the south side of the road and then moved over to the north side. I didn't expect to find anything I wanted to buy but ended up with some jewellery and some textiles. I guess that labour is very cheap and Burma is rich in precious stones so the prices on offer were very low by any standards. I was amazed at the low price of pearl necklaces and ended up buying a few. They looked very nice but I enquired as to whether they were real pearls. The lady assured me that was the case and took out a cigarette lighter and held under the pearls, which were totally unaffected by the flame. I got quite warm and sweaty in the hot morning but at least it wasn't raining. My impression is that the Burmese are good to deal with and essentially honest. After about an hour of walking around I took a cab back to the hotel and went for a swim and relaxation at the hotel pool. Besides me and an Italian mother with two children, there were none at the two pools. After some swimming and a snack, I decided to take a mid day rest.

Later that day, my last day in Yangon, I took another trip to the city market in order to spend my remaining Kyats and ended up with a few things I am sure I could do without but which may make good presents. I walked back stopping for a beer at a pretty basic restaurant and managed to fit a last swim in before getting ready for dinner. And I read a bit in my new book, 'Burmese Days' by George Orwell, which I bought in the hotel shop the day before. To read a well known author commenting on the foreign place you are just visiting can add a lot to the total experience, making you wonder if the country is still suffering from its birth complications. I loved the book which highlighted how condescendingly many British treated the native locals in the colonies.

For the evening, I had asked the hotel to put me on a tour with dinner and local dancing but they said that the only local dancing show they were aware of was right at this hotel, so I decided to attend that. I and seven more people dined in a hall for at least fifty and after dinner the dancers and musicians performed their whole program for us. The low attendance must reflect the off season and the Monsoon rains. The dancing was very pleasant and similar to local dancing I have seen before in Indonesia and Thailand. Very colourful costumes, beautiful dancers, and drum dominated music.

After dinner I sat down to read my book for a while in the hotel lobby where a pianist every evening spread easy music. He played 'As Time Goes By' and some other tunes of that era. I was feeling quite tired and was to depart Myanmar the next morning so I decided to retire to my chambers rather early. On the way to my room I saw the magnificent golden cupolas of the Shwe Dagon Pagoda to the west and the equally impressive golden ship (in the Kandawgyi Lake), both illuminated and glowing in the dark night.

My impression of Myanmar, which gained independence from Britain in January 1948, is of a rich land – rich in agriculture and raw materials - which has fallen behind because of poor governance. As with most places, people are friendly and keen to be part of the world and pushing for improvements. Tourism should have quite a potential to grow but this may necessitate some investment and also more open government. Three days is of course too short for any deeper understanding, but I find that a visit increases my sense of kinship and desire to learn more and perhaps help promote a country and its people.

In the days of empire building, nations were trying to lever off other nations to create superior wealth for themselves, pursuing one sided gain. Nowadays one would hope that nations will behave better than that even if one has to wonder in the case of American policy in Latin America and the Middle East. In future, policy and actions must be based on the endeavor to extend empathy, care and interest to all, regardless of nationality, race or religion. This I believe to be the only way to move towards sustainable peace and prosperity.

At 9.55 AM the following day Thai Airways flew me out of Yangon to Bangkok and later to Auckland. I feel very privileged to be able to travel and see new places every year. At the same time, it is great to arrive back home after a long trip.

22nd August 2007

A few notes on my trip to Shanghai May 2008

Sitting down at Pundang airport in Shanghai I have just received a piece of Swartzwald cake and a cafe latte after an effortless check-in. The taxi driver must have thought that I was in a great hurry because he drove like a car thief all the 50 kms to the airport. Occasionally he slowed down mysteriously but I soon figured out that he knew where the speed cameras were. His zig zagging between lanes reminded me of the guide's comment yesterday that approaches to fine buildings are often made to zig zag in China as the belief is that ghosts can't follow a zig zag. The check-in counter hadn't even opened when I arrived so I queued up and got into a conversation with a nice young German girl. She had spent six weeks in China supporting a mobile German trade fair. She had loved the experience and was hoping to come back for more China experience. I said I thought Shanghai interesting and good to have a little bit of first-hand experience of. But I found commercialism very dominant and thus it felt a little spiritually flat. Perhaps that is inevitable for a place that has grown so fast and leading China economically out of third world status towards first.

On my last day in Auckland, Thursday 15th May 2008, I went to work a little late as I had a few chores to attend to at home. My flight was only at 23.15 so there was plenty of time to do ordinary things during the day. I had been invited to an investment seminar with lunch and I went to that at 11am after checking mail and email etc. As my friend Dermot worked next door to the Investment seminar I brought a map of Stockholm for him and we had agreed to get together there three weeks later. When I realized the investment seminar would last to 2 PM I left at noon feeling a bit too high pitch to sit out the whole program. At the seminar I was told that energy will become more precious in future and that it is good to be reasonably cashed up for future opportunities. I agree with that. When seeing my friend at his 25th floor reception area he joined me for a brief meeting and I gave him the map and showed him the street of his hotel. As he was travelling to Shanghai two weeks after me he wished me a good trip and asked if I had all things in order including a Chinese visa? Visa?! I didn't even know it's required! I wonder if I can get a visa this very afternoon or if my travel plans need to be re-jigged. Dermot thought it took three days but that there may be some express option available as well.

He offered me to ring my travel agent from his office but I said I'll walk over to my office and deal with it there. And I thought; why didn't the travel agent tell me? And Dermot reminded me that last year when he and his wife were destined to Shanghai they had to settle for Phuket instead, because his travel agent hadn't mentioned the need for visa. I called my travel agent and asked about visa. He called the Chinese consulate and found out that they opened again after lunch at 2 PM. I went home and grabbed my travel documents and hotel reservation to be equipped for the visa application if they would accept my late arrival. I got there 1.30 PM and it was closed. A sign said open for applications 10 – 12 and for pick up of passports <u>only</u> 2 – 4 PM. I thought this is not going to work. The bureaucrats will probably not make a special case for me. I would loose my prepaid hotel and try to reschedule my trip. I went to a nearby cafe and had some Thai Chicken salad for lunch, returning 1.55 pm to the consulate. At 2 pm they opened the doors and about 20 people moved in with me at the front. I got up to the counter and said I have a problem because I am flying out tonight to Shanghai and I don't have a visa. Why didn't you come in the morning? I only found out I need a visa at lunchtime. Fill in the visa form and go to counter six and someone will help you. I filled in the form and got someone to take on my case, saying that it would cost me the express fee of $ 120. He also wanted a copy of my ticket and hotel reservation to keep in the file. He said to come back an hour later at 3.30pm to pick up the passport. I felt greatly relieved, called my travel agent (and Dermot) and said it was ok but I needed a new printout of the ticket and hotel reservation. I got back home, took the dog for a walk, picked up my new printouts and got back in time to pick up my passport. And breathed a sigh of relief! I had told myself not to get upset if it didn't work because in the greater scheme of things it was a triviality, but it also felt quite irritating that I might miss out on a trip planned for three months because of a small oversight. A little bit stressful but not too bad! Four days later I had a meeting with my wife in Rome but I felt confident that even if China didn't happen this time I could still make it to Rome in time.

Andre' took me to the airport and I offered to buy him dinner but he was going to see a friend so declined. Flight was smooth and uneventful. I saw the Kite runner movie which failed to make any deeper impression on me. In Shanghai customs and luggage handling was efficient and I was in a taxi on my way to the hotel within half an hour, arriving at the hotel 9.30 am. And as luck would have it my room was available so I could check in, take a shower, and hit the streets of Shanghai. I started with a walk around the hotel which is right on the river, but there wasn't much there so I took a taxi to Nanjing Road, the premier shopping street in China. It was lovely spring weather with 25 degrees daytime. Shanghai is full of high rises of 50 stories or more, most of them residential and some also for business. There is such a multitude of them so the mind and eye quickly adjusts to the fact and the sensation of it all fades out of mind. Streets are very busy, mostly cars – whereas when I was in Beijing 18 years ago it was 50 bicycles to one car but here the car dominated. And buses! I learned that there are 18,000 buses in Shanghai, many of them Volvo. And the number of cars is growing very fast although car buyers must now bid for a licence plate as a means to try to reduce car ownership. With a population exceeding 20 million and economic growth at 10 % pa, pressures on infrastructure and environment are bound to mount.

Half of Nanjing Street is pedestrians only. I walked around a bit and bought a few things. There were plenty of street peddlers selling watches and fake branded bags and hand bags. I avoided those as I don't want anything fake for myself and it is hard to explain to a friend why you thought a fake item would be good enough for him or her. I think there are enough people reasoning like me that the real brands won't be seriously threatened by these violators of intellectual property.

I had lunch at a Chinese restaurant and the best thing was a 60 cl Chinese beer. Throughout I found the food bland, not bad, but not worth remembering either. Perhaps that is because I didn't know what to order or where to find the better places. Italian, French and Japanese food I find more appealing. At the end of Nanjing road is the great river and along the river a promenade. It is quite spectacular to look at the big busy river with all the sky scrapers on the other side. Particularly at night the sight is very impressive. But unlike walking along the Thames or The Seine there is nothing but cheap tourist gadgets available along the river. One fake Mont Blanc pen for RMB 200!? No! Ok 100? No! And finally five for 100? And if you do buy at that stage, which I did, after the transaction I was offered another 10 for 100. So the only way to deal with it is to look the other way and not engage. And inevitably reflect that street selling must be a hard way to make a living. After some strolling around I got back to the hotel by 3 pm and slept deeply for three hours.

Wishing to see a bit more of the surrounds I booked a full day guided tour to Hangzhu for Saturday and a half day city tour for Sunday. I asked the front desk for tips on where to have dinner and they directed me to a nearby street with plenty of activity, shops and restaurants. I strolled around a bit and found somewhere to eat and again the meal wasn't bad but devoid of any deeper sensations. As the Hangzhu tour had a 7 am start I took an early evening. The TV offered CNN and Bloombergs like any other modern hotel. The three key news items were the severe Chinese earth quake, the flooding of south Burma and the soaring oil prices. The free availability of internet and international TV channels as well as travel for those who can afford it - together with foreign investment, trade and inbound tourism -must have significantly changed the awareness of the outside world to Chinese people. This century will no doubt bring both China and India into the community of advanced and integrated states.

Up early to join the tour. The bus was there at seven with only a few passengers and we spent nearly two hours collecting other passengers around Shanghai. A little over three hours later we arrived to the park area outside Hangzhu with hills and trees and a large partly manmade lake. The area is a beautiful imperial park dating back hundreds of years with greenery and wilderness on one side and the skyline of the City on the other. We learnt that Hangzhu has five million people and yet I must admit I hadn't heard of it before my arrival. Outside India and China I think I could name all world cities over a couple of million but the detailed lay-out of these major countries have been hidden in the dark for a long time. At least as far as I am concerned! When we arrived at our destination the guide said to observe the look of his flag and for the group to please stay together. There were people and busses everywhere. Marco Polo had visited the place five hundred years earlier and called it 'Paradise on Earth'. The place was quite scenic, pretty and historic but inevitably the abundance of people is the dominating impression. I befriended a couple of co-travellers; a male engineer from Wisconsin and a female communications expert from California. They were both working in China temporarily and used the week end to see a little of the country.

We had another stop for lunch which worked well and was taken in tranquillity away from the crowds, and one in a beautiful tea village where we had a tea ceremony. From my time in Japan I know that tea is surrounded with a lot of ceremony – my deputy in Japan had been attending a three years tea serving course – and we had a lot of things explained about tea here as well. It was suggested that once you have put the tea leaves in the glass you pour just a little water in the glass to allow the enjoyment of the fragrances before more water is added for drinking purposes. There are different teas for different times of the day and to achieve different effects like nausea or energy. We were also offered to buy nicely packed precious tea which I didn't do knowing how I would fall into the established low-culture habit of using a tea bag instead.

Then the long trip back and the dropping off of all the people at various hotels and I think I was back at eight o'clock. Rather a long day. Interesting, fun, but not sublime. From time to time during this trip I thought: 'Ok, that's fine, but what's the big deal.' I was wondering whether what I was seeing was bland or if I was in some kind of mood when nothing seemed to impress me? Perhaps it was the travelling on my own that influenced my mood. Being alone can be fun, but only if you meet somebody interesting. And of course, then you are not alone anymore. No man is an island! I had dinner and a nice foot massage and went to bed quite exhausted.

Next day I had a short city tour and that was essentially to the old town and to a large pearl shop. The old town is a busy tourist market but most if not all is not old at all but newly constructed. During the Cultural Revolution anything old and cultural was seen as standing in the way of socialism and progress so was either destroyed or had to give way for modern structures. These were dark times for China and many innocent people suffered and were harassed and killed. In the book I read 'Mao, The Unknown Story' by Jung Chang and Jon Halliday, Chairman Mao is depicted as a self-serving, power hungry executioner with no redeeming features at all. As I have wondered how the Chinese see Mao's legacy I asked several people about it. I guess that the synopsis of the answers I got was – yes, times were cruel and hard and many suffered and starved, but it also set the stage for modern China. My impression is that Mao has not be reassessed the same way Stalin and Lenin have, but he remains sort of a founder and hero in the eyes of the multitude. I may well be wrong and times may change this, but at this stage Chairman Mao continues to be revered.

The tour finished abruptly in the middle of nowhere and I tried to walk towards Nanjing Road. After a while I felt hungry and went into a local restaurant I happened to pass by. Not much English spoken there but I asked for chicken rice and a beer and think I was understood. A group of ten sitting at a round table next to mine started to try to communicate with me and gave me some of their food whilst I was waiting for mine. Very warm and friendly people and laughed and drank together but none of us understood a word of what the other was saying. The only word we both understood was 'campei' for skål or cheers.

After lunch I realised my Hush Puppie leather shoes were falling apart so I looked for a shoe repairer. After a while I found a guy in an alley. He looked at the shoe and probably considered it quite complicated but he did apply some superglue at the front. I asked him how much and he said 2 rembi which is NZ 35 cents. I gave him 3 rembi but he only wanted 2 so I put the third on the counter where I left it. (And four weeks later the shoes are still fine after intense use in Italy, Sweden and Thailand.)

I walked and walked but couldn't really make out if I was walking in the right direction so after a while a stopped a taxi and asked him to take me to old town which I wanted to explore further. I looked around a bit more but the number of people reduced the pleasure a little. And the weather was getting dark and windy. As I was buying a pair of shoes two young girls came to my assistance saying they liked my red cap. I asked if they belonged to the store but they just wanted to help, and they were part of an arts exhibition in the next building. I followed them there and looked at the art which was nice and interesting but more suitable to an eastern home than a western. We parted as friends exchanging email addresses to continue our friendship on cyber basis.

As I got out on the street again it skies were dark and it had started to drizzle. I looked for a taxi but in the rain there wasn't any. Instead I saw a rickshaw and asked how much he would charge to take me to my hotel. He said 30 Rembi and although I thought that 50 % more than a taxi would charge I said ok. The only trouble was that it rained on me all the time. When we got to the Hotel I offered him 50 Rembi but he wanted 60. I said no and left it at that.

After some rest I met up with my friend Lillian Xia. She was head of Commonwealth bank in Tokyo when I was head of National Australia Bank and we became good friends. I knew she had moved to Shanghai so I called her and invited her for drinks or a meal. As she had other visitors in town she could only see me for pre-dinner drinks. So we each had a drink in the hotel lobby and talked about life post Tokyo and post Australian banking. It is lovely to see an old friend like that in a strange place and meeting a good friend makes the strange place feel a lot less strange. She was now working as senior vice president for a Japanese Bank and found it slightly daunting to be head of a group of males in Japanese bank. We compared notes on our careers and vowed to continue to stay in touch. After an hour she needed to move on and I walked out to have dinner. It was still wet but I didn't have to go very far.

As I would be travelling on the next day I retired to my room after dinner. I had now acquired a little bit of a feel for what Shanghai is. Interesting trip, I thought, even if I didn't feel any urge to return in a hurry. Tomorrow would be a long flight to Rome via Frankfurt. I arrived in Rome by midnight the next day.

June 2008

Cambodia August 2008

Lovely little hotel, La Maison d'Angkor, in Siem Reap! Only seventeen rooms grouped around a lush garden with a 25 by 8 meter pool. The interior and exterior are exquisite in brown wood and white. All staff are softly spoken, smiling and friendly. Just had a beer at the bar and talked to the bartender. He was born 1978 just at the end of the Khmer Rouge rule which killed his parents so he was brought up by his sister. Earlier today I bought a book about the murderous period that killed a bigger portion of Cambodia's people than even Mao and Stalin managed to kill in their respective countries. And this is in a lovely little country which looks like paradise epitomized. How do these things happen?

When I arrived at the airport in Siem Reap, I had filled in all the immigration documents, there were three of them, (Sweden has none) and I realized I didn't bring any photo for the Visa application on arrival. But I decided not to worry about it because I am not the first who arrives without a photo. I got in line for visas which cost US $ 20 and for anyone who didn't have a photo the cost was an extra $ 2 so again it was confirmed that seldom is what we worry about worth worrying about. I changed $ 50 at the airport and got 190,000 local currency, meaning that one dollar equals roughly 4,000. Subsequently I learned that the local economy more or less runs on US$ with Thai Bath also being quite fungible.

Through the immigration I had a choice of three transport means to the city. Taxi at $ 7, Bus at $ 5 or motor cycle at $ 2! Because it felt like such a wonderful day (after an exceptionally wet and cold couple of winter months in New Zealand) with about 26 degrees at 9 PM I decided on motor bike. The driver put my moderate piece of checked luggage in front of his knees and I wore my back pack and we were away. He introduced himself as Kumara and said that he would be my driver for my two days in Siem Reap for $ 30. That seemed like a good deal to me.

Before we went for all the temples I did some laps in the pool and reviewed my emails. I brought my sunglasses for my second bike trip partly for the sun but also to keep flies and particles out of my eyes. Like India, Cambodia charges some fees for access to historical sites towards the expenses of maintaining and keeping them. One day access to all the temples is $ 20 and three days is $ 40. As we drove around the greater Angkor Vat area I was struck by how beautiful it is with a small paved road and very green and fertile vegetation all around. There are also lots of water and a lot of peddlers and eateries to cater for the great stream of visitors. I learnt that winter is the big season here whereas summer is low season as it is too hot and the majority of the world's population living in the northern hemisphere are in summer holiday mode at home then.

Everything was so beautiful and tranquil getting me into a really good mood, realizing how lucky I am to be able to make a couple of trips like this every year. The other tourists I ran into were from Japan, Italy, Germany, UK, USA as well as some from down under. Everyone looked happy in this historical setting and in the glorious weather. The temples seem to go on forever. What struck me as most amazing is how giant trees were just growing on the Angkor Vat rocks and walls. Huge trees with enormous roots on top of the ancient walls with roots seeking the way to the ground on either side of six feet high walls! It looked like an impossibility and yet it was there right in front of my eyes. And the trees themselves must be hundreds of years. Walking up to the main Angkor Vat temple gave me the same feeling as approaching Taj Mahal. Just mind-blowingly ancient, impressive and beautiful! Although I don't need anything I manage to buy a few presents from some of the keen vendors en route. After three hours of very hot weather and a lot of monuments and stones I felt templed out and ready to return to the hotel.

I did another round of laps in the pool, read a little in my Pol Pot book and cleared the emails. I also went to bed to catch up on some sleep, but after half an hour the phone rang (with no-one at the other end) and my nap got a little shorter than intended. But that just means it will be easier to sleep well in the evening.

For the evening my motorcycle friend picked me up and I took me to a restaurant with local dancing. There was a big table with buffet food and I helped myself to what I thought looked appealing. I had a reasonable meal with the local beer, Angkor. The restaurant was rather big – too big for any sense of intimacy or cosiness- with a stage at one end. I looked at a few dances and they were nice but the distance to stage was too great. And the many tourists standing up to take pictures reduced the spiritual value of the experience. When I finished my meal I left in the middle of the performance and went for a walk. Siem Reap is not really much of a walking city but I did find the night market and managed to buy a few more things I don't need. I guess most well off westerners including myself don't in fact buy real goods but feel goods. It is a pass time and as such it can be quite pleasant, particularly when you buy presents, which tends to be the majority of what I buy.

The history of politics in Cambodia is explained in the book I bought 'First they killed my father' by Loung Ung. Led by prince Sihanouk, Cambodia, then a French colony since about 100 years, became an independent nation in 1953. Throughout the 1950's and 60's, Cambodia prospered and became self sufficient. However many people were not happy with Prince Sihanouk's government. Many regarded the Sihanouk government as self serving and corrupt, where the poor got poorer and the rich got richer. Various nationalistic fractions sprang up to demand reforms.

One of the groups, a secret communist faction – the Khmer Rouge – launched an armed struggle against the Cambodian government. The war in Vietnam spread to Cambodia when the United States bombed Cambodia's border to try to destroy the North Vietnamese bases. The bombings destroyed many villages and killed many people, allowing the Khmer Rouge to gain support from the peasants and farmers. In 1970, Prince Sihanouk was overthrown by his top general, Lon Nol. The united states-backed Lon Nol government was corrupt and weak and was easily defeated by the Khmer Rouge. This is another example of where US foreign policy has gone disastrously wrong and achieved exactly the opposite of what it was purported to achieve, ostensibly driven by ignorance and arrogance and US domestic political agendas.

The second day I did my laps in the pool at 6.30AM and then had a wonderful South East Asian breakfast with an assortment of fresh fruits, pineapple juice, an omelette and coffee with toast. And I was enjoying the breakfast under the palm trees in the courtyard of this tastefully designed small hotel – with a French general manager. After working through my private and work emails I met up with the driver and went for another temple treasure hunt. I asked him where I could find stamps so he took me to the main post office and then to the agency selling tickets for the boat ride to Phnom Penh the next day. Once that was completed we were out in the Angkor Vat area again. None of us had any helmets and I saw his speedometer was dead, but he drove cautiously along with the rest of the traffic at 30 -40 km per hour. Everything seemed to move fairly slowly here – and especially perhaps in the tourist and leisure industry, hurrying defeats the purpose. So I sat back and enjoyed the green countryside and spotted some rice fields and also some farmers ploughing with a one bill plough and an ox. Quite a primitive and inefficient way to farm but perhaps the cultivation of good rice needs to be small scale.

I saw another string of fascinating temples in the vast temple area. I learned that it was all built as Hindu temples between the years 900 and 1200 but later were abandoned after Cambodia lost a war with the Thais. The Hindu emphasis was later changed to Buddhism one guide explained to me. I said that as Buddha was a Hindu that may not have involved too great a change. The guide didn't understand what I was talking about. Particularly I found the way the ruins are integrated with nature very fascinating. The abundance of grass areas and trees everywhere reminded me of my great liking of Ostia Antiqua and Hadriani Villa outside Rome for the same reason. These are also in full symbiosis with nature such as to make the experience a combination of history and a great nature outing.

I bought a few more things from the many clever children selling T-shirts and other garments. Seeing a stall owner without his right hand I asked what happened to you? He said he was cutting trees and when he set his hand down on the ground for support he put it on a land mine which blew his hand away. Thousands and thousands of these landmines have been cleared but as many or more remain unaccounted for. It is puzzling, disappointing and tragic that human beings can get so misdirected and cruel, as to focus on malice and causing each other harm rather than on love and peace.

Saturday was an early start to get to the lake and take the boat due to depart for Phnom Penh at 7 AM. The boat was nearly full with a group of Japanese youngsters and some Australians and Europeans. It looked a bit crowded but once we were in motion, most passengers went out and sat on the roof of the boat. I did some of that too, a little bit cautiously, trying to avoid too much sun and sea exposure. The combination can cause sunburn quickly and often you don't realize it until it is too late. I talked to one man from Perth who had his passport stolen at the market place so he needed to go to Phnom Penh to get a new one. And then I spoke to several of the Japanese youngsters with what little Japanese I know. When in Japan I had one or two language lessons per week for two years so I can say some phrases in Japanese and I think I sound ok but once they start converse with me I am lost. But they also spoke English so we had some good discussions. I was asked for advice on the best way to achieve fluency in English. I suggested living in an English speaking country for a year for study or work, and finding an English speaking girlfriend or boyfriend. They found the last part particularly appealing. One of them asked me how big my group was. What group I asked. When I understood that he meant my travel group I said one. There were 18 in their group.

The trip was very pleasant with the boat moving about 25 knots per hour for six hours. The draft when outside was just right to keep one from feeling too hot. We passed lots of little fishing boats and many wooden houses on stilts to protect them from shifts in the water level. There was also lots of greenery floating around everywhere but the boat just cut right across all that. I managed to write a few postcards and also to finish the book I bought two days earlier with the eye witness account for the Pol Pot era. As I read a book about the Lodz Ghetto annihilation on my flight to Asia a few days earlier, I found the horror stories not too dissimilar. How utterly ruthless human beings can be and in the name of some glorified cause commit the most despicable atrocities. When power and weapons are in the wrong hands and fear rules, the result can be hellish. Neither book was very uplifting but perhaps they serve as a reminder that times haven't always been good and we should try to safe guard civility and courtesy and live in love and peace. I think president Truman is quoted as saying that the only thing you can be sure to prevent by war is peace. Past horrors can also serve as a reminder to appreciate every day free of fear, want and sacrifice.

The Khmer Rouge closed the cities and said everyone has to till the earth. Much of what was produced in harvests was exported, causing famine, in order to buy arms. Anyone perceived to be, or have the potential to be, anti government were shot. And often the family members were shot too as a precaution against revenge. A third of the population perished before Vietnam invaded Cambodia and defeated the Khmer Rouge. The story teller in the book mentioned has given a real, detailed and vivid account of what actually happened to her during those years. She had her father and mother and little sister killed by the Khmer Rouge and an older sister died from malnutrition. Reflecting on the horrors I think the murdering by Hitler of so many Jews was even worse as it was a universal death sentence of a whole race. But then I am not sure that it is meaningful to grade or compare such unfathomable horrors. Later, the last day when I visited the killing fields at Choeung Ek Memorial, one of the signs there suggested that this was worse than Hitler in as far as each murder was designed to cause as much pain and suffering as possible.

We arrived just before two o'clock to the pier in Phnom Penh and were overwhelmed by TukTuk drivers who wanted to drive passengers to the hotels. I picked a driver who I asked to please collect my suitcase from the boat and in so doing he delivered real value to me and I was happy to award him with the drive and not negotiate the price. I put my feet up in the TukTuk and sat back and enjoyed the busy street activity around me. When I had checked in at the Kabiki Hotel and showered and had a little snack, it was already half three. I got a map in the reception and was told the National Museum is only 15 min walk away. I noticed that the museum closed at 5 PM but reckoned that if I was there by four I would have an hour and few museums can keep my interest for more than an hour anyway. As I seemed to lose my way a little I stopped a MC and asked him to take me to the museum. I paid the entrance fee of three dollars and looked at the many Buddha statues and bronze weapons and utensils but as anticipated, the law of diminishing utility became apparent after a while. Although the museum was well laid out and not un-interesting, I was ready to leave after half an hour. The hot weather is another reason to not keep doing anything for too long.

I walked the streets back to hotel, stopping at a nice bar for a bit of rest and a beer. One nice custom in Cambodia is that at all restaurants and bars you get more than you pay for, i.e. there are always small extras delivered to keep you delighted and happy. I have come to believe that generosity not only makes social sense, it also makes perfect business sense. Most companies talk about customer focus but all incentives are then designed for the immediate gratification of shareholders rather than customers, with the result that both in the long run get short changed. Very narrow minded!

As I started the day with a wake-up call at 5 AM I felt a little tired and went to bed for a pre dinner nap. I slept like a log until 9.30 PM and drowsily considered whether it was worth going out again. But I thought that this Saturday evening in Phnom Pen is a unique happening in my life so go for it! I showered and took an MC to the riverside restaurants downtown. I stepped into the Bougainville restaurant and had a light supper with salmon and a couple of glasses of white wine. After dinner I wondered about a bit and then went back to the hotel. Not really a bristling night life but somewhere in between Vientiane and Saigon.

The last day I woke up at seven and once I wake up and it is daylight I never try to prolong sleep, no matter how late I went to bed. That is just the way I am wired. I took my breakfast at the pool side and realized that the pool was more attractive than it looked the day before. Outside the hotel I found another MC and said I want to go to the market and then to the Choeung Ek Memorial and pointed to the picture and text on my map. The driver didn't know the second place so I gave up and asked to be taken to the central market. There were just endless counters with cheap clothes and shoes and kitchen utensils, and various foods, none of which attracted my interest. But the jewellery I found quite amazing, the most attractive little pieces of rubies and aquamarine at perhaps ten or twenty percent of the cost in Sweden or New Zealand. Hard to resist buying under those circumstances!

Twenty minutes of the market was enough for me and I wanted to find someone who could take me to the Choeung Ek Memorial. When asked if I wanted a ride I said yes but I want to go here pointing on my map. The driver took the map and consulted with a Chinese shop owner who explained where it was and we agreed a price of $ 10 for the round trip including the wait at the memorial. This driver had a helmet for himself but not for his passenger. I was just as happy because in the heat a tight fitting metal helmet is like a mini sauna. I looked at all the people on their MC's, often a full family, sometimes a very pretty girl. I was thinking that it would be fun to just spend a month photographing pretty girls in South East Asia. There are so many exquisite and beautiful faces and the little children are so endearing. But that will probably only remain a dream.

I was also thinking that people aren't particularly service minded even if soft spoken and ostensibly kind. Why is it that communist countries or countries with previous socialist experience frown upon good service? As I sat there on the bike I think I found a reasonable answer. If service is required from only one 'class' of people who have been abused and taken advantage of for generations, often under conditions near slavery, service and slavery become almost synonymous. If you get just reward for your service either in the way of appreciation or remuneration, of course it is great to be of service. If, as in the case of historic Russia, the majority of people were serfs for hundreds of years, owned by their landlords and forced to serve long days for compensation, barely enough for sustenance, no wonder they came to resent service.

It took us half an hour to get to the memorial where I paid for the ticket and also engaged a guide. The first exhibit you see is a 17 floor glass monument filled with craniums recovered from the mass graves at the spot. The guide showed me how the craniums bore marks of swords, hammers, and scythes even if most victims were electrocuted. All corpses had their arms tied behind their backs and women corpses were still wearing their jewellery. Teachers, lawyers and doctors and their families! The guide said I could take a photo of the monument but I declined the offer. What would I do with such a picture? There were bones and clothes remnants everywhere. A big tree had a sign that this is where the children were killed by the executioner hitting their heads against the trunk. Totally incomprehensible that this has happened in our time! An estimated two million people succumbed, a quarter murdered and three quarters worked and starved to death. Perhaps it is a little macabre that it now constitutes a tourist attraction. But the reason for the memorials is what is written on all war memorials in New Zealand: Lest we forget!

On our way back we saw a collision between two motorbikes with six people in an intersection. But due to the low speed in intersections I don't think there was any lasting damage. I asked the driver to stop by the Independence Monument which is only a few minutes' walk from my hotel. I paid the driver and thanked him for his kind services. As I stepped into the big green Freedom Park I thought of Uhru Park in Nairobi, Uhru meaning freedom in Swahili. I saw this great green space and at the end of the green it melded with the blue sky and some beautiful white clouds. I felt very happy and thought that great parks are 'freedom'. Freedom for souls and people to play! We need the parks to help remind us that nurturing the spirit is one level higher than giving all your life merely to utility. This is what makes us human.

Back at the hotel I went to the pool and managed to get my laps in, as all the swimming children seemed to have a break and, as always, it felt great. With check out time at two I planned to stay in my room to that time before making a last tour of the city prior to departure. As I was typing away at this story the heavens opened and it rained buckets full for about an hour. I thought it was lucky I didn't get caught out on the motorbike and I also thought that with some further luck it is all over by 2 PM as I need to check out then. And sure enough, I was lucky twice. I checked my luggage at the hotel reception and looked for a taxi to take me to the riverside eateries.

Once down there I found a little restaurant with a nice Cambodian waiting lady who kept me company during my meal. She said both her parents succumbed during the genocide. She was 30 and building a new life with smiles and happiness. I had spring rolls and then fried noodles and a big bottle of beer to go with it, watching the slow moving traffic and the boats on the river outside. There were massage studios on either side and I asked her which was best. I went to the one she recommended after finishing my meal and paying, leaving her the change. The massage was great, an hour of kneading all the muscles after lots of walking and climbing. The music and lighting was low to help create spirit and soul.

My last agenda point was a visit to the genocide museum a few kms away. I bought my ticket and started to walk from room to room in this prison which used to be a school, looking at torture cells and photos of people who went there but never came out. Although one could easily have spent hours there I was overwhelmed by how horrible and depressing it all was so I left after fifteen minutes. Another MC took me to Independence monument and I walked back to the hotel. The taxi ordered for 5 PM arrived half an hour early and after a glass of fresh pineapple juice I said goodbye, took my things and went to the taxi.

The trip through town to the airport on a Sunday afternoon showed lots of activity. All park areas were buzzing with people enjoying their outing on the Sunday. The roads were full of families on motorbikes. I was leaving Cambodia very impressed with all the beautiful things I had seen including the people and the remarkable way in which they seemed to have put the unspeakable horror of the Pol Pot era behind them.

31st August 2008.

Philippines July 2009

Ralph, my old friend from Wellington appearing at the gate for the flight to Hong Kong! What a coincidence. I am actually not going to Hong Kong said he, but to Manila. How interesting, then we will be on two consecutive flights together as I am going there too. Ralph is going for reasons of business related to smart card payment systems and I am just stopping for a week's holiday on my annual trip back to Sweden. With the whole world between my two home countries, New Zealand and Sweden, it makes a lot of sense to try to see a little of it all as one is passing by. Waiting for the boarding call we had a chance to cover lost ground as to the whereabouts and occupations of family and friends. Ralph has a house in Wellington and Sardinia, where his wife Letizia originates, and we have similarly two fix points at the opposite ends of the globe. Good to catch up with an old friend!

Andre', my youngest son, was driving me to the airport and having driven half way I said I think I forgot something, can you please turn around. What did you forget? My phone! Can't you travel without it? I looked at my watch, realized there was enough time and said for him to please go back as I would need the phone in Sweden. I knew I had the Swedish chip in my luggage so I could always buy a new phone but that would seem a bit wasteful. Andre' drove back, I got the phone, and we got to the airport 2hrs and 20 min before departure. As I approached the check-in queue I saw it looked like half an hour's worth of queuing, but the nice lady at the passengers-only-beyond –this-point said 'please come with me.' She took me to the Business Class check in and I thought this a good omen. It is useful to travel in good dress such that you may look like a business class passenger without really being one. So I ended up with two hours to spare before take-off.

Going through customs the young lady official asked where I was going and I said Manila and she said for what purpose? Holiday! Why would you want to go to Manila for a holiday? And you went to Thailand last year? I explained I have never been to the Philippines but to Thailand many times as I try to break up my annual trip to my country of origin, Sweden, with a stop-over in the middle, to rest and relax and see something new. I am not sure what went through her mind but she stamped my passport and gave it back.

Entering the plane I picked up two Financial Times, one for Ralph and one for myself. Ralph was ten seats behind me. I had the aisle seat 57 c and I wondered who would be next to me in 57a. After a while this young Chinese lady comes and indicates that she has the window seat next to mine. I help her stow her back pack and shopping bag over-head and let her into her seat. I see her passport is from Republic of China so I am guessing she is from Taipei. I ask her and she says she is from Kaohsiung which is the second biggest city in Taiwan with a population around 1.5 million. She has been on a working holiday sorting kiwi fruit in the small New Zealand town of The Puke, the kiwi fruit capital of the world, not far from Tauranga. After a visit back to her home country for the summer, she is going back to New Zealand for six months. She says she is a nurse and I comment that there is a shortage of nurses in New Zealand. Yes, but with a foreign nursing education you cannot work in New Zealand without a special licence.

I introduce myself and she says she is Hisao Chieh Wen, called Jay Wen. Her name means the quiet and mild one which I think quite lovely. It is interesting how Chinese names usually seem to have a meaning like that. I show her the book I am reading: 'A Leaf in the Bitter Wind' by Ting-Xing Ye, set in the time of the Cultural Revolution. Though I have read about this period before, I am again horrified and moved by the ruthlessness of that time in China and the indescribable suffering of the people. The author says that the Gang of Four who after Mao's death were denounced and punished should really have been the gang of Five and have included the biggest marauder of them all, Mao himself. And till this day Mao remains a hero in China although he caused so much starvation, persecution, death and destruction. History is a strange thing. Two nice lines in Chinese in the book are: *shan-meng-hai-she* witnessed by the mountains and the sea (referring to the pledge of eternal love) and *shu-dao-hu-sun* – when the tree falls the monkeys scatter (referring to the fate of all the political opportunists surrounding Mao). Jay wen provided tremendous company and we had a lot of fun talking to each other in pidgin Japanese as she knew a little and I knew a little. Her mother tongue is Mandarin but she has never been to China, i.e. mainland China. She has picked up Japanese from Japanese TV channels that can be received in Taiwan with its closeness to Japan.

When on the next flight I was upgraded to business class (as the flight was full) I reflected that cattle class with a nice person sitting next to you beats business class with no-one to talk to. From Jay wen I learned that she had visited Japan and Thailand, that she is 27 years with a two years younger sister who works in Taipei in a jewellery shop, that her parents work for the government, the family car is a Mitsubishi, she has three living grandparents, the eldest of whom is 92, and she likes to bicycle and go for walks but isn't much for sport. The population of Taiwan is 23 million with 3 million in Taipei at the northern end, 250 km from Kaohsiung at the southern end. With 250 km between them they are connected by a Japanese style bullet train. Jay wen didn't think the country would ever be joined with The People's Republic but she also didn't think there would be any war between the two. The trend is for more openness and co-operation. It is amazing how much ground you can cover during an eleven hours flight. And still I read half a book and sleep for a few hours. At the airport in Hong Kong we said good bye and hugged and said we could be cyber friends.

So what do I know of the Philippines? The Philippines has 7,000 islands of which 2,000 are populated. It looks like a big octopus on the map. It is a little bit behind many of its neighbours in terms of affluence and economic development. Politically it has been unstable and some guerrilla activity on Mindanao Island has gone on for a long while. There is a female president for the second time, **Gloria Macapagal-Arroyo.** The population of the country is 80 million with another 40 million Filipinos living outside the country. Manila has 14 million people living in 16 'cities.' The Philippines is the number one country in the world for inbound remittances – total world remittance industry is around $ 300 billion a year - from its diaspora. Filipinos are known in the region for joy and happiness and music and singing. A significant part of the Tokyo entertainment industry is populated by Filipino talent. I have had a few Filipino friends and also maids when living expat life in Singapore and Tokyo.

This morning of the second of July 2009 I woke up early because of the time differences so 6 AM her is 10 AM in New Zealand. I got my PC up and running and connected to the world and went for breakfast. I contracted a driver for a three to four hours' City tour. The morning was nice and sunny and about 30 degrees. The driver Ramil came in a small bus for ten people but there was only he and I there. Ramil is the father of two little girls, he showed me the photo of his family, and he said life was pretty hard. He drove towards the harbour and the new developments there. Traffic was intense just before 10 am so it all moved rather slowly. He explained to me that here is Shangri-la, The Renaissance and the Pan Pacific and all the other fine hotels which didn't impress me too much. What I did notice is that the city looked neat and tidy and modern – not quite to Singapore or Tokyo standard but ahead of many of the capitals of South East Asia.

We looked at the new huge shopping mall near the sea and I went in there for a little while but it just seemed vast and deserted. I assumed that it might be a destination for the week-ends as it is all cool and nice and offers something for every taste including things for children. I was interested in the forex shop but there was a group of ten Japanese tourists to be served ahead of me and I didn't have the time to wait them out. The rate was 47.80 as opposed to the hotel rate of 45 pesos to the US $. We drove along the sea shore of Manila Bay which made me think of history and the challenges there – like the devastating final battle before the Japanese withdrawal from the islands after general Douglas McArthur's famous return.

The driver stopped by Fort Santiago and I went in to have a look for half an hour. The grounds were meticulously kept and there were some nice shops and restaurants and lovely music covering the whole area The location is just at the mouth of the river Fasig and it all looked quite tranquil and idyllic. Not far from the fort is the old cathedral, but when the driver heard I wasn't catholic he didn't bother stopping there.

If you are not catholic, what are you? I shrugged my shoulder and said I beli still part eve in love and peace.

From the fort he drove to the museum. A sign there suggested that the greatest treasure resource in the world is the sea and the objects at the museum were from discovered ship wrecks. Most of the items were from the battle ship San Diego which sunk Dec 14, 1600. It reminded me a little of the Wasa Museum in Stockholm, the difference being that ths Swedish museum actually holds the entire ship as it sunk 400 years ago. Here it was just chattels but interesting all the same. And that was the end of the tour – not in itself something to fly across half the world for but still part of building an impression of a large country East Asian country, new to me.

On the way back we drove by a market place and as it was close to the hotel I asked to get out, paid the driver a tip and went to have a look at the market. Half of it was food market and that was probably the better half. But as I needed neither food nor any of the junk in the rest of it, I walked to the hotel. For lunch I had soup and Hainan Chicken which reminded me that Jay wen told me the day before that Hainan is called paradise for men. Interesting! My impression of Hainan which I have never visited is that it is a little like the Crimea in Russia (or now Ukraine) in that it provides a warm pleasant resort for the many northerners within the confines of their respective country – offering the excitement of something quite different without going abroad. The food was good and I had a couple of beers to help send me into a deep sleep at my upcoming siesta.

In the evening I went to a restaurant with a dance and music performance and it was all quite pleasant. As I had read in the paper that today is Imelda Marcos 80th birthday, I asked my evening driver how she was seen and he said both she and her husband were well regarded. This also went for Corrie Aquino who currently is struggling against malign cancer. And the murder at the airport of her husband Ninoy is among the many world unresolved mysteries, although it is generally thought that this act was masterminded by President Marcos. I also asked how Americans were viewed in the country and he made a gesture which I interpreted as so and so. And when I asked the same question for the Japanese he said they were well liked. No resentment because of the Second World War? No he said, the past is the past and we are forward looking. And he said to their credit, Japanese people never argue about money.

When I took a bath before dinner I couldn't get the water out of the tub. As there was no lever to push or pull or turn to have the plug come out, I tried with my nails but to no avail. I thought most plugs leak a little anyway and in the morning the water would probably be gone. But no, in the morning the water was still there and I wasn't overly keen to go into the same water again. That's when I got a bright idea! The rubber mat in the bath tub had sucking cups underneath to prevent it from sliding. If I put one of those cups on the plug and pushed it down hard to connect well, and pulled, that might do the job. And lo and behold, it worked and I could have a fresh shower. The key agenda item for this day was my flight to the island paradise of Boracay. The morning paper said that the Philippines now is the number one country in south Asia for Influenza (AH1N1) cases ahead of Thailand. With 77,000 cases worldwide and the death toll at 330 the mortality incidence equates to 0.42 % or one in 240. Not enough of a risk for me to lose sleep over!

The airport at Caticlan was closed because of an accident last week so the flight was diverted to Kalibo on the other side of the island with a two hours bus trip to get us to Caticlan. Less than one kilometre from the airport is the ferry terminal for transit to the smaller island of Boracay. The two hour bus trip meant that I would get an extra sight-seeing trip, all free of charge, and as I didn't have any appointed time for arrival it didn't bother me. On the flight south it struck me how happy/ lucky I was to be able to do all these things and have so few worries. Thinking about it I reflected that life had never been much better. I finished reading my book on the flight and found it beautifully written and very memorable. I also finished another shorter one on the bus trip.

The bus drive across the island showed up a lovely countryside and a nicely sealed road with people walking alongside. It looked like paradise with green rice fields on either side of the road and palm trees and mountains in the distance. But I also know that many people are quite poor here and struggle to make a living. When we arrived at Caticlan I had to buy three tickets in three different windows to board the ferry. One ticket was terminal fee, one was environmental fee and one the ferry charge and once I had bought these three there was a fourth person checking I had it all and a fifth checking my luggage. Why have one person selling tickets when you can create work for three or four?

The ferry proved to be small thing accessible only over a long unstable plank. I got on board safely and put my suitcase down and sat on an empty seat. I asked the girl sitting next to me how long the trip was. At first she didn't seem to understand but after a while she said just ten minutes across. I asked her if she was from here which she confirmed. Her name was Sheryl and she was twenty-three and teaching kindergarten children English. She laughed at everything I said – she must have thought I was funny. As the boat pulled out people put on life vests. I seem to recall that it is quite a frequent occurrence in the Philippines that a ferry is lost in a storm. With so many islands there must be a great number of ferries and perhaps it is not so strange. But today was calm in protected waters so I had no concerns.

Sheryl of course couldn't swim and said she was afraid of water. I promised that if we sink I would save her and at that she laughed and seemed happy. I asked her what happens on the other side and she said there would be taxis and tri cycles. I said I would be happy with a tricycle – it is like a cabriolet. Ha, Ha! Once ashore we shared the tricycle and she instructed the driver. As she was going a shorter distance than I, she asked the driver to stop after a while and I got out to say good bye, and continued to my destination. The road we were on was a back road and the driver stopped by an alley and said this is it. So I walked the 70 yards down the alley way and found that at the end there was a sand boulevard with no vehicles but lots of people walking and most hotels fronted that walkway.

My hotel is The Red Coconut and I was well received and got a nice frontal room with a great view over the mighty ocean. At this time it is nearly five o'clock but I thought the first thing to do would be to go for a swim in the sea. I did that and the water temperature was just marvellous – it felt good to be alive. There were no big waves and also no corrals so very pleasant swimming at both high and low tide. High tide made the beach almost disappear but at low tide there were lots of people playing games and walking the two mile beach. All hotels were small enough to fit under the trees so from a distance you could have believed that it was a desert island – very nicely and cautiously done, small scale, warm and human!

I asked the hotel for internet and they said it is available at all rooms free of charge. I tested this and it worked, even if it was a little slow. It is good to be able to service my three email addresses even if there isn't much traffic when people know you are away. I showered, unpacked, washed my shirt and then went out for dinner. I took dinner at the hotel on the beach and decided on soup, salad and mackerel. It was happy hour for drinks so I got two of the local specialties for the price of one. It was all good and nice but after the meal I felt a bit stuffed so went for a long walk to remedy that. By this time it was quite dark but all the little shops and stalls along the sandy boulevard were open. This five meter wide road of sand between the hotel fronts and the line of palm trees marking the beach was just divine. For some reason it made me think of Via Apia in Italy which is also such an inviting road made for people and horses and carriages and not monstrous vehicles.

I stopped in a small shop to get a pedicure and after that I had a local massage. The lady doing the pedicure said she was alone in bringing up an eleven year old boy. The father had a new family in Manila. She earned a total of five thousand pesos a month or just over US$ 100. Getting on to the massage, the masseuse asked me if I wanted hard or soft, and I said hard, and she meant hard. I am sure it is healthy and feels good, particularly afterwards, but when my calves are under attack, just under the knee, I must admit I am in agony. The masseuse, second in a lot of five children, was 18 and from Cebu Island. Having fallen asleep twice during the massage, in spite of its brutality, I realized it was probably time to call it a day and return to the hotel room.

In the morning I woke up with the light just after six and after a while I went for a morning swim followed by breakfast. All the sailing boats of yesterday were gone so I concluded they must be harboured somewhere else over night and then brought back later. At around nine they all started to come back and I negotiated to pay 1000 pesos or US $ 20 for three hours. I love being out on a sail boat with no sound, tropical warm water, lovely views and total tranquillity. It turned out to be a little too tranquil so the three sailors brought out paddles and paddled for an hour until some wind again appeared. These were out-rigger sail boats of ancient model and I was directed to sit on a surface above the water outside the boat. As it was so slow I lay down and fell asleep twice, probably only for five or ten minutes each time. I think a brief nap daytime equates to low stress and quality of life. If you can sleep like a child by just lying down, life can't have been too hard on you. I felt happy.

A huge dark cloud, indicating bad whether to come, had developed with rumbling thunder in the distance. Luckily it never reached us though, and we returned at one pm rather than at noon. I said thank you to the captain and paid fifty percent more than agreed and all were happy. Although I had tried to sun screen most of my body, inevitably there were some gaps which were now quite red. Luckily I wore my shirt all the time and if I hadn't I would have been really sick. I just need to be careful tomorrow and make sure red parts are covered when out in the sun.

I swam again in the afternoon and wrote a few postcards. I took dinner at the hotel restaurants on one of the table on the sand boulevard watching people strolling by. One of the nice looking waitresses patrolled the boulevard with a menu and solicited suitable targets to come and have dinner at the restaurant. After eating fish for several days, I decided on spare ribs and salad this evening. Even if ribs are a bit messy to eat they taste well and it is something I wouldn't cook myself so several good reasons for the choice. After dinner I shopped some pearls which seemed to be the local merchandise and then ventured to a karaoke bar. The bar was not very busy. I ordered three songs please and a beer to go with it. After singing 'Diana,' 'Yesterday' and 'What a Wonderful World' I broke up and decided to call it a day. My best score for singing close to the original was 94% for Paul Anka's Diana. Reflecting on the day I thought I had met none but lovely, friendly people and the slow pace and music and boating and swimming made this place something very special.

Sunday all sunny and sparkling! When going into the sea this morning I thought it is amazing how cooling it feels in spite of being around 30 degrees – 'mud, mud, glorious mud, nothing quite like it for cooling the blood' rang in my head. Although the water was clear and not muddy at all. After breakfast and finishing off some postcards I again met Edgar, the owner of the sailing boat, and agreed to a twelve noon lunch excursion. By starting later I hoped the wind would be up a little and also wanted to have the morning free to try to locate Patrick. Patrick is the brother of Mary who is a friend from the tennis club and she had encouraged me to seek up Patrick when on Boracay. Patrick has a hotel called Butterfly Gardens on Bulabog Beach on the other side of the island, perhaps 400 meters across from my hotel. I took a tri-cycle there and walked fifty meters along the beach to get to the place. I saw someone sitting in the office typing away and thought that must be him. I walked right up and said, 'Dr Livingston I presume.' I didn't really say that but rather 'are you Patrick' which he confirmed. I introduced myself, and after a few seconds the penny dropped and he realized the connection. He invited me to sit down to have a drink and a chat. His hotel had a nice green lawn with low buildings on either side with the endless ocean at the end of the u-shaped configuration – very charming and idyllic.

Patrick said half the year the wind blows from the east and half from the west making one side always calm. He bought the place a few years ago and it has proven a great investment with annual average occupancy of 67 %. Patrick has lived all over Asia for many years and thought this the best place. Very easy living, even if dealing with the authorities often was frustrating. They are slow and enigmatic and have very little feel for and understanding of environmental concerns. Boracay had attracted a lot of Filipinos to come for work and those who couldn't find work would sometimes resort to crime, so good security and night guard was essential. Patrick looked well and healthy but said he had developed a stomach problem which he would have fully diagnosed and analysed in Manila next week. I wished him good luck and said it was very nice to meet with him and his Doberman dog, Kiwi. (Sadly Patricks sister, Mary, emailed me two weeks later saying Patrick died in hospital in Manila – it is hard to believe that someone you met two weeks prior, looking so full of life, could be gone!)

I walked back and then went to the Barber for a tidy up which was done well and with panache. When the barber asked for 100 pesos for the job, I doubled it, thinking that it was well worth four US$. Next was another sailing trip. I had to be careful to not expose my red parts again but solved this by wearing socks rather than barefoot as my biggest problem was the top of my feet. I wasn't sure if the idea was to have lunch on the beach but realised after a while that this was not the case so my lunch today would consist of one can of beer which I brought. I quite enjoy under-eating as a contrast to the bigger problem of overeating. The pleasure of being really hungry seems rarer and rarer in western civilization. The two last words brought to mind Ghandi's answer to the question: "What do you think about western civilization?" And his answer was 'That would be a good idea!'

Edgar, the captain, had the idea to go to the other side of the island to offer me some snorkeling. That seemed ok. We didn't travel fast and between the two islands we had quite a strong current against us so I talked to Edgar and slept a little too. Edgar taught me a few words in Filipino and the only one I remember is *maganda* for beautiful. It has a nice ring to it and made me think of princess Kunigunda who married Bernard, the King of Italy in 813 and I am sure she was very beautiful. I asked Edgar how tourists from different countries behave. He seemed to like all tourists but did say that the Chinese had a hard time parting with money, the Germans were too disciplined and serious, the Americans gave a mixed impression and the Koreans and Japanese were ok. It seems that the dominance of Japanese tourists earlier had been replaced by Chinese and Koreans and much fewer Japanese were now travelling. Edgar said there were also many Russians during peak season and also Israelis. The latter were often into drugs he said. Another piece of information he volunteered was that Koreans and Chinese make a lot of noise during sex. I am not sure if he meant both genders and also not sure how he obtained that information or how I might benefit from it, but who cares. The sun was shining, the water crystal clear and warm and people everywhere seemed quite happy and waved to us as they passed by in their motorboats.

We got to our destination and I put the snorkel on and he threw some broken crackers into the water. And hundreds of beautiful little fish appeared totally oblivious of my presence. Quite spectacular really! I have snorkelled before in Bora Bora, Fiji and Malaysia and this experience was right up there. One must marvel at the gorgeous colouring of these little tropical fish – and the same goes for birds and butterflies for that matter. I am not sure that Darwin's evolutionary hypothesis covers beauty as well – how is it that these creatures are so stunningly perfect and beautiful? I swam with the little fish for twenty minutes but was then exhausted. I saw a silver coin at the bottom of the sea and dived for it and picked it up – a treasure of 20 cents I think.

The return trip to the beach took half as long as the outward trip because we were going with the current this time. Edgar told me his wife works in Bahrain as a domestic helper and they communicate via texting because she doesn't have a pc. She is part of the extensive Philippine diaspora. The many offices of Western Union in almost every street corner is a reminder of how these people have spread over the world. I paid and said thank you to Edgar and his two mates – we were old friends by now. On the return trip we also got into singing. Edgar played the guitar, although not on the boat. A nice acquaintance and some very friendly people!

I went for another swim and then found time for a snooze as well before the evening program. I thought I'd have a massage before dinner and did so. Great masseuse from Manila! She said she was 18 and I said I was 19 which made her laugh out loud. Massage is such a nice thing and again I nearly fell asleep. When I dressed, my glasses flew onto the floor and I picked them up. I paid my due and gave the girl a good tip and said thank you. I was again asked to write my impression on a piece of paper and I did it with accolades as she delivered great value.

I went back to the hotel restaurant by the sand street next to the ocean and ordered a Pina Colada and a Lobster. This was my last night! After twenty minutes my lobster thermidor arrived and I was wearing my glasses in order to be able to see the delicacy. It struck me that my left eye didn't see much at all so I thought there must be a film on the glass or some dirt. I took my glasses off and intended to polish the left glass – only to discover it was gone. It must have fallen out on the floor when I dropped my glasses at the massage place. After the delicious dinner including two glasses of white wine, I walked back to see if I could recover my lost glass – and there it was still lying on the floor and as luck would have it no one had stepped on the glass. I took the glasses to an optician, open at 9 pm on a Sunday night, and the girl refitted the glass in no time at all. My lucky day! I always bring a pair of reserves but I was still very pleased to have my favourite pair restored. Another great day in paradise and tomorrow I would return to Manila. The nearby airport in Caticlan was still closed so the return trip would require a two hour land transport to get to the airport. In writing this it reminded me to charge up my i-pod for the bus trip.

Last day I did my morning swim and a walk on the beach and then had a big breakfast realizing I probably wouldn't see food again for ten hours, which turned out to be more like twelve. I took a tricycle to the ferry landing and sailed across and another tricycle took me to Caticlan airport. I checked in and had to wait for ninety minutes for the two hour bus trip to Kalibo. And when I got there the plane was delayed so another two hours' wait for take-off. The flight was only 50 min and baggage handling was quick but then the Manila traffic and a driver who didn't know where to go took another two hours out of my schedule. Fortunately I had nothing really to hurry for as I didn't have a schedule so I just read my book, listened to music and relaxed.

At the hotel, The Richmonde where I now felt at home, I asked for internet connection to be set up and ordered some room service food. The day was more or less lost to travel anyway as my travel from Boracay to Manila took twice as long as normal. Lost to travel? If life is a journey, as if often claimed, lost to travel seems a bit of an oxymoron. You do see a lot of fellow travellers and some you exchange a word with, and for some others, your imagination has you guessing as to their delights, lives and character.

This last day in the Philippines I went for a walk after breakfast to what looked like a shopping area. I had a hunch shops wouldn't open before 10 am but I couldn't restrain myself so arrived half hour before opening of the big nearby Mega Mall. To fill out the time gap I sat down on the edge of the pavement and read the last part of my book Brida by Paul Coelho. I liked his first book, The Alchemist,' and this one was an equally warm nice read. Just before the shop opened I read: "Never be ashamed. If it wasn't for shame, God would never have discovered that Adam and Eve had eaten the apple. Accept what life offers you and try to drink from every cup. All wines should be tasted; some should be sipped, but with others, drink the whole bottle. Good wine you can only know if you have tasted the bad one."

At ten sharp the doors to the mall opened and the small group of people outside went in. There was a brief security check of bags at the entrance – lots of security checks in the Philippines but they are rather superficial and quick. No need to take the computer out at the airport and no need to take metal off your clothes. One thing they did do at airports was to have you show your luggage tag and see that it corresponded to the baggage. This mall was huge and I thought I will never find anything here. But after five minutes I found some T-shirts I felt would make good presents – the text on the shirt, very delicately written, said 'I am a pinoy.' I asked what a pinoy is. It means a Filipino. Ah, again I had extended my vocabulary with a new piece of valuable information. I bought a few of those and outside there was someone doing tailor made luggage labels and I found those irresistible as well. Further on I stumbled onto a mango yoghurt stand and thought, yes that is me.

Barely had I finished the yoghurt before I found another nice polo shirt for my Swedish friend and also a pair of Levi's blue jeans. Each of the people I dealt with offered me friendship and smiles and I danced in between shops to the music from the loudspeakers. And I reflected on my previous management thinking that people buy as much the person as the goods. If anyone is trying to sell me something, I am likely to be disinterested, but if someone looks like offering friendship, I am very happy to buy anything. An hour went by in a flash and I walked back to the hotel for my 12 noon pick up – now in a very good mood.

As I had seen the obvious sights in Manila the week earlier I decided to take the advice of my driver and go and have a look at Angeles City. I had been informed it was two hours away but again, time didn't seem to have much essence. Angeles City was established 1796 and has gradually become known as Luzon Islands entertainment capital. The City was badly affected by the Pinatubu volcano eruption in 1991, the biggest one in the world in the last century. Five billion cubic metres of ash and debris were ejected from the mountain and the eruption killed nearly one thousand and displaced a million people. Angeles City, besides entertainment, also has some historic buildings, shopping and good restaurants. Two hours to get there, some time to look around and have a good meal, and two hours back and I would be in good shape for a sensible early night given the need for a 3.30am wake-up call and arrival in London 20 hours later. I thought if I make a visit daytime before all the bars have opened I would avoid temptation. This last word reminded me of the saying 'Don't worry so much about avoiding temptation when you are young, as you grow older temptation will avoid you.'

Suddenly I got a call from Nora, wife of Edwin, the driver, saying he may be slightly late due to heavy traffic but he was there spot on time. We drove towards Angeles first in the city of Manila and then on the toll road between the two cities. The landscape was quite flat with a mountain range and volcano in the distance. It all looked quite idyllic and not many people to be seen. In ninety minutes we were in Angeles and I asked to be shown around the sights first. Edwin said there weren't many other than a generous park in the middle and the huge ex American air base to the right, now taken over by Philippine security forces. The town was pretty basic with lots of little hotels and bars/nightclubs and quite active foot traffic along the key roads.

The driver left me on a street corner and we agreed to meet up at the same corner at an appointed time. I went to have a hamburger and a beer as I now had become a little bit hungry again. I walked the streets in the scorching heat and I gave all my coins to a few beggars. Two shoe shine boys pointed to my red leather shoes and said they looked like in a bad need of a polish for 100 peso. I gave them my shoes and walked a little further to a bar counter and sat down and ordered a beer. There were also two guys from Darwin there and we got talking for a while. One of them was a builder and they were staying in Angeles for two weeks. I can't quite imagine how anyone can go on bar hopping for that period of time but obviously people do. I learnt that government driven building activity in Darwin is formidable and no recession is in sight there. And I commented that New Zealand is very lucky to have Australia as a neighbour.

At that time my shoes were ready and I said good bye to my new friends and moved on, stopping into another couple of bars briefly before it was time to go back. One thing I did notice was that it all seemed very peaceful and friendly. Everyone was kind and smiling. But I still wasn't quite sure I understood how people could fly into the Philippines just to spend a whole holiday in this place. The trip back to Manila took only an hour but negotiating the rush hour traffic in Manila took another hour. I had a good dinner at the hotel and went to bed early. When I settled my account the lady at the front desk said they could bring me breakfast at the same time as the wake-up call 3.30 am. I said thank you and was quite impressed with this useful service.

The next day my driver didn't show up for some reason and after waiting fifteen minutes I caught a taxi on the street to take me to the airport. I read the news paper and one article said Robert McNamara died on Monday aged 93. The article also said that the former Defence Secretary was famous for saying about the Vietnam War – which he was responsible for - that 'it was a terrible mistake' (what an unmitigated tragedy in our time with almost two million dead for no sensible reason) and also that if the US had lost the war those responsible for the firebombing of Tokyo would no doubt have been convicted of war crimes (Tokyo suffering more bomb casualties than Hiroshoima and Nagasaki put together). And these are supposed to be the good guys?

Six days in the Philippines! I felt I had had a great time and that I knew a lot more now about the country than I did before. My impression was of a friendly, gentle people who know how to lead a happy life even if many are not far away from the poverty line. How nice it is to have the chance to see new places and get acquainted with people you haven't met before.

7th July 2009

Hong Kong / Macao July 2009

I started out my day of travel in Stockholm by washing sheets and towels and then a last cycle tour around the centre of Stockholm. It felt nice to break out for a little while and not dedicate the whole day to travel and utility. I caught the 1 pm Arlanda Airport Express and checked in by the machines, but had to queue a little to get rid of the bag. All worked out well and I fell asleep twice on the London flight. The machine gave me my second boarding pass to HK as well so lots of time to relax in London. Security in London confiscated my umbrella explaining that only umbrellas which fit into your hand luggage are permitted. Somewhere in my subconscious I almost anticipated that. I wonder what they do with all confiscated goods?

I finished my Dostoevski book, 'Winter Notes on Summer Impressions' where he particularly pokes fun at the French and their inflated view of themselves and their country. At the end of this book there was an account for Dostoevski's life which of course included confinement to prison for a while, constant lack of funds and a corresponding indebtedness, the odd epileptic attack, and also unhappy love. The account also said a number of prominent writers didn't think much of his writing, whereas Sigmund Freud saw him as the best. Personally I hold Dostoevski very high – particularly The Idiot and The Karamazov Brothers are amazing.

On the full flight to Hong Kong of nearly twelve hours I slept a little and then felt very sick. Fortunately the feeling gave way after a few glasses of water. I am glad I felt better upon arrival as the HK and China authorities quarantine people who arrive feeling sick with reference to the Swine flu. I sat next to a boring guy who didn't say anything, but I slept most of the time anyway so it wasn't too bad. In HK I took the Hotel Shuttle bus serving several adjacent hotels, taking a little extra time but then I got to see more of town and I wasn't in any real hurry. We did pass through the Disneyland complex which has several hotels. The Ramada Kowloon is a pretty inconspicuous hotel but well located and of decent standard which is all I was looking for. I got into internet, checked my mail and let people know my new abode. I showered and walked out to see a little of Kowloon street life before it got dark. These Hong Kong streets are amazing with all the colourful signs with Chinese characters filling up most of the space above the traffic between buildings.

My first visit to HK was in May 1968 when I was twenty. Then we stayed at Repulse bay hotel on the island. And it was also a poor country at that time whereas now average income is higher than in many western countries. There are still many poor, perhaps due to the constant influx from China of people who seek better fortunes. The new airport and the infrastructure in terms of roads, bridges and mass transport is absolutely world class. I have subsequently visited HK many times on my travels to Asia and also during my time as an expatriate in Singapore and Tokyo. But there is still the excitement of discovery, learning and finding things out.

I bought a few presents including some for myself and had dinner at a small Chinese restaurant, duck, pork, rice, vegetables and a large local beer. After dinner I walked another hour in the hectic foot traffic before settling in for the evening. I felt I had got quite a lot out of the few hours of my first day here. The second day I planned to go to Macao and the third day I was giving a presentation to a group of philanthropists on the Island.

I woke up at 2.30 am feeling clear and awake so did some typing and reading and tried to sleep again an hour later. When I woke up I looked at my watch and the hour hand had disappeared. Finally I detected it under the minute hand and it was 12 noon. I don't think I ever have slept that long. I showered and dressed and started to walk towards the 1 PM ferry for Macao. After some wrong turns I was there just before one only to discover that departure was 1.30pm. This gave me the chance to have a light Starbucks breakfast. Tickets were HK$ 320 return and the service is hourly all day. Since the distance is about 60 km and the time just over an hour the speed must be just over 30 knots. Sailing out of Hong Kong offered up some spectacular views and en route we met a lot of ships and the odd one overtook us as well. Because these territories, Hong Kong and Macao, are like different countries there is full immigration documentation going and coming.

Once through all the processes in Macao a local guide offered me a tour of Macao for $ 600. I said no and he asked how much I wanted to pay and I suggested $ 300 which he accepted. His name was Chou Hon Choi and he was from Burma. I asked him where I could get some stamps for the postcards I wrote on the ferry and as luck would have it there was an open post office right there. The lady behind the counter informed me that postage was five HK $ so I bought the stamps and posted the cards. Macao has its own currency but HK $ is of the same value and also accepted. Then we went to see some of the sights including the Mount Fortress, the Ruins of St Pauls and a few others.

The driver, who emigrated from Burma a few years prior, was like an old encyclopaedia. He said the population of Macao is half a million and the area is 28 sq miles, compared to 7 million and 382 sq miles for Hong Kong. Tourist visits to Macao are 23 million a year, half from Hong Kong and Half from China. There are 30 casinos of which three are Las Vegas owned and one Australian. The gambling industry raises 100 Billion annually of which 40 % goes to the government leading near nil tax for the citizens. In fact $ 6,000 a head is recycled to needy every year. The driver suggested that Macao shopping was cheaper than HKK due the absence of taxes in Macao. He also said he had two children, one daughter studying the arts and a son attending a hotel management education in Los Angeles. Given the political mess in Burma he was very happy in Macao for the foreseeable future. He said Macao is friendly and now free of the mafia since the Chinese took over – everything is now looking pretty good for those who live there. Business had dropped 10 % in response to the general global downturn.

My impression was that people looked very well-to-do and happy this Saturday afternoon, shopping, strolling, eating and just enjoying life. I was thinking that these people never had it as good as today. Shop assistants were happy and friendly and it was with delight I purchased a few Items I probably didn't need for myself and others. Particularly the area around Senado Square looked very attractive. I decided on a meal there and found a nice little restaurant called Wong Chi Key, just across from the Scottish restaurant which is almost everywhere around the world.

I ordered beef and fried noodles and learned that China started to make noodles during the Han Dynasty. Cantonese noodles are different from others being fine as silk, smooth and springy. The golden era of noodle eatery was 1920 – 1930 when Canton was rapidly developing. This I learned from the table mat. I had a great meal in this rather traditional looking Chinese restaurant. The noodles were truly delicious. As darkness settled on Macao all the casino signs came on and it looked a little like Shanghai or Las Vegas. When I decided to return to the ferry at eight pm the streets were still full of pedestrians trying to make the most of their Saturday.

The second taxi driver said he was born in Macao and that life was better than in HK because of a slower pace. He was 61 and said I was lucky to get him as 95 % of drivers in Macao can't speak English. He much enjoyed life in Macao. I felt it was a very worthwhile visit to Macao that I would recommend to anyone going to Hong Kong. The area is currently under a fifty year transitory government before a full China take over. Back in Hong Kong I walked slowly to the hotel stopping in one bar for a night cap. It had been quite a long day so I retired to the hotel and made some pre-arrangements for the next day's early check out.

By eight am the next day I was on my way to the Star Ferry terminal. As I saw I had plenty of time before my 9.30 am rendezvous at the peak tram station, I stopped in a café' for a quick breakfast. The Star Ferry cost $ 2 for the crossing and it is quite a charming option as the boats look like they have been doing the crossing for at least one hundred years. I was early at the tram station sweating heavily as it was a very hot day. After a while my friend Sou showed up plus a few other friends and we went up the tram. It is quite steep and the vegetation around very lush. And it is quite fascinating that the extreme high rises by the sea can be looked down upon from the peak. At the top our hostess Vishaka Hussein met us and our group gathered for a walk around the peak. It continued to be very hot and in spite of my trying to keep the sweat away with towels it just kept coming. The walk was fantastic and I chatted to a couple of our group making it quite swift and easy, disregarding the humidity and heat.

After perhaps forty minutes walk we turned towards Vishaka's house at the peak. She and her husband, who had been home cooking a fine brunch, have a beautiful house with views over the sea and hills of Hong Kong. We ate various Indian dishes and also salmon and Makademia nuts and lots of fruits, sitting in a ring around the table. One couple had just spent time as volunteer lecturers at the Woman's College in Chittagong helping out with lectures in Psychology and finance. I said I had just visited Macao and was impressed by how tidy and affluent it seemed. The husband, an economist, said that there are some problems there too. China is being more restrictive in letting people through to Macao and one of the casinos is about to go bankrupt for lack of business.

The hostess Vishaka wished all welcome and suggested all introduce themselves before the speech and when that was done, Sou introduced me and I talked for thirty minutes about Enviroschools as well as about ethics and leadership and motivation. I felt privileged to be invited to address such a group of distinguished people of international background in Hong Kong. One person was a Doctor of Medicine, his wife and Odontologist, one was a lawyer, two were civil engineers, one an economist. There were Chinese, Middle Eastern, Indian, American, Portugese, and some others represented. I also sent around business cards and said I would be happy to link up with anyone on any issue after the meeting.

I sang a couple of songs as well and spoke about music and singing and the need to stay positive and optimistic about the future in order to enlist support and achieve change. I spoke about how the divide between Philanthropy and Business needs to be bridged as all activity including corporate needs to align with what is good for the people. The only sound relationship principle is the win-win philosophy as anything else will reduce wealth and happiness. I felt it was a good group to talk to and all seemed very positive.

After the presentation there were coffees and teas and continued discussions in smaller groups. At around two o'clock the party was over and we moved back to the tram station to get back to city level. Sou wanted me to bring a letter to New Zealand so we went to her office too fetch it. En route we stopped in to see the Aviary which is huge and very well done. It was still incredibly hot and humid with the mercury hitting 37 degrees that day. At the office Sou explained to me that her project involved making the legal system more accessible to ordinary people. She said there are a lot of people who are not poor enough to get legal aid but yet not wealthy enough to run a court case on their own and she was now trying to build a low cost arbitration process in order to make justice more available. Sou has her home in NZ but has taken a one-year job in Hong Kong where she has worked before as a prosecutor.

We then walked together to Star Ferry and I am glad she accompanied me as walking paths are elevated with many twists and turns to get to you destination. On Sundays, the whole city centre is full of Philippine maids sitting on a piece of plastic or cloth or cardboard on the ground everywhere. They like to gather with their friends to play cards, chat, and sometimes sleep. I said to Sou that the not so nice thing about this phenomenon is that is easy to feel that they are almost another species than full human beings. Sou said many are also treated as lesser citizens, and some are very well educated. The minimum wage law in Hong Kong excludes maids and domestic workers and she said that if that weren't the case, maids would need to be paid about three times current pay levels.

We got to Star Ferry and I bought my token, we said good bye and I thanked Sou for her support and kindness. I enjoyed the sailing and was across the harbour in ten minutes. On the Kowloon side I bought a cold drink to try to cool down a little. I later learned that it had been the hottest day of the year. I had a pick up at the hotel at four forty and about half an hour to spare before I needed to go there. I thought I would buy some more things, particularly small presents, but I couldn't find anything suitable and gave up and went to the hotel to get my things. With fifteen minutes to spare I took out some dry clothes and changed trousers and shirts after a quick wash up and that felt really good. I got to the airport a full three hours before take off with plenty of time to type a little and look at all the shops. The things I saw at the shops in town were twice the price at the airport which put me off buying anything. Likewise the currency buying and selling was 10 % worse at the airport suggesting that it is wise to try to avoid any economic transactions at airports. Otherwise the airport is modern and efficient with plenty of clean toilet facilities.

The flight went well in spite of some bad weather along the route. I arrived in Auckland after some delay and felt very happy about my nearly five week's holiday. I also felt keen to see family and friends again and get stuck into my New Zealand life.

August 2009